Appearance and Reality

Appearance and Reality

A Philosophical Investigation into Perception and Perceptual Qualities

P. M. S. Hacker

Fellow of St John's College
Oxford

Basil Blackwell

Copyright © P. M. S. Hacker 1987

First published 1987

Basil Blackwell Ltd
108 Cowley Road, Oxford, OX4 IJF, UK

Basil Blackwell Inc.
432 Park Avenue South, Suite 1503
New York, NY 10016, USA

British Library Cataloguing in Publication Data

Hacker, P. M. S.
    Appearance and reality : a philosophical investigation
into perception and perceptual qualities
    1. Reality   2. Perception
    I. Title
    153.7   BD331

ISBN 0-631-15704-2

Library of Congress Cataloging in Publication Data

Hacker, P. M. S. (Peter Michael Stephan)
    Appearance and reality.

    Includes index.
    1. Perception (Philosophy)   2. Senses and sensation.
I. Title.
B828.45.H33 1987   121'.3   87-11667
ISBN 0-631-15704-2

Typeset in 10½ on 12½ pt Bembo
by Alan Sutton Publishing
Printed in Great Britain by
T. J. Press, Padstow

For Julie

For there is no friend like a sister,
In calm or stormy weather . . .

Contents

Acknowledgements

I am much indebted to institutions, audiences and friends for various forms of assistance and support given to me while I was writing this book.

The British Academy elected me to a Research Readership which, by relieving me of teaching, enabled me to concentrate my efforts on completing this project without unduly neglecting my main work with my colleague Gordon Baker on Wittgenstein's *Philosophical Investigations*. My college St John's, as always, gave liberally of its many facilities and tolerated my absence from teaching.

Early drafts of various chapters were read as occasional papers at the Universities of Nijmegen, Michigan, Yale, Maryland and Georgia State. The testing questions put to me by my audiences were of great utility in helping me to clarify my thoughts. Swarthmore College invited me to deliver a set of six lectures on the themes of this book in the Fall Semester of 1986, and I benefited greatly from the ensuing discussions. I am particularly indebted to Hans Oberdiek, who arranged my visit and made it so delightful, and to Hugh Lacey, who kept me on my toes. The probing questions put to me by participants in my Friday evening graduate seminars on perception at Oxford always sent me scurrying back to the drawing board first thing on Saturday morning. I am grateful to all, but especially to Oswald Hanfling.

Gordon Baker, Raymond Frey, Herman Philipse and Joseph Raz all gave me the benefit of their time and wit. Their detailed comments on my typescripts were invaluable, and the many hours of cheerful and stimulating discussion were memorable. John Cottingham kindly commented on chapter 1. To Bede Rundle I owe a special debt. His encouragement has sustained me at times when my spirits flagged and my will faltered, and I cannot count the number of fruitful ideas which originated in the smoke-laden corners of the Gardeners' Arms where we meet. My greatest debt is to John Hyman. His enthusiasm was infectious, his fascination with the problems inspiring, and his penetrating and constructive criticisms prevented me from error again and again. One of the many delights of philosophy is the excitement of discussion with a sympathetic listener who can weed out the nonsense without destroying, but nurturing, the seeds of sense. I have been fortunate in having so many who were willing to listen to me.

P. M. S. Hacker
St John's College, Oxford
1987

The evolution of the higher animals and of man, and the awakening of consciousness at a particular level. The picture is something like this: Though the ether is filled with vibrations the world is dark. But one day man opens his seeing eye, and there is light.

Our language primarily describes a picture. What is to be done with the picture, how it is to be used, remains obscure. Quite clearly, however, it must be explored if we want to understand the sense of what we are saying. But the picture seems to spare us this work: it already points to a particular use. This is how it takes us in.

Wittgenstein

1

Appearance and Reality

1 The origins of an illusion

For twenty-five centuries questions about the relations between
Appearance and Reality have fascinated, obsessed and bewildered
philosophers. A multitude of very different issues lay intermingled
under the heading of this pair of abstract nouns. Some concerned the
nature of the empirical in contrast with the a priori, others the
temporal as opposed to the atemporal; some concerned the nature of
the corruptible in contrast with the incorruptible, or the human and
the divine; and some concerned the relations between the world as we
perceive it to be and the world as it is in itself.

The latter kinds of contrast incorporate a battery of interrelated
problems about the nature of the physical world we inhabit, our
modes of apprehending its features and the limits and constraints
upon the possibility of attaining empirical knowledge. We are
creatures with perceptual capacities, i.e. capacities whereby we can
discern, discriminate or detect features of the world surrounding us.
But our perceptual capacities are limited; eagles can see farther, dogs
can smell better and bats can hear more acutely than we can. We often
err in our perceptual judgements concerning how things are in our
environment. Moreover, we are subject to occasional illusions and
hallucinations. And not everything in the world manifests its true
nature to casual perception, for things are sometimes different from
the way they perceptually appear to be.

For those in whom philosophical questions strike a responsive
chord awareness of these simple truisms suffices to raise a variety of
prima facie puzzling questions. Does perception reveal to us the
world as it really is, or only as it appears to us to be? Does it appear

differently to a creature with a very different sensibility? If so, can we determine how the world is independently of us? Or are we forever enmeshed within the veil of appearances, cut off from direct apprehension of the world as it is in itself?

Since the seventeenth century these puzzling (and not wholly clear) questions have been brought within the ambit of a fresh field of force. For thenceforth such questions about the relations between appearance and reality overlapped with questions about the relationship between the scientific characterization of the nature of the physical world and our ordinary (conceptualized) perceptual experience. From Galileo onwards the mainstream of scientists and philosophers contended that the deliverances of physics are grossly at odds with mundane experience. The world appears to be multi-coloured, noisy, many-scented, hot or cold, but in reality there is only the rapid moving of colourless, invisible particles, of waves of air or electromagnetic radiation. The doctrine of the subjectivity of secondary qualities, viz. colour, sound, taste, smell, heat or cold, and texture, was re-awakened from its post-classical slumbers and became a permanent feature on the European intellectual landscape. The conception was, to the unblinkered mind, a very strange one indeed, opening a vast and unbridgeable gulf between the world as we experience it as being and the world as it is in itself. Whitehead sketched it nicely:

bodies are perceived as with qualities which in reality do not belong to them, qualities which in fact are purely the offspring of the mind. Thus nature gets credit which should in truth be reserved for ourselves; the rose for its scent; the nightingale for his song; and the sun for his radiance. The poets are entirely mistaken. They should address their lyrics to themselves, and should turn them into odes of self-congratulation on the excellency of the human mind. Nature is a dull affair, soundless, scentless, colourless; merely the hurrying of material, endlessly, meaninglessly.[1]

How did this curious picture emerge? And by what strange movements of thought does it hold us in thrall?

The modern origins of this conception are to be found in the

---

[1] A. N. Whitehead, *Science and the Modern World*, Lowell Lectures 1925 (Mentor Books, New York, 1948), p. 56. He did not, however, endorse this picture!

writings of Galileo, in particular in *The Assayer*. When we conceive of a material substance, he argued, we are constrained to think of it as bounded, as possessing a certain shape and size, as being located somewhere in space, somewhen in time, as moving or motionless, as being in contact with other such bodies or not being in contact, as being one or many. However, there is no necessity to conceive of material bodies as coloured, emitting sound, possessing any taste or fragrance. Indeed, did we not sense these sensible characteristics, neither reason nor understanding would, by themselves, arrive at such notions. From these considerations Galileo drew dramatic conclusions:

I think therefore that these tastes, odours, colours, etc., so far as their objective existence is concerned, are nothing but mere names for something which resides exclusively in our sensitive body, so that if the perceiving creature were removed, all of those qualities would be annihilated and abolished from existence. But just because we have given special names to these qualities, different from the names we have given to the primary and real properties, we are tempted into believing that the former really and truly exist as well as the latter.[2]

The picture had and retains a certain perverse charm. Think of a thunderstorm on a desert-island: huge trees are uprooted in the raging wind which blows in gusts of 50 mph but whistles not; they topple slowly, but soundlessly, to the ground; forks of lightning bathe the forest in light-waves, but the trees are not green – they merely reflect electro-magnetic radiation of between 575 and 491 nanometres!

Galileo's argument, however, is defective. From the fact that our very general concept of a material body is that of a *space-occupant,* and that this concept implies shape, size, spatio-temporal location, capacity for motion and contact with other bodies, as well as (he should have added) consisting of matter of one kind or another and hence as excluding other bodies from simultaneous occupancy of a given space, does not imply that material bodies are not coloured,

[2] Galileo, *The Assayer* (1623), excerpt trs. A. C. Danto, repr. in A. C. Danto and S. Morgenbesser (eds) *Philosophy of Science* (Meridian Books, Cleveland and New York, 1960), p. 28.

fragrant, noise-emitting or flavoured. At most it implies that we can conceive of a colourless, soundless, odourless and tasteless material object. But if we can conceive of a colourless material object, we can also *conceive* of a colourful one. Indeed, if it *makes sense* to say of an object, for example a piece of glass, that it is colourless, it must also *make sense* (although it may be false) to say of it that it is coloured. Only what can be coloured can be colourless. Of such things as numbers, aches and pains, rights and duties, indeed of events and actions it makes no sense to say that they are coloured (a colourful event is not a red, blue, or white happening) and hence too it makes no sense to say that they are colourless. For to deny of something that it is coloured is to imply that something would *count* as its being coloured. Hence even if it be true that possession of primary qualities is definitive of our formal concept of a material object, it in no sense follows that material objects, in themselves, are not coloured, noisy, smelly, etc.

It might, of course, be objected that this 'bipolar' principle of sense is incorrect. It surely makes sense, one might argue, to say of a rod that it has a length, of a lump of wood that it has a mass, or of an electron that it has an electric charge. But it makes *no sense* to deny such propositions; their negations are not false, but *nonsense*. If it were merely *false* to say 'I have a rod at home which has no length', then something would count as its being true; and someone who holds it to be false must explain what it would be for it to be true. But there is no such thing as a rod without length (an electron without charge or lump of wood without mass). Does this not show the principle to be wrong? No, it does not. We must distinguish between 'This rod has a length, namely eighteen inches' and 'This rod has a length'. The former seems to imply the latter, but it does not. 'This rod has a length, namely eighteen inches' is an empirical proposition which is false if the rod is more or less than eighteen inches long. It is equivalent to 'This rod is eighteen inches long, and eighteen inches is a length'. The second conjunct here is a purely grammatical proposition, which adds nothing to the first (hence the conjunction is comparable to '$p \& (q \vee \sim q)$'). But neither 'This rod has a length, namely eighteen inches' nor its equivalent 'This rod is eighteen inches long, and eighteen inches is a length' implies that this rod has a length. 'This rod has a length' should not be confused with the distinct grammatical proposition 'Every rod has a length', which expresses a *rule* of grammar, namely that anything that can be said to be a rod can also sensibly be said to have a certain length (and cannot sensibly be denied to have any length). The negation of a grammatical proposition is not a 'false' grammatical proposition; it is not a grammatical proposition at all. 'No rod has a length' does *not* express a rule of grammar. But note that '*This* rod has a length', unlike 'Every rod has a length', is not the expression of a rule for the use of 'rod' and 'length'. It is not an empirical proposition either, for could this rod have *lacked* a length? Indeed, it is best dismissed as nonsense.[3]

A defender of Galileo might see this exclusion of true grammatical propositions from the scope of the principle of 'sensicality of contradictories' as a concession. For now, he may say, he can surely argue that indeed it makes no *sense* to attribute colours, etc. to objects, just as it makes no sense to attribute pains to sticks or colours to numbers. But this is a Pyrrhic victory. First, his thesis ceases to be empirical. He can no longer claim to be penetrating the veil of appearances and achieving an insight into the true characteristics of objects in the world. At best he can claim a surview of a segment of our grammar, i.e. not a fresh achievement in physics at all. (Of course, he might be recommending a *different* grammar in the belief that it better reflects the nature of things. This cul-de-sac will be explored later.) Secondly, his contention would amount to the claim that it is a rule of our grammar that anything that can be said to be a material object *cannot* also be said to be coloured (or, indeed, colourless). But this is just wrong, indeed as wrong as the claim that it is a rule of our game of chess that the chess king moves four squares at a time. (He might *recommend* that we play such a game, or adopt such a grammatical convention. But if we did so, the king would not be what we call 'a chess king' and the game would not be our game of chess; and if we adopted his new style of speech, we would not be talking of *colours* at all.)

Indeed, one can go further. Far from his claim achieving a surview of our grammar in this respect, it completely misconstrues it. It is no

---

[3] This brief argument is derived from L. Wittgenstein, *Philosophical Investigations* (Blackwell, Oxford, 1953) §§ 251–2 and *Philosophical Grammar* (Blackwell, Oxford, 1974) p. 129. For more elaborate treatment see G. P. Baker and P. M. S. Hacker, *Wittgenstein: Rules, Grammar and Necessity* (Blackwell, Oxford, 1986), pp. 263–347.

less part of our concept of a material object that it be either coloured or colourless (i.e. transparent and without colour), odorous or odourless, flavourful or tasteless, than that it possess primary qualities, for example be in motion or be motionless. What is, of course, true is that whereas a material object can be colourless and motionless, like the glass paperweight on my desk, it cannot lack length, height and breadth, i.e. extension in three dimensions, nor can it fail to consist of matter. For then it would no longer be an occupant of space.[4] The *possibility* of being coloured, like the *possibility* of moving, is definitive of our concept of a material object, but it is the *actuality* of some extensive qualities (not their mere 'possibility') that is partly constitutive of such objects.

The defect of Galileo's argument was perhaps masked from view by the fact that it was interwoven in the same discussion with a different consideration. Perceptions, he argued, are produced through *impact* of bodies (or waves) upon our sensitive organs. If we pass a feather over a body, whether inanimate or sensitive, the mechanical action of the feather on the body will be identical. But if the feather be passed over the nostrils or eyes of a sensitive creature, it will produce 'an almost intolerable titillation'. It is obvious, Galileo argued, that

this titillation is completely ours and not the feather's, so that if the living sensing body were removed, nothing would remain of the titillation but an empty name. And I believe that many other qualities, such as taste, odour, colour, and so on, often predicated of natural bodies, have a similar and no greater existence than this.[5]

Galileo applied this reasoning not only to tactile qualities in general, but to the other sensible (secondary) qualities. Tastes and odours *are caused in us* by the impact of minute particles upon the tongue or

---

[4] What of atomic and sub-atomic particles? They surely are space-occupants, and yet it makes no sense to attribute secondary qualities to them, or to claim that they consist of some stuff or other – on the contrary, it is of these that all stuff is constituted. This is correct, but precisely because of this they are doubtful members of the category of material objects (in this respect, though for different reasons, they are like shadows, rainbows, images in mirrors). Our categorial concepts were not tailored by an Invisible Hand to fit the contours of the meaning-body of terms in particle-physics.

[5] Galileo, *The Assayer,* pp. 28–9.

nostrils. Sounds 'are produced in us and felt' when a rapid vibration of air causes motion of our eardrum. In all such cases, a sensible affection is generated in us by the movement of objects outside us,

But I cannot believe that there exists in external bodies anything other than their size, shape, or motion (slow or rapid), which could excite in us our tastes, sounds and odours. And indeed I should judge that if ears, tongues and noses be taken away, the number, shape and motion of bodies would remain, but not their tastes, sounds and odours. The latter, external to the living creature, I believe to be nothing but mere names, just as . . . I asserted tickling and titillation to be, if the armpit or the sensitive skin inside the nose were removed.[6]

Similar considerations apply, he argued, to heat, which is wholly 'subjective'. There exists in a fire a multitude of particles with shape, number, movement, power of penetration and contact, but no *further* quality which we call 'heat'.

It is this nascent and, in Galileo's day, speculative empirical theory of perception that provided the fulcrum to prise apart appearance and reality. Analysis and criticism of this conception will be deferred until a more complete picture has been elaborated, but it is worth noting some of the salient features of Galileo's account.

First, to perceive is to have sensible excitations caused in a perceiver by the action of material objects. The empirical, causal, explanation of perceptual mechanisms seemed to force the conclusion that the perception of an object or perceptual quality of an object is the final link in a causal chain commencing with the impact of an object or of 'corpuscles' or waves upon the body and perceptual organs of the perceiver.

Secondly, the paradigm of perception is taken to be sensation resulting from mechanical action (for example tickling). Feeling tactile qualities such as roughness or smoothness and other textural properties is held to be no different in principle from feeling tickles and like sensations. Furthermore, hearing sounds, tasting tastes, smelling smells are severally conceived on the model of tactile perception.

---

[6] Ibid., p. 30. Note the odd vacillation between 'our tastes . . .' and 'their tastes . . .'

Thirdly, sensible qualities such as colour, taste, smell, sound and heat or cold are conceived to be 'in us'. They are produced in us by the action of objects on our sense organs. Hence they are not in any sense real properties of objects. Independently of perceivers, nothing in the world can coherently be thought to be hot or cold, coloured, smelly or noisy.

Galileo's conception greatly influenced Descartes, who expanded and enriched it. As empirical scientist he made considerable strides forward in investigating the mechanisms of perception, especially of vision. As philosopher and metaphysician he elaborated Galileo's rudimentary remarks in his sophisticated dualist picture of the relation between the mental and the physical and in his representative theory of perception.

Like Galileo, Descartes held that objects in themselves have only geometrical and numerical properties. The essence of body is extension. Material objects have extensive magnitudes, size, shape, are in motion or at rest. They are composed of (infinitely divisible) material parts *(partes materiae)*, the shapes and motion of which give rise to our varied perceptual experiences. Sensory perceptions are causal consequences of the mechanical action of bodies (including sound-waves or 'vibrations' in the air and light rays) upon our organs of perception. Like Galileo, Descartes drew no sharp distinction between sensation and perceptual experiences, between having tickles, twinges or pains and seeing (or, more accurately, seeming to see) objects, hearing (or seeming to hear) sounds, and, *mutatis mutandis,* tasting, smelling or feeling. That which has sensations or perceptions is not the sensory organ, nor is it the body, but rather the soul: it is the soul which sees, and not the eye, and 'it does not see directly, but only by means of the brain'.[7] The principal seat of the soul, Descartes held, is in the brain, and it 'will have different sensations corresponding to the different ways in which the entrances to the pores in the internal surface of the brain are opened by means of the nerves'; thus injury to the body causes 'a movement in the brain

[7] Descartes, *Optics,* repr. in *The Philosophical Writings of Descartes,* trs. J. Cottingham, R. Stoothoff, D. Murdoch (Cambridge University Press, Cambridge, 1985), vol. 1, p. 172; AT VI, 141. (Subsequent references will be abbreviated to CSM 1 or 2 and references to the Adam and Tannery edition *Oeuvres de Descartes* (revised edition, Paris: Vrin/C.N.R.S., 1964–76) will be abbreviated to AT and given in parentheses.)

which gives occasion for the soul . . . to have the sensation of *pain'* and 'according to the various other ways in which they are stimulated, the fibres will cause the soul to perceive all the other qualities belonging to touch in general, such as *moisture, dryness, weight* and the like'.[8] Similar reasoning was, rather perfunctorily, applied to our perception of other sensible qualities.

What is the relationship between the sensory perceptions of the soul and the properties of the objects that cause them? Descartes employed much the same reasoning (and examples) as Galileo to show that the sensory perceptions need not, and often do not, resemble that in the object which causes them. If we pass a feather over our lips we feel ourselves being tickled, but no one thinks that the 'idea' of tickling we experience resembles anything in the feather. A strap pressing harshly into our flesh produces in us a sensation of pain, but there is nothing in the strap which is like the felt pain. So too, nothing in a hot object resembles the sensation of heat it gives us, rather 'this sensation may be produced in us by anything that can set up various motions' in our body.[9] Sensations are best thought of as *signs* of that which causes them, and *qua* signs they need not, though they may, resemble what they signify. Descartes articulated this conception in a simile which was to echo down the ages:

if words, which signify nothing except by human convention, suffice to make us think of things to which they bear no resemblance, then why could nature not also have established some sign which would make us have the sensation of light even if the sign contained nothing in itself which is similar to this sensation? Is it not thus that nature has established laughter and tears, to make us read joy and sadness on the faces of men?[10]

Nevertheless, some kinds of sensory perceptions do resemble their causes in objects, and others do not. In particular, our perceptions of

[8] Descartes, *Treatise on Man,* CSM 1, pp. 102f. (AT XI, 143–4).
[9] Descartes, *The World or Treatise on Light,* CSM 1, p. 84 (cf. p. 82); (AT XI, 10: cf. 6)
[10] Ibid., p. 81 (AT XI, 4). The suggestion that a neural stimulus which causes an idea in the mind stands to the idea in a similar (but non-conventional) relation to that between a word and the 'idea' it signifies was picked up by Glanvil, Cudworth and Bonnet. See J. W. Youlton, *Perceptual Acquaintance* (Blackwell, Oxford, 1984), pp. 27ff.

secondary qualities (to use non-Cartesian terminology) do not. To perceive light, colour, smell, taste, sound, heat or cold is to have certain sensations. Are the objects we perceive then *not* coloured, odorous, noisy, flavourful, hot or cold? In one sense, Descartes, like Galileo, was convinced that they are not. There is no need to suppose, he argued, that 'there is something in the objects which resembles the ideas or sensations [of light and colour] that we have of them',[11] indeed, 'if the sense of hearing transmitted to our mind the true image of its object then, instead of making us conceive the sound, it would have to make us conceive the motion of the parts of the air which is then vibrating against our ears'.[12] Unlike Galileo, however, Descartes added a further element to the emerging picture. Although colours, sounds, tastes, etc. do not exist in objects as we apprehend them, nevertheless they can be said to be 'simply various dispositions in those objects in the shapes, sizes, positions and movements of their parts which make them able to set up various kinds of motions in our nerves [which are required to produce all the various sensations in our soul].'[13] This articulation introduces an ambiguity in the alleged meanings of predicates of secondary qualities which was to loom large in the writings of Descartes' successors. On the one hand, names of secondary qualities signified those properties we experience in perception precisely as we conceive them to be, only contrary to our ordinary beliefs they are not properties of objects but of our 'subjective' perceptions. On the other hand they signify properties of objects as we take them to, only those properties are not at all as we conceive them to be, but are rather the particulate structure (disposition or manner of arrangement) and motion of the constituent parts of an object in virtue of which it has the power to affect our sensibility in such-and-such ways.

Primary qualities, however, are on a different level. Our perceptions of shape, size and movement do correspond (at least some of the time) with objective, mind-independent, features of

---

[11] Descartes, *Optics,* CSM 1, p. 153 (AT VI, 85)

[12] Descartes, *The World or Treatise on Light* CSM 1, p. 82 (AT XI, 5).

[13] Descartes, *Principles of Philosophy,* CSM 1, p. 285 (AT VIII A, 323). The final bracketed clause is not in Descartes' original Latin text of 1644, but was added, probably with Descartes' approval, in the 1647 French translation of the *Principles* made by Claude Picot.

objects. Descartes' overt arguments for thus distinguishing matters were three.

First, we can detect size, shape and motion with more than one sense, viz. sight and touch (and in the case of motion, also hearing), whereas the other qualities can be detected only by one sense.[14] This is roughly correct, but one may well have qualms. One can surely see that a red-hot poker is hot or that it is a cold day outside (snow is falling and the window is frosty). Do objects not look hot or cold occasionally, and does ripe fruit not look sweet? A defender of Descartes might concede this, but insist that in these cases we are dealing with an inductive correlation between visual features and thermal or gustatory properties that are *essentially* felt or tasted and not, strictly speaking, seen. Indeed the inductive correlation (viz. when bananas are *sweet,* they typically look like *that* ↗) presupposes this very point, for it could not be established independently of tasting the gustatory quality or feeling the thermal one. We might concede that it is a grammatical truth that one cannot feel the cold (beyond the window) with one's eyes or taste the fruit by looking at it; and we might also grant that the use of 'looks sweet' (said of edibles) or 'looks cold' presupposes the use of 'sweet' and 'cold' in gustatory and tactile judgements. We need not concede that one cannot see heat, but only that we see heat in the sense in which we see danger ahead. Shelving these qualms, however, we should query why the detectability of a perceptual quality by one sense alone (as explained) is thought to imply the mind-dependence of the quality or to suggest that the quality as we apprehend it is really a property of our sensations. In the world of the blind would a Cartesian philosopher be disposed to argue that size and shape are mind-dependent or subjective? Accessibility to more than one sense is not obviously a sufficient condition of objectivity either, for is it not possible to have a hallucination that is both tactile and visual, or both olfactory and gustatory? That a certain property is detectable only by one sense does not mean that it is 'subjective'. *Ex hypothesi* the confirmation of a judgement about the instantiation of such a property cannot be by way of an alternative sensory modality. But it does not follow that such a judgement cannot be checked, for example by looking again in better light, or asking someone else.

[14] Ibid., p. 286 (AT VIII A, 323–4).

Descartes' second argument was that the primary qualities can be distinctly imagined and understood by us, whereas the 'images' we have of the other qualities 'are always confused, and we do not know what they really are'.[15] The argument is opaque. Elsewhere Descartes argued that the ideas of heat and cold lack clarity and distinctness, in as much as we cannot detect from them whether cold is merely the absence of heat or heat the absence of cold, whether both are real qualities or neither are.[16] Evidently absence or presence of clarity and distinctness here cannot signify resistance to Cartesian doubt, since perceptual error with regard to shape or motion is common. It seems rather that the absence of clarity and distinctness signifies the fact that secondary qualities are not susceptible to mathematicization. In the *Principles of Philosophy* he argued: 'The only principles which I accept, or require, in physics are those of geometry and pure mathematics; these principles explain all natural phenomena, and enable us to provide certain demonstrations regarding them.'[17] Descartes' conception of a purely quantitative science of nature, like Galileo's, presaged the development of modern physical sciences, but is there any reason to suppose that susceptibility to numerical measurement is a mark of objectivity? The idea is clearly an ancient one, with powerful Pythagorean and rationalist appeal. Plato argued in this vein in the *Republic* (602d–603a):

> And have not measuring and numbering and weighing proved to be most gracious aids to prevent the domination in our soul of the apparently greater or less or more or heavier, and to give the control to that which has reckoned and numbered or even weighed.
> Certainly.
> But this surely would be the function of the part of the soul that reasons and calculates.
> Why, yes, of that.
> And often when this has measured and declares that certain things are larger or that some are smaller than the others or equal, there is at the same time an appearance of the contrary.
> Yes.

[15]   Ibid.
[16]   Descartes, *Meditations on First Philosophy*, III, CSM 2, p. 30 (AT VII, 43–4).
[17]   Descartes, *Principles of Philosophy* CSM 1, p. 247 (AT VIII A, 78).

And did we not say that it is impossible for the same thing at one time to hold contradictory opinions about the same thing?

And we were right in affirming that.

The part of the soul, then, that affirms in contradiction of measurement could not be the same with that which conforms to it.

Why no.

But, further, that which puts its trust in measurement and reckoning must be the best part of the soul.

This reasoning must have appealed to Descartes. He delimited the domain of science to the investigation of space-matter (*res extensa*), the essence of which is extensive magnitude and motion or rest. He characterized its method as essentially quantitative. The previously quoted passage from the *Principles* continues boldly:

I recognize no matter in corporeal things apart from that which the geometers call quantity, and take as the object of their demonstrations, i.e. that to which every kind of division, shape and motion is applicable. Moreover, my consideration of such matter involves absolutely nothing apart from these divisions, shapes and motions; and even with regard to these, I will admit as true only what has been deduced from indubitable common notions so evidently that it is fit to be considered as a mathematical demonstration. And since all natural phenomena can be explained in this way, as will become clear in what follows, I do not think that any other principles are either admissible or desirable in physics.

Finally, like Plato, Descartes thought that the faculty that is concerned with quantity and quantitative relations is epistemically superior to the senses, that are concerned with appearances. But this vision, fruitful though it has been for the progress of the physical sciences, is rooted in confusion. It is true that apparent magnitude (something's *looking* larger, more distant, etc. than something else) is checkable and correctible by measuring. But, of course, measurement is only possible if the measuring device is itself perceptible, and if it is perceptibly applied correctly to what is measured (see below, p. 119). Apparent colour, taste or sound is, as previously noted, checkable (and errors of judgement correctible) by looking again in better light, etc.; absence of a metric is irrelevant. Furthermore, Descartes clearly erred in supposing that because physics employs mathematical techniques it enjoys the certainty of mathematical propositions, and was equally wrong in supposing that no judgements concerning non-quantifiable qualities could possess that sort of certainty. The certainty of the propositions of pure mathematics *excludes* doubt by the fiat of a norm of representation (mathematics is the *grammar* of measurement), whereas the certainty of well-established propositions of physics (which is not of a lesser *degree,* but rather of a different *kind) refutes* doubt by observation, experiment and explanation. Propositions of applied mathematics, being empirical, do not partake of the 'certainty' of mathematical propositions which are norms of representation. On the other hand, propositions such as 'Red is darker than pink', 'Nothing can be red and green all over simultaneously', 'There is no transparent white glass', although they are concerned with colours, do have the 'certainty' which mesmerized Descartes, for they too are expressions of norms of representation. Lastly, it is surely a confusion to suppose that susceptibility to measurement is a mark of objectivity. The measurement of preference or of popularity ratings (of politicians, books, etc.) does not make the likings or dislikings any the less 'subjective'. And conversely, the fact that indefinitely many empirical propositions do not mention or involve any measurement does not derogate in the least from their 'objectivity'. What is, however, true is that the terms 'objective' and 'subjective' are exceedingly opaque, ambivalent and best eschewed.

Descartes' third argument paralleled Galileo's, viz.

that nothing whatever belongs to the concept of body except the fact that it is something which has length, breadth and depth and is capable of various shapes and motions; moreover, these shapes and motions are merely modes which no power whatever can cause to exist apart from body. But colours, smells, tastes and so on, are, I observed, merely certain sensations which exist in my thought, and are as different from bodies as pain is different from the shape and motion of the weapon which produces it.[18]

This, as we have seen, is unsatisfactory. That possession of extensive magnitudes partially defines the concept of body does not show that being coloured is not a property of (most) bodies. It is not true that *only* bodies have extensive magnitudes (that shape and motion are

---

[18] Descartes, *Replies to the Sixth Set of Objections,* CSM 2, p. 297 (AT VII, 440)

always and essentially the shapes and motions *of* some body), since rainbows have a shape, shadows can move, and spaces between bodies have length or breadth.[19] Similarly, colours are typically colours *of* bodies, but a red object may cast a pink shadow on an adjacent white surface, rainbows exemplify all the colours of the spectrum, and the sky is blue.

These three arguments supporting Descartes' distinction are patently feeble. It is arguable that what moved him was the much more general underlying vision of the nature of physics on the one hand and a model of perception on the other. The former has been noted above: Descartes' commitment to mathematical physics, his vision that all natural phenomena can be explained in arithmetical and geometrical terms, that mechanical motion is the fundamental principle of the physical universe, provided one main motive for arguing that secondary qualities are not, as we apprehend them, objective properties of objects. The second general consideration parallels Galileo's argument. It is the belief that the mechanisms of perception can themselves be explained in mechanical terms. To this extent, the conception of perception was tailor-made for the vision of physics, of method in the physical sciences, and for the Cartesian conception of the relation between the mental and the physical. It is important that the paradigm which guided Descartes' thoughts on this subject is that of the causation of pain:

A sword strikes our body and cuts it; but the ensuing pain is completely different from the local motion of the sword or of the body that is cut – as different as colour or sound or smell or taste. We clearly see, then, that the sensation of pain is excited in us merely by the local motion of some parts of our body in contact with another body; so we may conclude that the nature of our mind is such that it can be subject to all the other sensations merely as a result of other local motions.[20]

Galileo's paradigm was the sensation of tickling caused by impact, and he modelled his schematic account of the perception of colour,

---

[19] This criticism is not wholly fair to Descartes, since he equated space and matter. But that is no merit in his position, merely a further confusion.
[20] Descartes, *Principles of Philosophy*, CSM 1, p. 284 (AT VIII A, 321); see also, with particular reference to the sensation of tickling, Descartes, *The World*, CSM 1, p. 82 (AT XI, 6–7).

sound, taste and smell on this model. Descartes' paradigm is likewise a *sensation*, similarly caused. We shall see later that this assimilation of perception to sensation is pregnant with confusion.

According to Descartes our perceptual experiences are caused by impact and motion upon our sensory organs, which generate a pressure or movement in our nerves which is immediately transmitted to the brain. In the brain, Descartes identified the pineal gland as the organ which receives and 'synthesizes' the impressions or images transmitted from the sensory organs. It is in the pineal gland that 'the two images coming from a single object through the two eyes, or the two impressions coming from a single object through the double organs of any other sense [for example hands or ears], can come together in a single image or impression before reaching the soul, so that they do not present to it two objects instead of one'.[21] These images or figures 'which are traced in the spirits on the surface of the gland' are 'the forms of images which the rational soul united to this machine will consider directly when it imagines some object or perceives it by the senses'.[22]

Descartes cautioned against two errors. First, one should not assume that in order to have sensory perceptions, the soul must contemplate images transmitted by objects to the brain as conceived by scholastic doctrines of 'intentional forms'. On that conception, the object perceived must, in some sense, form an image, transmit it to and impress it upon the sense organ, which in turn must convey the image along the nerves to the brain. This 'intentional form' must exactly resemble what it is an image of. Descartes objected to this on three grounds: (i) the supposition that there are, as he put it, 'little images flitting through the air',[23] struck him as absurd. What passes through the air are light rays which by means of pressure produce an image on the retina, but the light rays are not *vehicles* for images; (ii) the production of a corresponding image on the pineal gland is not effected by a *transportation* of an image along the nerve fibres, rather, 'when an external organ is stimulated by an object, the figure it receives is conveyed at one and the same moment to [the locus of the

[21] Descartes, *The Passions of the Soul*, CSM 1, p. 340 (AT XI, 353).
[22] Descartes, *Treatise on Man*, CSM 1, p. 106 (AT XI, 119).
[23] Descartes, *Optics*. CSM 1, p. 154 (AT VI, 85).

'common' sense in the brain,[24] viz. the pineal gland] without any entity passing from the one to the other',[25] just as the motion of the point of a pen while writing is transmitted simultaneously to the whole pen without any entity moving through it; (iii) an image does not have to resemble what it represents in all respects, but only in some. Descartes did not doubt that images *are* produced in the pineal gland. The problem, as he conceived it, is not how the images can resemble objects, but rather 'how they can enable the soul to have sensory perceptions of all the various qualities of the objects to which they correspond'.[26] He intimated (but did not elaborate) that it suffices that the neural image have the same 'logical multiplicity' as what it represents: 'This is what occasions his soul to have sensory perceptions of just as many different qualities in these bodies as there are differences in the movements caused by them in his brain'.[27]

Secondly, Descartes warned that although the picture generated in the brain does bear some resemblance to its cause, viz. the object perceived, the resultant sensory perception is not caused by the resemblance. For that would require 'yet other eyes within our brain with which we could perceive it'.[28] Rather, it is the movements composing the picture which, by acting directly upon the soul which is intimately connected with the pineal gland, cause the soul to have the sensations it has.

The warnings are apt, but the caution is insufficient. Descartes was right in thinking that perceiving involves stimulation of the nerves of the perceptual organs, that the stimulus causes changes in the brain even though no image moves along the nerves, and right in conjecturing that our perceptual capacities depend on the functioning of localized groups of cells in the brain. He was wrong to identify the pineal gland as the locus of 'common' sense, and wrong to think that an image corresponding to and resembling the retinal image is reconstituted in the brain. These are errors of fact. He was right to caution that whatever occurs in the brain that enables us to see what

---

[24] The 'common' sense was conceived by Aristotle as the faculty which synthesizes the impressions received by the five senses, see *De Anima*, III, I, 425ª 14.
[25] Descartes, *Rules for the Direction of the Mind*, CSM 1, p. 41 (AT X, 414).
[26] Descartes, *Optics*, CSM 1, p. 166 (AT VI, 113–14).
[27] Ibid., p. 166 (AT VI, 114).
[28] Ibid., p. 167 (AT VI, 130).

we see, our seeing cannot be explained by reference to *observation* of brain events (such as the conjectured appearance of an image on the pineal gland), since that would require 'yet other eyes within our brain'. He was, however, conceptually confused in suggesting (i) that 'images' or 'impressions' coming from double organs of sense must be united in the brain *in order that* the soul should not be presented with two objects instead of one, or that the soul 'considers directly' the forms or images in the brain when it perceives an object, and (ii) that it is the *soul* that perceives.

The first error presupposes precisely what he had warned against, for only if the images or impressions are *perceived* by the soul would there be any reason for supposing that the two images would result in double-vision or 'double-hearing'. But since neither images nor neural excitations are perceived by the perceiving agent, it is not *necessary* that there be one image, or, indeed, *any* image. What precisely occurs in the cortex is a matter for factual investigation.

The second error is to attribute perceptual predicates to the *soul* (or the mind, or the brain). The conceptual confusion involved has been picturesquely named the 'Homunculus Fallacy' by Anthony Kenny.[29] Kenny's insight was inspired by a remark of Wittgenstein's: 'only of a living human being and what resembles (behaves like) a living human being can one say: it has sensations; it sees, is blind; hears; is deaf; is conscious or unconscious'.[30] Wittgenstein was drawing our attention to the fact that we say of a creature that it perceives or lacks perceptual capacities, is conscious or unconscious only if it is of a kind that does or can display certain patterns of *behaviour* in complex circumstances which constitute grounds for saying that it sees or hears (and the different patterns of behaviour license the judgement that it is blind or deaf). Scientists can, to be sure, investigate the organic perceptual mechanisms of a perceiving creature, but to do so they must first establish that the creature they are investigating *can perceive*. For this it is not sufficient to establish the sensitivity of a given organ to, say, light or sound; rather one must establish that it is a *perceptual* organ. It must be an organ the creature uses in discerning features of its environment as it pursues its goals and shuns those

---

[29] A. J. P. Kenny, 'The homunculus fallacy' (1971), repr. in his *The Legacy of Wittgenstein* (Blackwell, Oxford, 1985).
[30] Wittgenstein, *Philosophical Investigations,* § 281.

things it apprehends as dangerous or threatening. That a creature can perceive is established by observing its behaviour, its discriminatory, conative and affective responses to visibilia, audibilia, etc., its use of its perceptual organs in discerning objects, sounds, smells or warmth in its environment. It is not the eye, brain, mind or soul that perceives, but, as the Aristotelian tradition prior to Descartes insisted, the living creature; and we determine *that* it perceives by observing its *behaviour* in appropriate circumstances. It is the behaviour of the animal that logically (or grammatically) justifies us in saying of the animal that *it* sees, hears or feels. Kenny extended this insight: one commits the homunculus fallacy when one extends predicates which can only intelligibly be applied to a human being (or sentient creature) as a whole to parts of the creature. Some predicates, of course, can intelligibly be applied to a whole creature and to its parts: if I am sunburnt all over, my limbs are sunburnt too. Some predicates can, in certain contexts, be *extended* from application to the whole creature to its parts: if I grip the banisters tightly, my hand can be said to grip the banisters tightly (though note that if my hand moves, it does *not* follow that I moved my hand). Psychological verbs, however, are perspicuously different. From the fact that I want something, it not only does not follow that some part of my body wants something (although it may *need* something) but it does not make *sense* to attribute a desire to anything short of the creature as a whole. When I am angry or joyous no part of me is thus overwhelmed with emotion, although my face and demeanour will express anger or joy. (But a joyous face is not a face that feels joyful, it is a face that manifests a person's joyful feelings.) Similar considerations apply to perceptual verbs. Descartes contravened the bounds of *sense* in claiming that it is the *soul* that sees, hears, tastes, smells and feels pains. Neither the soul nor the mind can manifest visual discriminatory behaviour; the soul cannot look, peer, spot or glimpse and the mind cannot sniff, savour food upon the tongue, finger the soft texture of velvet. The 'cannot' here is *logical*, signifying not *inability*, but senselessness, i.e. there is no such thing as a mind or soul acting thus. It is noteworthy that the homunculus fallacy is rife in the writings of contemporary psychologists and neurophysiologists who endeavour to explain the mechanisms of perception by attributing cognitive capacities and their exercise to the *brain*.

Descartes conceived of the soul as a part or constituent of a human person, for he thought of a person as a combination of two substances, the material body and the immaterial soul, which interact inexplicably via the pineal gland. The moderns conceive of a person as a single material substance, but endeavour to explain a person's perceptual capacities and their excercise by fallaciously attributing cognitive predicates which can only intelligibly be predicated of persons to their brains and indeed parts of their brains. In this sense modern science has replaced Cartesian mind/body dualism with an isomorphic 'brain/body dualism' which perpetuates the Cartesian fallacies.

2 The British contribution

In a brief remark in the 'Reply to the Sixth Set of Objections', Descartes railed against the doctrine of *real accidents*. Accidents are modes of substances, not substances in their own right. They cannot exist save as qualifying a substance, and hence cannot be 'separated' from the substance which is their 'subject'. The idea of a 'real accident' conceived as an independent entity, separable from the substance whose accident it is, is incoherent. The doctrine which Descartes was criticizing is not to be found in Aristotle or in Aquinas (who, indeed, emphasized this very point),[31] but in the writings of Descartes' contemporaries. Alchemists and latter-day schoolmen misinterpreted Aristotelian analytical claims concerning the persistence, change, transformation and dissolution of substances, transforming these conceptual contentions into putative empirical explanations of change. Descartes had little to say on the issue, but it looms large in the writings of Robert Boyle, in particular in his work *The Origin of Forms and Qualities according to the Corpuscular Philosophy* (1666). This work is the fountainhead of the British empiricists' preoccupation with the doctrines of primary and secondary qualities.[32] What Boyle added to the Galilean and Cartesian

---

[31] Cf. A. J. P. Kenny, *Descartes* (Random House, New York, 1968) pp. 210ff; Kenny is, I think, mistaken in suggesting that this is an argument in support of the 'subjectivity' of secondary qualities in Descartes.
[32] P. Alexander, *Ideas, Qualities and Corpuscles; Locke and Boyle on the External World*

conceptions was a more elaborate corpuscularian foundation for the kinds of physical explanations they had envisaged for physical phenomena and our perception of them.

Conceiving of a property or 'accident' of a substance which can change without the substance ceasing to exist as one of its 'forms' which 'inform' its matter, and of that feature of it without which it will not be what it is as its 'substantial form', the seventeenth-century 'schoolmen' offered explanations of why a certain substance has a given property by reference to the presence in it of a 'real accident'. Transformation of substances (stuffs) was conceived to be effected by inducing the qualities of one substance to transfer to another. Thus if lead was to be transmuted into gold, it had to have super-added to its existing qualities of being metallic, heavy and malleable the further quality of, for example, being yellow. The alchemists thought of their quest as the discovery of techniques for *transferring qualities* from one substance to another. Boyle's criticism of this doctrine of 'real accidents' was that illegitimately reified properties were treated as if they were Aristotelian *substantial forms* which make a thing what it is. It will not do to offer as an explanation of what makes white things white that they contain the form of whiteness which makes whatever it is joined to white.[33] This is not only vacuous, but also it is tantamount to treating qualities or forms as if they were constituents or ingredients of a stuff, i.e. as if they were themselves substances (and in this sense 'real' accidents).[34] It is this misconception that generates the mistaken idea that transformation of substances is explicable by the transference of qualities. Change is *described* by the substitution of predicates in the description, as when we say that the leaf was green and is now yellow, but it is not *explained* but merely *redescribed* by saying that the greenness was replaced by yellowness.

The purpose of Boyle's treatise on *The Origin of Forms and Qualities according to the Corpuscular Philosophy* was to replace the schoolmen's

---

(Cambridge University Press, Cambridge, 1985) is most helpful on Boyle and his influence on Locke.

[33] Boyle, *The Origin of Forms and Qualities according to the Corpuscular Philosophy*, in *Works*, vol. II (London, 1744), p. 459.

[34] It is important to note that the contrast between accident or quality and 'real' accident or quality is not between merely apparent and actual qualities, but rather between the concept of a quality and the pseudo-concept of a substantial, reified quality.

degenerate Aristotelianism by physical (mechanical) explanations of a genuinely causal character. To this end Boyle developed what was in effect a wholly a priori theory of the corpuscularian structure of matter. Although it turned out to be far from the truth (being essentially mechanical rather than chemical), it paved the way for the later development of fruitful scientific hypotheses which led in due course to the emergence of modern chemistry.

Matter and motion are 'the two grand and most catholick principles of bodies', Boyle argued; each fragment of matter must have some shape and size, and must be capable of moving. The smallest corpuscles Boyle called *minima* or *prima naturalia*. They have shape, size and mobility, and though divisible 'in thought' (unlike the Democritean atom) are physically indivisible or 'impenetrable' in as much as there are no spaces within them by the penetration of which they might be divided. In this sense they are absolutely 'solid' or dense. These characteristics are the *primary qualities* of all matter, i.e. qualities attributable to every particle of matter. All other qualities and 'forms', Boyle held, are explicable in terms of arrangements of corpuscles possessing these primary qualities. In particular, *texture,* i.e. the structure of an array of corpuscles, will explain the overt properties of perceptible material objects (although, since 'texture', thus conceived, is not a property of an individual corpuscle, it is not a primary quality). It was in terms of this a priori theory of matter[35] that Boyle defended the claim that the sensible qualities (i.e. the qualities *as sensed* by us) of colour, taste, odour, sound, heat or cold are not qualities (let alone 'real accidents') of bodies at all:

we have been from our infancy apt to imagine, that these sensible qualities are real beings in the objects they denominate, and have the faculty or power to work such and such things . . . whereas . . . there is in the body to which the sensible qualities are attributed, nothing of real and physical, but the size,

---

[35] Understandably it never occurred to Boyle or to anyone else at the time that the properties of having a shape or consisting of matter are no more absolutely dissective than the property of being a certain colour, warmth or taste. It is noteworthy that the a priori theory of matter was *one* ground for the misconceptions concerning the status of secondary qualities. It is even more important to note that our contemporary well-established *empirical* theories of matter do *not* confirm the seventeenth-century conception of (secondary) perceptual qualities, but are rather enmeshed in the very same *conceptual* (non-empirical) confusions.

shape and motion or rest of its component particles, together with that texture of the whole, which results from their being so contrived as they are; nor is it necessary they should have in them anything more, like to the ideas they occasion in us.[36]

His reasoning here wrongly presupposes two theses. First, that it *makes sense* to ask whether the colour we see, the sound we hear, the taste we taste *resembles* a quality in the object perceived. Secondly, because we can explain the mechanisms involved in our perceiving what (properties of objects) we perceive by reference to *other* properties of objects, for example propensity to reflect certain kinds of light, therefore there is no need to suppose that the perceived objects have the properties we perceive them as having. Both theses are misguided.

It makes sense to ask whether this leaf resembles that leaf in colour, or whether the two leaves have the same colour. It makes sense to ask whether this apple tastes the same as that apple, or whether it has a similar but not identical taste. It does not, however, make sense to ask whether the colour I saw when I looked at the leaf *resembles* the colour of the leaf or even whether it is *the same as* the colour of the leaf. For if I saw the colour of the leaf, then the colour I saw was the colour of the leaf, not the colour of some other object that might resemble or be the same colour as the leaf. (It makes no sense to say of the colour of the leaf that it resembles itself, let alone that it is the same colour as itself.) Of course, when I glanced at the leaf it may have looked dark green to me, even though it is light green. And surely dark green resembles light green (and does not resemble red)! Indeed, but it does not follow that the colour I saw resembles the colour of the object I saw, but only that the colour *as* I saw it, i.e. as it struck me or appeared to me, resembles the colour of the leaf. Here the characterization of the leaf I saw as dark green and the characterization of how it struck me, viz. as light green, bear a resemblance. But this 'resemblance' is an affinity between two *concepts* (viz. light green and dark green) *not between two coloured objects,* for, of course, there is only one coloured object in question. (To make the same point slightly differently: the 'resemblance' in

---

[36] Boyle, *Origin of Forms,* p. 466.

question consists in the internal relation between light green and dark green, and that in turn is constituted by the grammatical fact that both are determinates of a single (relative) determinable.) Berkeley criticized a similar move made by Locke on the grounds that an idea can resemble nothing but an idea, and in particular cannot resemble, in respect of a perceptible quality, something in principle imperceptible. I am suggesting the converse of this, viz. that one coloured *object* may resemble or be identical with another in respect of colour; that, in a different sense, one colour may resemble another (as red resembles pink), but that *in neither sense* can something's looking green to a person be said to *resemble* its being green. Of course an object may look to A exactly as it is; alternatively, how it looks to him may approximate to how it is. But that is ill-expressed by saying that how it looks to him *resembles* how it is. (My conjecture may approximate to the facts, but it does not *resemble* them!)

The second flaw in Boyle's reasoning is the supposition that, because we can explain the physiological processes requisite for our perception of colours, tastes, sounds, etc. by reference to 'textures' or corpuscularian (molecular) structures, light- or sound-waves, *therefore* there is no need to attribute such properties to the objects perceived. Many confusions are interwoven here, and they will be examined at length in the sequel. For the moment two observations must suffice. First, the corpuscularian explanation which Boyle sapiently envisaged is meant to explain, without reference to occult 'real accidents', what makes white things white, sweet things sweet, warm things warm. The fact that such explanations are effected in terms of molecular or atomic structures and their properties does not explain away or show to be merely apparent the perceptual qualities in question. In his eagerness to prove that colours, smells, tastes, warmth or cold are not 'real accidents' of objects, Boyle was induced to think that they are not really accidents. And that conclusion, as will be argued throughout this book, is wholly misguided. Secondly, the fact that an explanation of our perceptual mechanisms is likewise effected in (neural, electro-chemical) terms that themselves involve no perceptual qualities of the kind in question does not show that what we perceive in perceiving noisy, odorous or colourful objects are not precisely those perceptual qualities of the objects themselves.

In support of his claim Boyle appealed to much the same arguments as had been rehearsed by Galileo and Descartes, assimilating (as they had done) perception and sensation. Thus, a pin run through one's finger causes pain, but 'there is no distinct quality in the pin answerable to what I am apt to fancy pain to be', but rather the qualities of the pin, viz. its being slender, stiff and sharp, are such that when it is impressed upon the finger 'by reason of the fabrick of the body and the intimate union of the soul with it, there ariseth that troublesome kind of perception which we call pain'.[37] It is the 'local motions' of some part of the brain that is the immediate cause of our sensations of colour, and though these are typically caused by light affecting the retina, they can be caused otherwise, in dreams, by sudden blows on the head, etc.[38]

Boyle did, however, exploit the ambiguity introduced by Descartes between perceptual (secondary) qualities conceived as sensations and such qualities conceived as corpuscular structures (or 'dispositions') in virtue of which objects have the power to affect our sensibility:

Colour may be considered, either as it is a quality residing in the body that is said to be coloured, or to modify the light after such or such a manner; or else as the light itself, which so modified, strikes upon the organ of sight and so causes that sensation which we call colour . . . this latter may be looked upon as the more proper, though not the usual acceptation of the word colour . . . the more immediate cause of colour [is] the modified light itself, as it affects the sensory: though the disposition also of the coloured body, as that modifies the light, may be called by that name metonymically.[39]

Galileo had argued that 'if the perceiving creature were removed, all of those qualities would be annihilated and abolished from existence', but Boyle, capitalizing upon the metonymical use of names of secondary qualities, demurred:

I do not deny but that bodies may be said, in a very favourable sense, to have those qualities we call sensible, though there were no animals in the world; for a body in that case may differ from those, which now are quite devoid of quality, in its having such a disposition of its constituent corpuscles that in ~ duly applied to the sensory of an animal, it would produce such a

nere are derived from Descartes, cf. *Optics*, CSM 1, pp. 167–8.
imental *History of Colours*, in *Works*, vol. II, pp. 6–7.

sensible quality, which a body of another texture would not: as though, if there were no animals, there would be no such thing as pain, yet a pin may, upon the account of its figure, be fitted to cause pain in case it were moved against a man's finger.[40]

Colours, therefore, in so far as objects *can* be said to be coloured, are such corpuscularian structures (dispositions of corpuscles) as have the *power* to cause sensations of colour in us. Conceiving thus of colours, Boyle was able to answer to his satisfaction a question that had plagued classical philosophers, namely whether objects are coloured in the dark:

if colour be considered as a certain disposition of the superficial parts of the object to trouble the light to reflect after such and such a determinate manner, this constant . . . modifying disposition persevering in the object, whether it be shined on or no, there seems no just reason to deny, but that in this sense, bodies retain their colour as well in the night as day; or, to speak a little otherwise, it may be said, that bodies are potentially coloured in the dark and actually in the light.[41]

This is misguided, for it is surely not licit to say that objects are potentially coloured in the dark and actually coloured in the light. If 'colour' signifies a corpuscular array, an object is *actually*, not merely potentially, coloured in the dark. If colour signifies a dispositional power to affect us, then it has the power whether it affects us or not, just as (a given quantity of) cyanide is poisonous (for human beings) whether we consume it or not. The power is actualized in the light *if* an observer is present, but the object is no more *potentially* coloured in the dark than cyanide is potentially poisonous in a bottle. To be poisonous (and, according to the conception of colour as a power, to be coloured) *is* a potentiality. A 'potential power' is either a pleonasm, or a second order power, i.e. a power to acquire a power. (A substance is potentially poisonous not if it is poisonous but not consumed, but rather if it is edible but may *become* poisonous, for example as a result of rotting. But a poisonous substance tautologically has the potentiality to poison a person who consumes a

[40] Boyle, *Origin of Forms* p. 467.
[41] Boyle, *The Experimental History of Colours,* p. 19.

sufficient quantity of it.) We shall see later that conceptual confusions about the relationship between colour, darkness and perception of colour persist to this day.

Boyle's investigations into colour were surpassed by Newton's great work *Opticks: or, A Treatise of the Reflections, Refractions, Inflections and Colours of Light*. Although published only in 1704, hence *after* Locke's *Essay*, one passage from it is worth noting at this juncture. Newton enshrined, indeed canonized, the conceptual structure that had informed the thought of his predecessors. Since his investigations into light formed the foundations of subsequent scientific research, his preconceptions and misconceptions informed most later writings, and are as widespread today as ever. In a brief passage he clearly articulated the now triumphant seventeenth-century conception:

a sound in a bell or musical string or other sounding body, is nothing but a trembling motion, and in the air nothing but that motion propagated from the object, and in the sensorium 'tis a sense of that motion under the form of sound; so colours in the object are nothing but a disposition to reflect this or that sort of rays more copiously than the rest; in the rays they are nothing but their dispositions to propagate this or that motion into the sensorium, and in the sensorium they are sensations of those motions under the forms of colours.[42]

Here we have a threefold differentiation between what might be called the material grounds of a secondary quality, viz. the structure or mechanical action of an object, for example the vibration of a bell or string; the quality as it is in the object, viz. a power or disposition in virtue of its material structure or action; and the quality as we apprehend it, viz. a *sensation* in the sensorium. It is noteworthy that like his predecessors Newton was enmeshed in the homunculus fallacy, speaking of the images which are 'carried through the organs of sense into our little sensoriums [and] are there seen and beheld by that which in us perceives and thinks'.[43]

Locke's *An Essay Concerning Human Understanding* (first edition,

---

[42] Newton, *Optics: or, A Treatise of the Reflections, Refractions, Inflections and Colours of Light*, 4th edn (William Innys, London, 1730), p. 109.
[43] Ibid., p. 345.

1690) articulated a metaphysics and epistemology of corpuscularian physics. It became the primary source of empiricist reflections on perception and perceptual knowledge for the next century. It is striking that on the specific matter of the character of perceptual qualities Locke added very little to Boyle; rather was it that through the immense popularity and influence of the *Essay* Boyle's conception of primary and secondary qualities and of our apprehension of them, as presented by Locke, became the received wisdom of European science and a permanent, though occasionally contested, feature of subsequent philosophy.

As in Boyle's reflections, so too in Locke's the argument in favour of the curious picture delineated was largely an a priori theory of matter, a speculative theory of perceptual mechanisms, and an array of dubious conceptual presuppositions. What are sometimes taken to be the main arguments in favour of the subjectivity of colour, taste, smell, sound, heat and cold, and which were so treated by Berkeley, are in Locke's discussion largely *illustrations* of the explanatory force of the corpuscularian hypothesis. By the time he gets around to the examination of particular cases, all the crucial moves in the conceptual conjuring trick have already been made, all the crucial questions have been begged.

Like his predecessors, Locke took it for granted that it is the soul or *mind* that perceives:

Our Senses . . . convey into the Mind, several distinct *Perceptions* of things, according to those various ways, wherein those objects do affect them: and thus we come by those *Ideas,* we have of *Yellow, White, Heat, Cold, Soft, Hard, Bitter, Sweet,* and all those which we call sensible qualities, which when I say the senses convey into the mind, I mean, they from external Objects convey into the mind what produces there those *Perceptions.* (II–i–3)

The nerves are the 'conduits' which convey ideas 'from without to their Audience in the Brain, the mind's Presence-room' (II–iii–1).[44] Bodies produce ideas in us by impulse, which is 'the only way which we can conceive Bodies operate in' (II–viii–11). The impulse is

---

[44] Locke was careless here, since on his own account ideas are not conveyed by the nerves, but generated in the mind as a result of motions of the animal spirits in the nerves which affect the brain.

transmitted in the form of motion of the nerves or animal spirits to the brain, where ideas are produced in the mind. How this latter causal transaction is effected was as much a mystery to Locke as to his predecessors (and successors).

Like them, Locke assimilated having pain, feeling tickles and twinges, i.e. sensations properly conceived, to seeing coloured objects, hearing noises, smelling odours, i.e. perceiving. The 'idea' of pain, as Locke puts it, is produced 'in us' by, for example, a knife cutting our flesh, i.e. by motion of matter upon our sensitive organs. 'Ideas' of colour, sound, smell, etc. are produced in us, no *more* mysteriously, by the motions of imperceptible particles upon our eyes, ears and nose.

Following Boyle, Locke identified as *original* or *primary* qualities of objects those features of a material object as

are utterly inseparable from the Body, in what estate soever: such as in all the alterations and changes it suffers, all the force can be used upon it, it constantly keeps; and such as sense constantly finds in every particle of matter, which has bulk enough to be perceived, and the Mind finds inseparable from every particle of Matter, though less than to make itself be perceived by our Senses. (II–viii–9)

These qualities are: solidity, extension, figure and mobility. Note that the last three are not absolute and invariant, but rather essential determinables of any conceivable body the specific determinates of which (under those determinables) are *accidents,* whereas solidity, as Boyle argued, is absolute and invariant. These are qualities which every particle of matter must have to be a material object or space-occupant. Concatenations of particles possess the further crucial feature of *texture,* i.e. corpuscular structure, which Locke also includes in most of his confusedly varying lists of primary qualities, even though it is not a feature of a single particle. (Number notoriously occurs on his list too.) The conception of 'body' and its 'original' qualities emerges from wholly a priori considerations concerning the concept of space-occupancy (and the explicitly anti-Cartesian differentiation of *space* from an *occupant* of space).

Secondary qualities of objects 'are nothing in the Objects themselves, but Powers to produce various Sensations in us by their *primary Qualities, i.e.* by the Bulk, Figure, Texture, and Motion of their insensible parts, as Colours, Sounds, Tastes, *etc.*'(II–viii–10). If by 'power' Locke means what he seems to mean,[45] then he has made an emphatic step beyond Boyle in *explicitly* identifying secondary qualities with relational powers or dispositions to affect sentient creatures rather than with the corpuscular structure which is the 'ground' of this power.

The primary qualities, Locke emphasized, may be called *real qualities* for they *really exist* in the bodies (II–viii–17). But colour, heat or cold, sound, scent and taste are no more really in objects than is pain. They are, properly speaking, ideas caused 'in us' by the corpuscularian action upon our sensory organs. To be sure, objects produce in us ideas of primary qualities no less than ideas of secondary qualities, but

Ideas of primary Qualities of Bodies, *are Resemblances* of them, and their Patterns do really exist in the Bodies themselves; but the *Ideas, produced* in us *by* these *Secondary Qualities, have no resemblance* of them at all. There is nothing like our *Ideas,* existing in the Bodies themselves. They are in the Bodies, we denominate from them, only a Power to produce those Sensations in us: And what is Sweet, Blue, or Warm in *Idea,* is but the certain Bulk, Figure and Motion of the insensible Parts in the Bodies themselves, which we call so. (II–viii–15)

Like Boyle, Locke held that predicates of sensible qualities of colour, smell, taste, sound, heat or cold signify, properly speaking, sensations or ideas in us, and apply only metonymically to the objects that cause these sensations. Thus, he notes, '*Flame* is denominated *Hot* and *Light: Snow White* and *Cold; and Manna White* and *Sweet,* from the *Ideas* they produce in us' (II–viii–16). What *corresponds* to these ideas in us are the secondary qualities in objects, viz. their powers to produce the ideas, and the structural grounds or basis of the powers, viz. the 'texture' of the body in question.

Locke was, of course, aware that the picture which he had delineated runs against the grain of the way in which we conceive of objects in our environment and of our apprehension of them. Hence he gave a handful of examples the analysis of which was intended to take the edge off natural objections to his corpuscularian conception

---

[45] For a quite different view, see Alexander, *Ideas, Qualities and Corpuscles,* ch. 7.

and its attendant metaphysics and epistemology. Subsequ
especially in Berkeley's hand, these examples were to be
primary arguments in favour of the assimilation of sensible qual
to ideas. However, even in his presentation of these analytical
examples, Locke misrepresented the 'realist's' case. We attribute
colours, thermal qualities, tastes to, for example, fire or manna
metonymically, i.e. from the ideas they produce in us: 'Which
Qualities are commonly thought to be the same in those Bodies, that
those *Ideas* are in us, the one the perfect resemblance of the other, as
they are in a Mirror: and it would by most Men be judged very
extravagant, if one should say otherwise' (II–viii–16). But this is *not*
what is 'commonly thought' at all. We do not think that our
perceptions, i.e. our seeings, hearings, smellings, tastings or feelings of
these sensible qualities of objects *resemble* the qualities of the objects
perceived. My seeing Michelangelo's *Last Judgement* today may
resemble my first seeing it twenty years ago, in as much as it may
occasion the same sense of awe and excitement, my pulse now as then
may beat faster; as on the first occasion, tears may spring to my eyes,
for familiarity has bred no contempt and my responses have not been
tarnished with age. But my seeing the great fresco cannot *resemble* the
fresco seen. *A fortiori,* my seeing the colour harmonies and
disharmonies of this proto-Mannerist painting cannot *resemble* the
colours seen. Similarly the imitative sound of a starling may resemble
that of a blackbird, as the tones of a late Mozart symphony may
resemble those of an early Beethoven one, but my hearing Mozart's
41st cannot be said to *resemble* or to fail to resemble the symphony
itself.

It is, of course, true that perception may be accurate or inaccurate,
correct or incorrect, that one may see, perfectly accurately, how
something *merely* appears as opposed to its true character; something
may appear to one other than as it actually is, and one may suffer
hallucinations. But misperception is not erroneous because of a lack
of *resemblance* between the perceiving of a colour and the colour
perceived, or the hearing of a sound and the sound heard. If I look at a
piece of material in neon light it may look bluish-green to me; when I
take it out into the sunlight I see that it is green. To be sure, things do
not always look as they are, not only in respect of colour, but also of
shape and length. But if I see the green cloth and it looks bluish-green
to me, it is not the case that my seeing the green cloth fails to

resemble the green cloth, nor is it that my seeing the green cloth *as* bluish-green fails to resemble the green cloth. Rather, it strikes me as bluish-green, even though it is not; I may, going by mere appearances under non-optimal conditions, take it to be bluish-green, and if so, I will be wrong. But the falsity of my judgement does not turn on the fact that my perception does not resemble the object perceived.

This might be conceded, but a defender of Locke may still insist that a respectably cogent point is being made. Our perceptual experiences have an 'experiential content'. When I see, hear, or smell something it looks, sound or smells somehow or other to me. What I see, hear or smell may not be as I see, hear or smell it to be, but it really does look, sound or smell thus-and-so to me. How it looks, sounds or smells to me is the *content* of my perceptual experience, or, to use different jargon, 'the intentional object' of the experience.[46] If so, then to say that our ideas of sensible qualities do or do not resemble the qualities of objects perceived is just to say that what is perceived is or is not as it looks, sounds, smells or tastes to a person.

This is misleading in as much as it harnesses a partial truth to a misconception. To talk of 'experiential contents' or 'intentional objects' of perceptions is to talk of certain kinds of answers to the question 'What did A perceive?'. Such a 'content' or 'intentional object' is not a phrase or word, but nor is it something (a kind of 'entity') for which the phrase or word cited in answering the question stands;[47] for if, at the oculists's, I am asked what I see written on the bottom line of the chart and I answer, 'I see only a black blur', then the 'content' of my seeing (its 'intentional object') is given by the specification 'a black blur', but this phrase in this context does not 'stand for' any entity at all.

The dominant use of perceptual verbs does not admit an intentional (or merely intentional) object. If a child reports seeing a unicorn at the zoo, we correct him: 'No – you can't have seen a unicorn, there is no such animal. What you saw may have been an oryx.' I may exclaim, 'I heard a gunshot.' 'No,' you reply, 'it was the car back-firing.' I can feel the ground rocking during an earthquake, but stepping off a ship

---

[46] Cf. J. L. Mackie, *Problems from Locke* (Clarendon Press, Oxford, 1976) pp. 48ff.
[47] See G. E. M. Anscombe, 'The intentionality of sensation', repr. in her *Metaphysics and the Philosophy of Mind* (Blackwell, Oxford, 1981).

I cannot feel the ground rocking, since it is not rocking, but the ground will feel to me *as if* it is rocking.[48] This use of perceptual verbs admits only 'material' (non-intentional) objects of perception, and that A perceives M here entails that there is an M within view (earshot, etc). It is altogether natural that this use should dominate in as much as our perceptual faculties are cognitive faculties, capacities for discerning how things are in our environment by the use of our perceptual organs. We employ perceptual verbs thus in justifying our own cognitive claims ('The A is F.' – 'How do you know?' – 'I can hear it.') and in third-person reports. Hence too the propositional use of perceptual verbs in which they take propositional clauses (including *Wh*-clauses) as their grammatical objects entails that things are as the observer perceives that they are. If a person sees that the sun is shining it follows that the sun is shining; if he hears that the person in the next room is in pain, then that is how things are. Similarly, if he sees what is happening, what time it is, who is at the party, where the ball fell, then he sees that such-and-such is happening, that it is midnight, that John is at the party and that the ball fell in the bush.

Nevertheless, there is an important use of perceptual verbs which does admit intentional objects. It is perfectly licit to say that what I saw when the cricket ball whizzed by was a red blur, and that when I stuff earplugs in my ears on a transatlantic flight what I hear of the roar of the engines is a dull hum, or that after sunbathing the lukewarm water in the swimming pool feels very cold. Here the answer to the question of what I perceived is given by specification of an intentional object. But it is wrong to say that such 'intentional objects' or 'experiential contents' are 'just as we perceive them', that they are 'mind-dependent', that 'they exist only in and by being perceived'.[49] For 'intentional objects' or 'experiential contents' are not kinds of objects, any more than what I think, query, or answer is a kind of object. An intentional object or content of perception is not what a person perceives in the sense in which a material object of perception is. The latter can be specified by ostension, the former by a characterization of how something perceptually strikes a person. Hence in cases where a perceptual verb is thus used it can always be

[48] *Pace* Mackie, *Problems from Locke*, p. 48.
[49] Ibid.

paraphrased by 'It looked . . .', 'It appeared to be . . .', 'It seemed . . .', 'It felt as if . . .', etc.

It is, of course, quite correct to say that a perceived object typically is as it perceptually strikes one or appears to one to be on looking, feeling or listening. But that it is (or is not) as it thus appears to one to be is not a matter of a *resemblance* (or lack of resemblance) between two items that are both qualified by a common perceptual quality. A red gem may look red to me, but there are not two objects involved here, both of which are red, just as, if the ruby costs £100 and is worth only £50, there aren't two objects which fail to resemble each other in price. The resemblance between the appearance of a thing and the thing is not akin to the resemblance between two things in respect of a given property. It is, if anything, a relationship between two descriptions, between how it perceptually strikes one and how it is. Hence invoking the jargon of 'intentional objects' or 'experiential contents' does not vindicate Locke's description of 'what is commonly thought'. We do *not* commonly think that we *perceive* ideas, experiential contents or intentional objects. We think that we perceive objects (events, etc.) and their sensible qualities, not some surrogate for them. We do indeed think that objects are typically just as we perceive them to be or as they perceptually strike us as being, but we do *not* think that they are so because of a resemblance between, for example, the table's being square (or brown) and my seeing it as square (or brown).[50]

To vindicate his account Locke examined four examples intended to demonstrate that his position is not as 'extravagant' as it seems. First, he noted that as one approaches a fire, it produces in one initially a sensation of warmth, subsequently, and by imperceptible degrees, a sensation of pain. The 'idea of pain' is evidently not in the fire; why then should we think that the 'idea of warmth', which is produced in us in exactly the same way, is so? And what applies to warmth applies no less to, for example, the coldness and whiteness of snow (II–viii–16). This consideration, which was to loom large in Berkeley's *Dialogues*, will be examined in detail later (pp. 88–93). For the moment, it should merely be noted that the argument turns on assimilating sensation and perception, an assimilation facilitated by the example of tactile perception. For we speak indifferently of *having*

[50] Ibid. p. 49.

a pain and *feeling* a pain and of *feeling warm* and *having* a warm feeling; but we must take care not to assimilate feeling warm and feeling warmth. Secondly, Locke invited us to

consider the red and white colours in *Porphyre:* Hinder light but from striking on it, and its Colours Vanish: it no longer produces these appearances on us again. Can any one think any real alterations are made in the *Porphyre,* by the presence or absence of Light; and that those *Ideas* of whiteness and redness, are really in *Porphyre* in the light, when 'tis plain *it has no colour in the dark?* (II–viii–19)

Following Boyle, Locke argued that the corpuscular structure of an object is constant, and hence too the secondary quality which is a power to produce ideas of colour in us by means of light, 'But whiteness and redness are not in it at any time, but such a texture, that hath the power to produce such a sensation in us.' This too will be examined in the sequel. For the moment note again that perception, viz. seeing the red porphyry, is assimilated to sensation; furthermore, the example is misdescribed, since the colours of porphyry do not 'vanish' in the dark any more than its shape, they merely cease to be visible; finally, note again that the 'realist's' position is misrepresented in as much as he does *not* claim that, in Locke's jargon, the 'ideas of whiteness or redness are really in *Porphyre'* but rather that porphyry is mottled white and red, whether by day or by night. Thirdly, Locke points out that if one pounds an almond with a pestle, its taste and colour alter, but pounding thus can only alter the 'texture'. The implication suggested is that if alteration of texture is the cause of alteration of colour and taste, the colour and taste cannot be qualities of objects. This manifestly does not follow, for (i) the pounding does not alter *only* the texture, but also the colour and taste; (ii) that the change in taste and colour depends on the change in 'texture' no more shows the taste and colour to be mental than the fact that the change in the shape of a piece of wax depends on the heat of the fire shows that its shape is mental. Fourthly, Locke draws attention to the fact that lukewarm water may feel hot with one (cold) hand and cold with the other (hot) hand:

Whereas it is impossible, that the same Water, if those *Ideas* were really in it, should at the same time be both Hot and Cold. For if we imagine *Warmth,* as it is *in our Hands,* to be *nothing but a certain sort and degree of Motion in the minute Particles of our Nerves, or animal Spirits,* we may understand, how it is possible, that the same Water may at the same time produce the Sensation of Heat in one Hand, and Cold in the other. (II–viii-21)

Again, Locke's description and explanation beg the question. The 'realist' does not contend that the *perception* or 'Idea' of warmth or coldness are in the water, but rather that the water is warm, cold or lukewarm. While the water cannot be both hot and cold simultaneously, no antinomy arises from the possibility that it might *feel* hot and *feel* cold simultaneously to the same person in the circumstances envisaged. For there is no contradiction in something lukewarm feeling hot to a person with cold hands. Perception of thermal qualities is again wrongly assimilated to sensations of heat and cold. My feeling hot and the water's feeling hot are as different as my feeling a pain and my feeling a pin.

Locke's conclusion, like Galileo's, is that a world without sentient beings is a world without colours, sounds, smells, tastes, heat or cold. Or, more accurately, that the world as it is in itself consists only of particles, variously arrayed, qualified only by the *real* or primary qualities and (as Boyle emphasized) the resultant secondary qualities, conceived as mere powers to affect sentient creatures.

Light, Heat, Whiteness, or Coldness, *are no more really in* [bodies] *than Sickness or Pain is in* Manna. Take away the Sensation of them; let not the Eyes see Light, or Colours, nor the Ears hear Sounds; let the Palate not Taste, nor the Nose Smell, and all Colours, Tastes, Odors, and Sounds, as they are such particular *Ideas,* vanish and Cease, and are reduced to their Causes, i.e. Bulk, Figure, and Motion of Parts. (II–viii–17)

Locke's *Essay* provided all the pieces for a game which in all essentials is still being played upon a board which differs but little from that devised in the seventeenth century. His successors added little of note. Berkeley and Hume occupy a curious position in this tale, in as much as they put Lockean points to very different uses from anything he would have licensed. Berkeley in particular rejected the philosophical role of underlabourer for the sciences, envisaging the task of philosophy in this respect as being that of metaphysical (or, as we might put it, conceptual) critic of the sciences. The Galilean conception of the world struck him as wildly misconceived, and he bent his efforts to demonstrating its conceptual incoherence. One of the moves he made was amusingly subtle. The distinction between appearance and reality as represented by Galileo and his successors was rooted in an a priori theory of matter and a conjectural corpuscularian (physical) theory of perception. Its outcome was the contention that the 'real world' is altogether unlike the world as it appears to us to be. Berkeley found this picture absurd; as he rather charmingly put it, 'There are men who say there are insensible extensions, there are others who say the Wall is not white, the fire is not hot etc. We Irish men cannot attain to these truths.'[51] But far from denying the mentality or subjectivity of 'sensible qualities', Berkeley cut the argument free of corpuscularianism or any theory of matter at all. He focused sharply upon the examples which Locke had rehearsed to demonstrate the cogency of his conception of reality and, after elaborating them in much greater detail, used the conclusions to turn the tables against the representationalist, idealist, conception that had, by then, become the received metaphysical underpinning of the physical sciences. He endeavoured to show the incoherence of the conception of material substance which he discerned in his predecessors, the unintelligibility of the notion of an object qualified only by primary qualities, and that the arguments supporting the mind-dependence of 'sensible qualities' applied with equal force to the primary qualities. The story is familiar and needs no elaboration. From the point of view of our interests, Berkeley added nothing new to the pieces on the board. Nor, indeed, did Hume.[52]

3 A persistent tradition

In his *Inquiry into the Human Mind* (1764) Thomas Reid described the picture of perception and perceptual qualities that had emerged from the writings of philosophers (and 'natural philosophers') over the previous century and a half. The philosopher, he wrote in criticism, tells the common man

[51] Berkeley, *Philosophical Commentaries*, § 392, in A. A. Luce (ed.), *The Works of George Berkeley*, vol. 1 (Nelson, London and Edinburgh, 1948), p. 47.
[52] Save for his observation that solidity, in one sense of the term, is a *relative* property; see *A Treatise of Human Nature*, I-IV-iv.

that there is no smell in plants, nor anything but the mind; and that all this hath been demonstrated by modern philosophy. The plain man will, no doubt, be apt to think him merry; but if he finds that he is serious, his next conclusion will be that he is mad; or that philosophy, like magic, puts men into a new world, and gives them different faculties from common men. And thus philosophy and common sense are set at variance. But who is to blame for it? In my opinion the philosopher is to blame. For if he means by smell what the rest of mankind most commonly mean, he is certainly mad. But if he puts a different meaning upon the word, without observing it himself, or giving warning to others, he abuses language and disgraces philosophy, without doing any service to truth.[53]

This methodological observation is very nearly correct. We do not think, with Galileo, that 'these tastes, odours, colours, etc. so far as their objective existence is conceived, are nothing but names for something which resides exclusively in our sensitive body.' When we are not under the sway of the magic of philosophy and misconstrued natural science, we do not think that colours are but 'sensations in the sensorium', as Boyle and Newton claimed. On the contrary, we think that geraniums are red and delphiniums blue, and are amazed and baffled to be told that they are 'in and of themselves' without colour. Until the spell has been woven, and our intellectual faculties numbed, we must find it extraordinary to be told by Locke that '*Light, Heat, Whiteness* or Coldness *are no more really in* [bodies] *than Sickness or Pain is in* Manna. Take away the Sensation of them; let not the Eyes see Light, or Colours, nor the Ears hear Sounds; let the Palate not Taste, nor the Nose Smell, and all Colours, Tastes, Odors and Sounds, as they are such particular *Ideas,* vanish and Cease' (II–viii–17). Can he really mean, we wonder, that ice is not cold when no one feels it, that the summer sea is not warm until someone swims in it? Surely snow does not cease to be white when no one looks at it, but only when it is trampled into grey slush; and at dawn the landscape is bathed in light even though all viewers are yet abed. We must concede that there are indeed no unfelt pains, no unsuffered sickness; and though manna may cause pain and sickness, the manna does not suffer stomach-ache. But colours, tastes, odours, heat and

[53] Thomas Reid, *Inquiry into the Human Mind,* in Sir William Hamilton (ed.), *The Works of Thomas Reid* (MacLachlan and Stewart, Edinburgh, 1863) vol. 1, p. 112.

cold are not sensations or ideas, rather they are qualities of objects that persist whether sensed or not.

Nevertheless, Reid's remark is potentially misleading in invoking common sense. If we confront weighty scientific theory with common sense, we are liable to be 'twitted with vulgar prejudice, and asked how we distinguish the one from the other.'[54] Yet, as Hazlitt pointed out, 'There is nothing more distinct than common sense and vulgar opinion. Common sense is only a judge of things that fall under common observation . . . it anchors in experience.' The criticism of common sense by reason may be as severe as one pleases, he added, but it must be as patient as it is severe: 'Hasty, dogmatical, self-satisfied reason is worse than idle fancy or bigoted prejudice.' It is a matter of common sense, in a literal if slightly archaic acceptation of the word, that geraniums are red and delphiniums blue – just *look* and you will see! (Unless you are colour-blind, in which case you will *not be able* to see what the common run of humanity *can* see.) It is not, however, a matter of common sense whether colour words and other names of secondary qualities signify sensations and ideas, or rather powers in objects to cause sensations, or whether they signify particulate structures (dispositions of particles) of objects or publicly observable qualities of objects that persist whether perceived or not. That is a conceptual matter, to be investigated not by laboratory experiments and scientific theory-construction, but rather by patient examination of our use of the relevant expressions.

The proper criticism of the family of doctrines about the 'subjectivity' of secondary qualities is not a criticism of scientific theory in the name of common opinion. It is, after all, not an *opinion* that snow is white or sugar sweet! Nor is this task a defence of common sense against philosophical theorizing. For the claim that rubies are red and sapphires blue needs no defending. It is rather a criticism of a *conceptual incoherence* deeply embedded in such theorizing. These *philosophical* confusions were generated (partly) by the endeavours of philosophers and scientists in the seventeenth and eighteenth centuries to grasp the conceptual articulations between their revolutionary (and ultimately triumphant) physical theories and the form of repre-

---

[54] William Hazlitt, 'On genius and common sense' in *Table-Talk, Original Essays on Men and Manners*.

sentation we all, common men and scientists alike, employ in describing the objects of our perceptual experience, the natural world we inhabit.

The criticism of these confusions is not a defence or vindication of our common form of representation either. There is no such thing as vindicating a form of representation by reference to reality.[55] For any description of the facts, which is intended to show the form of representation to be true to reality, must already employ a given form of representation. If it employs the same form of representation as that which is being challenged, it cannot also justify it by reference to the facts described, since the description presupposes the very distinctions between sense and nonsense enshrined in the form of representation in question. And if it employs a different one, it makes no contact with that which it purports to justify. On the other hand, if 'vindicating a form of representation' signifies demonstrating its *usefulness,* then surely the utility of our rich and venerable vocabulary of colours, sounds, tastes, smells, etc. needs no vindicating – it speaks for itself in a thousand ways every day of our lives.

The result of our inquiries is not to *force* anyone to employ our vocabulary of perceptual qualities. He who wishes may eschew the use of colour names, names of smells or sounds altogether, although it would be prodigiously inconvenient in one's daily transactions. What he may not do, however, is to misuse them in scientific and philosophical speculation. The result of our inquiry is intended to be a *clarification* of this fragment of our form of representation, a clarification that will make perspicuous its abuse in science and philosophy. The consequences of such abuses of language are not merely the disgrace to philosophy and disservice to truth that Reid pointed out, but above all *nonsense,* a violation of the bounds of sense.

It is sad, as well as ironic, that Reid, having given so sapient a warning, should have succumbed to much the same confusions. He tried to reconcile what he conceived to be common sense with philosophical or scientific theory by pointing out an alleged ambiguity in names of sensible qualities

---

[55] Cf. L. Wittgenstein, *Philosophical Remarks,* ed. R. Rhees, trs. R. Hargreaves and R. White (Blackwell, Oxford, 1975), § 7.

The vulgar are commonly charged by philosophers, with the absurdity of imagining the smell in the rose to be something like to the sensation of smelling; but I think unjustly; for they neither give the same epithets to both, nor do they reason in the same manner from them. What is smell in the rose? It is a quality or virtue of the rose, or of something proceeding from it, which we perceive by the sense of smelling; and this is all we know of the matter. But what is smelling? It is an act of the mind, but is never imagined to be a quality of the mind. Again, the sensation of smelling is conceived to infer necessarily a mind or sentient being; but smell in the rose infers no such thing. We say, this body smells sweet, that stinks; but we do not say, this mind smells sweet and that stinks. Therefore, smell in the rose, and the sensation which it causes, are not conceived, even by the vulgar, to be things of the same kind, although they have the same name.[56]

Consequently, he argued, names of smells signify two quite different features. First, a mind–dependent sensation; and secondly, 'some power, quality, or virtue, in the rose, or in effluvia proceeding from it, which hath a permanent existence independent of the mind'. He applied similar reasoning to thermal perception. The vulgar are not as foolish as philosophers imply, for no one supposes the sensation of heat or indeed anything that resembles it to be in the fire. What is supposed is that there is some quality in the fire that makes us have that peculiar sensation. Generalizing, Reid stated: 'The names of all smells, tastes, sounds, as well as heat and cold, have a like ambiguity in all languages'; but, he noted, their primary application is to the cause of the sensation, i.e. to a mind-independent feature of objects. Echoing Descartes' analogy between sensations and linguistic signs, he argued: 'The sensations of smell, taste, sound, and colour, are of infinitely more importance as signs or indications, than they are upon their own account; like the words of a language, wherein we do not attend to the sound but to the sense.'[57] The reconciliation, however, was purchased at an excessively high price. First, on Reid's account all perception involves having sensations: seeing involves visual sensations of colour and shape, hearing involves auditory sensations,

---

[56] Reid, *Inquiry into the Human Mind,* p. 114.
[57] Note, however, that the analogy has shifted. Descartes compared the objective property (disposition of particles) and the corresponding sensation to sign and thing signified; Reid, more happily, reverses the relationship: it is the sensation which is a sign of the objective property.

and so on.[58] Secondly, the sensation felt and the quality perceived are always distinct. The sensations are signs indicating a quality of the object perceived. In the case of the secondary qualities, *we have no idea what the qualities perceived are*. Our senses 'inform us only, that they are qualities that affect us in a certain manner – that is, produce in us a certain sensation; but as to what they are in themselves, our senses leave us in the dark'.[59] Just as a pain signifies a disorder in the body, but does not indicate what that disorder is, so too seeing colours, hearing sounds, feeling heat signify qualities of objects but do not indicate what they are. They are merely unknown causes of sensations. It follows that in the sense in which we know what red is, *we do not see it,* and in the sense in which we perceive the red colour of the rose, we *have no idea what it is*. Thirdly, it also follows (although Reid did not realize it) that the concept of a sensation of red (or of noisiness, malodorousness, sweetness) must be logically prior to the concept of the allegedly unknown quality in objects that occasions it. The meanings of 'red', 'noisy', 'malodorous', 'sweet' as applied to objects perceived are given by explanations of the form 'the unknown quality in objects that causes in us a sensation of . . .'. Hence what might be called the 'objective meaning' perspicuously presupposes the 'subjective meaning'. This in turn raises the question of the determination of the meanings of names of perceptual qualities conceived as sensations. What are the rules for the use of these expressions, how are they given, what form does an explanation of what they mean take? These three difficulties will be confronted in the sequel.

It is noteworthy that nothing in Reid's remarks seriously conflicts with the representational idealists' conception of reality and our perception of it in respect of the issues at hand. Reid rightly objected to the claim that things are not multi-coloured, noisy or smelly, but sustained his objection only at the cost of admitting a systematic ambiguity in the meanings of names of secondary qualities, an ambiguity already emphasized (although not always consistently) by Descartes, Boyle, Newton and Locke. He rightly refused to ascribe to the common man the absurd idea that objects have 'in' them

---

[58] T. Reid, *Essays on the Intellectual Powers of Man*, in *Works*, vol. 1, pp. 310ff.
[59] Ibid. p. 313.

sensations of colour, sound, heat, etc. but attributed to the common understanding the equally absurd idea that names of secondary qualities signify 'for the most part'[60] unknown (and, in one sense, imperceptible) causes of these sensations.

Reid's conception became enshrined in the pioneering work done in physiological psychology in the nineteenth century. Thomas Young (1773–1829) first suggested (1802) the theory that colour perception was dependent upon only three kinds of colour receptors in the retina which are sensitive to three 'principal' colours: red, yellow and blue (he later suggested red, green and violet). Perception of the remaining colours must depend, he conjectured, upon a mixture of light to which pairs of receptors respond to give the appropriate *sensation of colour*. Clerk Maxwell, writing later in the century, observed:

It seems almost a truism to say that colour is a sensation; and yet Young, by honestly recognising this elementary truth, established the first consistent theory of colour. So far as I know, Thomas Young was the first who, starting from the well-known fact that there are three primary colours, sought for the explanation of this fact, not in the nature of light but in the constitution of man.[61]

Hermann von Helmholtz, the Newton of physiological psychology, further developed Young's theory (on the basis of work done by J. Müller in the 1840s). Like so many of the great nineteenth-century scientists, he was acutely conscious of the philosophical or conceptual framework of his theorizing. It is noteworthy that he claimed, 'In the writings of . . . Locke were correctly laid down the most important principles on which the right interpretation of sensible qualities depends.'[62] All that we apprehend of the world around us is brought to our consciousness by changes produced in our sensory organs by means of 'external impressions', i.e. by light-waves impinging upon

[60] Reid, *Inquiry into the Human Mind*, p. 14.
[61] C. Maxwell, quoted in R. L. Gregory, *Eye and Brain, the Psychology of Seeing* (Weidenfeld and Nicolson, London, 1966), p. 118.
[62] H. von Helmholtz, 'The recent progress of the theory of vision', *Preussischen Jahrbücher*, 1868, repr. in translation in R. M. Warren and R. P. Warren (eds), *Helmholtz on Perception, its Physiology and Development* (Wiley, New York, 1968), p. 101. Subsequent references to this collection will be abbreviated to WW.

our retinae, sound-waves upon our eardrums, heat radiation upon our skin, etc. These are transmitted to the brain by the nerves, and 'it is in the brain that these impressions first become conscious sensations.'[63] It is, however, impossible to sustain our 'natural and innate conviction that the quality of our sensations, and especially our sensations of sight, give us a true impression of corresponding qualities in the outer world.'[64] For whether the rays of the sun appear to us as colour, or as warmth, does not depend at all upon their own properties, but simply on whether they excite the fibres of the optic nerve, or those of the skin. Indeed, 'all properties ascribed to [the objects of the external world] by us only characterize *effects* which they exert either upon our senses or upon other objects in nature. Colour, sound, taste, smell, temperature, smoothness and solidity . . . characterize effects upon our sense organs.'[65] Hence 'the colours which we see are [not] attributes of bodies in themselves but are introduced by our eye into them.'[66] Like his predecessors, Helmholtz too echoed the Cartesian analogy between (secondary) perceptual quality and linguistic sign:

Our sensations are indeed effects produced in our organs by external causes; and how such an effect expresses itself naturally depends quite essentially upon the kind of apparatus upon which the effect is produced. In as much as the quality of our sensation gives us a report of what is peculiar to the external influence by which it is excited, it may count as a symbol of it, but not as an image. For from an image one requires some kind of a likeness with the object of which it is an image . . . But a sign need not have any kind of similarity at all with what it is the sign of.[67]

Colour, therefore, (like other secondary qualities) is, as we experience it, merely 'a sensible "sign" of certain external qualities, whether of light itself or of the objects which reflect it.'[68]

[63] Ibid., p. 82.
[64] Ibid., p. 99.
[65] Helmholtz, *Physiological Optics* (2nd edn), fragment repr. in translation in Helmholtz's *Epistemological Writings,* ed. R. S. Cohen and Y. Elkana, trs. M. F. Lowe, (Reidel, Dordrecht, 1977), p. 168.
[66] Helmholtz, 'The facts in perception' (1878), in *Epistemological Writings,* p. 123.
[67] Ibid., pp. 121–2. Note that, like Reid, Helmholtz inverts the original Cartesian analogy.
[68] Helmholtz, 'The recent progress of the theory of vision', WW, p. 102, cf. p. 106.

Thus far Helmholtz's conceptual observations move along well-worn tracks. In conformity with the representational idealist tradition, he argued that we never *directly* perceive so-called 'external objects'. What we perceive directly are 'invariably simply the nervous stimulations'.[69] The 'external world' is perceived *indirectly,* since our apprehension of it always involves *interpreting* the sensations produced in us, and *inferring* (unconsciously) the character of their causes. (Occasionally he went so far as to suggest absurdly that we interpret 'the retinal image of which we are actually conscious'[70] – absurdly inasmuch as one item of which we are *never* actually conscious is the reflected image on our own retinae.) Where he did make a new movement of thought was in confronting the question of whether our perceptual experience presents us with a deceptive appearance of reality. Under evident Kantian influence, Helmholtz distinguished between *phenomena* and *mere* appearances. Colours (and sounds, smells, tastes, etc.) are phenomena. However, 'a "deceptive appearance" is the result of the normal phenomena of one object being confounded with those of another. But the sensation of colour is by no means a deceptive appearance. There is no other way in which colour can appear . . .'[71] Consequently, it is senseless to ask whether, for example, vermilion (i.e. powdered mercuric sulphide) as we see it is *really* red, or whether this is an illusion. The sensation of red is the normal reaction of normally formed eyes to light reflected from this substance.

The central elements of Helmholtz's conceptual account, which he held in common with his predecessors, will be the concern of subsequent chapters. But a few points of detail merit comment here. They are confusions typical of the whole tradition that derives (*inter alia*) from Helmholtz in scientific writings on perception (and are sadly prominent also in philosophical writings)

First, the contention that external impressions are transmitted to the brain where they become conscious sensations is surely a misdescription of the phenomena. Physical stimuli upon sensory receptors

---

[69] Helmholtz, *Physiological Optics* (1866), repr. in WW p. 174.
[70] Helmholtz, 'The recent progress of the theory of vision', WW, p. 130, cf. p. 184. For criticism of Helmholtz's famous theory of unconscious inference in perception see P. M. S. Hacker, 'Helmholtz's theory of perception: an investigation into its conceptual framework' (forthcoming).
[71] Helmholtz, 'The recent progress of the theory of vision', WW, p. 101.

cause electrical discharges which are transmitted along nerve fibres. The resultant electrical activity in the appropriate part of the cortex is, however, mischaracterized as a 'transmitted impression', since it is not an 'impression' nor has any *thing* been transmitted from sense organ to brain. The neural network is not a transportation system and the triggering of a connected series of causal reactions is not the transference of some *thing* from receptor to cortex. On analogy with communication systems, the electrical impulse caused in the cortex is sometimes referred to as a 'message' or as 'information'. It is important to remember (since scientists often forget) that this is either a metaphor, or a technical term in information theory only tenuously if at all connected with the ordinary meanings of 'message' and 'information'. Furthermore, an electrical impulse in the brain cannot *become* a sensation. An appropriate set of electrical impulses in the cortex may be a causal condition for a person to have a certain sensation, but there is no such thing as transforming an electrical impulse into a sensation.

Secondly, while it is true that sunlight impinging on the skin in summer feels pleasantly warm, and that the sun is yellow (or fiery red at sunset), it does not follow that the truth of the propositions that it is warm in the sunlight and that the sun is yellow depends upon whether the radiation of the sun excites our thermal skin receptors or our retinal receptors. We feel the warmth of the sun with the exposed surfaces of our bodies, and see its colour with our eyes. (The *light* itself is rarely coloured in the primary sense of the term, but only in the derived scientific sense; moreover, in normal circumstancs, we do not even *see* the light of the sun, rather we see the objects in our environment *in* the light of the sun.) A condition of our perceiving those distinct properties is that our perceptual organs receive the appropriate stimulus, but *what is perceived* is the colour of the sun and the warmth of its rays, i.e. properties of the 'outer world', not their *effects* upon our sense organs, i.e. electro-chemical changes in sensory receptors.

Thirdly, a brief warning is appropriate about the use of the expression 'external world', ubiquitous in the writings of philosophers and scientists alike who write on perception. It originates in a misleading contrast between the 'internal world' of the mind, and the 'external world' of 'physical reality'. To the 'internal world' belong a person's thoughts and feelings, his motives and intentions, his mental images, fantasies and dreams. To the 'external world' belong material objects and their mind-independent properties. But this Cartesian dichotomy is altogether misleading. There is only one world, for the world is simply the totality of everything that exists, happens, obtains or goes on. It encompasses people (and animals) and their psychological features no less than inanimate objects and their physical features. The 'mental' is not *inside* anything, even though much that is, crudely speaking, mental can be concealed; and the 'physical' is not *outside* the mind, since the mind is not a space. I can sometimes conceal my thoughts and feelings, but not by preventing them from emerging from an inner world to an outer one; rather by not telling others what I think, by writing my reflections down in code, or by keeping my diary under lock and key, as I conceal my feelings by suppressing them or by dissimulation. But, of course, when I say what I think, sincerely confess my motives, publish my diary, give vent to my passions, I am not issuing emigration licenses to objects from the inner world to enable them to roam in alien territory.[72] By a natural extension this misleading Cartesian dichotomy is applied to a genuine contrast between what is inside the body (or one's own body) or brain, and what is outside the body or brain. But then, of course, it is false that perception informs us only of the 'external world'. For the insides of others are visible in the operating theatre or autopsy room, and palpable in the doctor's surgery (and elsewhere); and much of what lies within one's own skin is manifestly perceptually accessible to one's own ill-informed pokings and proddings as well as to the doctor's well-informed ones.

Fourthly, the dichotomy Helmholtz invoked between direct and indirect perception is equally misleading. It makes sense to talk of perceiving an object indirectly only if it *makes sense* to talk of perceiving it directly. One may say of a certain person that one could not, on a given occasion, see him directly but only *in a mirror*. But then, of course, it *makes sense* to speak of seeing him face to face. It is true that I cannot see the back of my head 'directly' but, of course,

---

[72] The above intimations of an argument are merely a gesture in the direction of Wittgenstein's wonderful explorations of the endemic picture of the 'Inner' and the 'Outer'. For a detailed examination of his ideas, see P. M. S. Hacker, *Insight and Illusion, Themes in the Philosophy of Wittgenstein,* rev. edn. (Oxford University Press, Oxford, 1986), ch. X.

others can. It is noteworthy that the idiom of 'direct/indirect' perception applies paradigmatically to vision, and there principally to cases in which the direct line of vision is (or is not) broken.[73] To hear something indirectly is to come to know of it by *hearsay;* and there is little if any use for the notion of smelling or tasting indirectly (which is not to say that it could not be *given* a use!) Helmholtz, in company with many philosophers, insisted that 'external objects' are *essentially* never perceived directly. But if so, then they cannot be said to be perceived indirectly either, for the intelligibility of this expression depends upon the availability of its complement.

The picture sketched by Helmholtz was perspicuously derived from a canvas painted in the seventeenth century. However, his great works in physiological psychology were of such moment that the conceptual framework he adopted has become received wisdom to this day among empirical scientists probing the psychology and physiology of perception (although there have been a few laudable dissenters). Some randomly chosen examples of contemporary writers should suffice to substantiate this.

Sir John Eccles, Nobel Laureate for physiology, writes:

There is no colour in the material world, only the emission of electromag-netic waves of various spectral composition. There is no colour as such in the brain, only modules responding selectively in their coded responses to visual inputs of various spectral characteristics. Colour is created by the reading out by the self-conscious mind of the responses of these 'colour-coded' modules.[74]

Conscious perception, he adds, 'gives us some symbolic image of the external world and of ourselves in relation to this world. Such qualities as light, colour, distance, spatial relations, sounds and smells participate in this symbolic image.'[75]

R. L. Gregory, a distinguished British psychologist of perception, observes that colour sensations (following Young's suggestion) are

[73] J. L. Austin, *Sense and Sensibilia,* ed. G. J. Warnock (Clarendon Press, Oxford, 1962), pp. 16ff.
[74] J. C. Eccles, *The Human Mystery* (Routledge and Kegan Paul, London, (1984), p. 179.
[75] Ibid., p. 161.

produced according to proportional mixtures of neural signals from three 'colour channels'. Hence

simple-seeming sensations may not be given by single signals but by complex mixtures of signals. Thus yellow is given by a combination of red and green signals; that is from channels tuned to red and green spectral wavelengths of light. Though yellow seems to be a simple sensation, it is physiologically complex. This implies that, in general, introspections of sensations are no sure guide to underlying mechanisms.[76]

American psychologists share the same picture coloured by preconceptions of so-called cognitive science. I. Rock writes:

The perceptual world we create differs qualitatively from the physicists' descriptions because our experience is mediated by our senses and constructed internally as a representation of the world. Thus we perceive colors, tones, tastes and smells – perceptions that either have no meaning in the world of physical reality or have a different meaning. What we perceive as hues of red, blue, or green the physicist refers to as surfaces reflecting electromagnetic waves of certain frequencies. What we experience as tastes and smells the physicist refers to as chemical compounds. What we experience as tones of varying pitch the physicist describes as objects vibrating at different frequencies. Colors, tones, tastes, and smells are mental constructions, created out of sensory stimulations. As such they do not exist outside of living minds.[77]

H. Rossotti, in a book intended to introduce the educated layman to contemporary findings on the subject of colour, beings by observing that 'we must recognize. . . that colour is a *sensation* produced in the brain, by the light which enters the eye',[78] and concludes on the penultimate page that 'today, we accept that colour is a sensation'.

This conception is transmitted to the educated public as a slightly startling, but well-established fact about the nature of things. Innocent art theorists adopt it on the authority of the scientists. F. Malins, in a book on the appreciation of painting, writes:

---

[76] R. L. Gregory, *Mind in Science* (Penguin Books, Harmondsworth, 1984), p. 205.
[77] I. Rock, *Perception* (Scientific American Books, New York, 1984), p. 4.
[78] H. Rossotti, *Colour* (Penguin Books, Harmondsworth, 1983), p. 16.

The word 'colour' is used to describe a sensation received by the brain when the retina of the eye is stimulated by certain wavelengths of light. Although we tend to refer to 'colour' as if it exists as an entity in the outside world, since it is a sensation, it only exists when there is someone present to experience the sensation.[79]

E. Newton, art historian and aesthetic theorist, proclaims:

what man calls 'colour', for example, is merely a sensation in the human eye caused by white light that has been interfered with in certain ways – usually by the molecular structure of the objects that reflect it. The nature of 'colour' depends on the construction of the eye. The word 'colour' can have no other meaning . . . [80]

This received picture, propounded by scientists and widely adopted in good faith by the gullible, is a well-entrenched piece of *mythology* based not upon scientific experiment and theory but upon conceptual confusion. This verdict will be substantiated in the sequel.

Contemporary philosophers should know better. The underlying misconceptions which hold these ideas in place were exposed in mid-century by Wittgenstein, Ryle and Austin. For those whose intellectual sensibility is attuned, the materials for the identification of the conceptual disharmonies involved in this venerable song are readily available. Unfortunately, philosophy in the late twentieth century is bent upon repeating the errors of its forebears. J. L. Mackie, the most distinguished of recent neo-classical empiricists, observed that in the development of physical theory 'it is simply superfluous to postulate that there are, in material objects, in the air or in the light, qualities which are at all like sounds as we hear sounds or colours as we see colours',[81] for these properties, like heat and cold, 'are not present in the things themselves in the same way as their shape (or . . . their mass).'[82] C. McGinn, writing in the same vein, contends that 'secondary qualities are thus subjective in the way

[79] F. Malin, *Understanding Paintings, the Elements of Composition* (Phaidon, Oxford, 1980), p. 96.
[80] E. Newton, *The Meaning of Beauty,* (Penguin Books, Harmondsworth, 1962), p. 13.
[81] Mackie, *Problems from Locke,* p. 17.
[82] Ibid., p. 34.

sensations are, even though they are ascribable to external things.'[83] And in an even more recent book, E. Prior argues that 'the secondary qualities are dispositional properties of objects . . . which are manifest when an observer experiences an appropriate sensation.'[84] Hence, 'what all purple items have in common is the power to cause a particular kind of visual sensation (one of purple) in a normal observer when they are illuminated in sunlight.'

It is evident that the conceptions and misconceptions of the heroic age of European science, dressed in modern garb, still soldier on. They are adorned with the trappings of twentieth-century science, talk of molecular and atomic structures replacing the older corpuscularian jargon, neural synapses and electrical impulses displacing animal spirits. Nevertheless, the picture has changed but little and the conceptual problems artfully concealed within it are not resolved. The insoluble problem of how the motion of animal spirits in the brain can produce a perception or sensation in the mind or soul is not resolved by jettisoning the soul and attributing sensations, perceptions, perceptual hypotheses or perceptual descriptions to the brain. The incoherence in denying sensible qualities to objects and assimilating them to sensations is not eliminated by identifying sensible qualities with perceptual 'contents' or 'intentional objects'. The absurdity of claiming that colours, sounds or textures as they are 'in' objects are merely powers is not reduced, but merely rendered more sophistical, by the contemporary philosopher's claim that to be coloured *means* to be disposed to cause a looking-coloured-experience to a human observer. The task of this book is to show how the seeds of seventeenth-century confusion still produce poisonous fruits in the twentieth century, and to expose the nonsense in prevalent conceptions of sense.

The purpose of the investigation is to break the spell of the scientific picture; not to abjure science, but rather to restrain it within the bounds of good sense. Science has replaced religion as the source and authority of truth. Yet every source of truth must, in the nature of things, be not only a source of falsehoods too, against which it

---

[83] C. McGinn, *The Subjective View, Secondary Qualities and Indexical Thoughts* (Clarendon Press, Oxford, 1983), p. 9.
[84] E. Prior, *Dispositions*, Scots Philosophical Monograph No. 7 (Aberdeen University Press, Aberdeen, 1985), p. 106.

must itself struggle, but also a source of mythology, against which it is typically powerless. One great and barely recognized source of mythology in our age is science itself. The unmasking of scientific mythology (which is not to be confused with scientific error or falsehood) is one of the tasks of philosophy. For philosophy is not the underlabourer of the sciences but rather their tribunal; it adjudicates not the truth of scientific theorizing, but the sense of scientific propositions. Its rewards lie not in furthering our knowledge, but rather in restraining us from nonsense and in giving us a proper understanding of what we know.

2

Sensation, Perception and Perceptual Qualities

1 Cracks in the surface

The sketch (and passing criticisms) of the origins and development of the well-entrenched conception that secondary qualities, in one sense of the relevant expressions, are but sensations in the mind suggests that not all is well in this scientific conception of the world and of our perception. The idea that colours (as well as other secondary qualities) as they are objectively are but dispositions (either structures of particles or powers of objects resultant upon such structures) and as we see (or, more generally, perceive) them are sensations has dramatic consequences. The gulf between appearance and reality is widened to an incredible degree. We can, on this conception, *never* perceive the world as it really is. No matter how carefully we check the conditions of observation, no matter how meticulously we monitor our perceptual competence (ensuring 20/20 vision) we *cannot*, in the nature of things, perceive objects as they are independently of us. While not as far removed from the human sphere as Kantian noumena, things as they are in themselves are truly accessible only to the probing eye of the electron-microscope or radio-telescope and to the theoretical constructions of contemporary physics.

The sensationalist conception of secondary qualities is complementary to an objectivist counterpart, which may be dubbed the 'dispositionalist' conception. Given the requisite ambiguity in the names of secondary qualities, one need not argue as Galileo did that 'if the perceiving creatures were removed, all these qualities would be annihilated and abolished from existence.' Rather, one will claim with Boyle, Reid and others that to attribute secondary qualities to objects *is* to attribute to them dispositions (powers), grounded in their particulate structure, to cause corresponding visual, auditory, etc. sensations in us.

The two complementary conceptions can be attractively synthesized into a unified account. This budgets for the circumstance-relativity and patient-relativity of dispositions (sugar, for example, is soluble, but not *at any* pressure or *in any* liquid; so too tomatoes are said to be red *in* normal light, relative *to* normal human observers). This synthesis may be called 'a reductive analysis'. On this conception, secondary qualities as perceived are held to be no more than *appearances* to normal observers under normal observational conditions. Hence, it is argued, 'for an object to be red is for it to present a certain kind of sensory appearance to perceivers.'[1] *Pari passu*, being B-flat is sounding B-flat to a normal listener under normal conditions, being sweet is tasting sweet to a normal taster under normal circumstances, and so on. Note that 'to present an appearance', to look red, sound shrill, feel smooth or cold, etc. are typically conceived here as *sensory states* or *experiences* of perceivers on the same level as *sensations*. Consequently it is claimed that this reductive analysis 'embodies what we might call the dispositional route from subjective experience [viz. appearing red, thus construed] to objective property [viz. being red, conceived as a power to cause a certain sensation or sensory state in a normal observer under normal conditions].'[2] All three (complementary) accounts will be examined in detail in later chapters. For the moment we shall take some preliminary steps towards clarifying the roots of their confusions.

If they are indeed confused, the confusion is a result (*inter alia*) of a misapprehension of the import of *empirical* theories of perception, viz. conjectural corpuscularian theories in the seventeenth century[3]

[1] C. McGinn, *The Subjective View* (Clarendon Press, Oxford, 1983), p.5.
[2] G. Evans, 'Things without the mind' in Z. van Straaten (ed.). *Philosophical Subjects, essays presented to P. F. Strawson* (Clarendon Press, Oxford, 1980). p.98.
[3] The corpuscularian theory of matter was, as argued in ch. 1, a priori in so far as it rested wholly upon a priori considerations pertaining to the *concepts* of space, space-occupancy, etc. The corpuscularian theory of perception was to a large extent a rudimentary empirical theory. Though interwoven with a misconceived *philosophical* causal analysis of the *concept* of perception, it was separable therefrom. Its ultimate fruitfulness for empirical research was independent of the misguided conceptual wrappings.

and well-confirmed contemporary empirical theories of physiological psychology. It is important to note that no empirical theory can show a *concept* not to be true to the facts, or to be mistaken. Nor can an empirical theory elucidate a concept, i.e. clarify the *grammar* of an expression. For the grammar of an expression is elucidated by describing the rules for its correct employment (in ascriptions *and denials* alike). Concepts are not true or false to the facts, rather they fix a logical space within which the facts may be determined by observation or experiment. An empirical theory may determine that things thought to be F are not actually so, but not that the concept of being F is 'false' or 'wrong'. Moreover no discoveries in physics or physiology can show that the *meaning* of 'red', 'sweet', 'shrill', 'acrid', 'torrid', etc. outstrips the understanding of competent users of the language, who must therefore wait upon science to reveal the real meaning of such expressions. At most what such discoveries could show would be that things which we take to *be* red, sweet, shrill, acrid, or torrid are not really so, i.e. an error of fact.[4]

Our apprehension of perceptual qualities (not only secondary qualities, note, but also primary ones) is explained in terms of the impinging of colourless, tasteless, odourless particles or radiation upon our sensory organs thus causing a neural excitation. It seemed to scientists and philosophers alike that it follows (i) that *what* we sense are not, or not 'directly', the objects themselves, but only their effects upon us; hence (ii) that the colours, tastes, sounds, etc. that we 'experience' are the final link in the causal chain commencing with the object's emitting or reflecting particles, radiation, etc.; and so (iii) that colours, tastes, sounds, etc. are not 'in' the object that affects us, but rather 'in' us. A detailed analysis of the misapprehension of the conceptual structure of physical and physiological explanations of perception of secondary qualities and its relation to ordinary descriptions of perceiving and its objects would be necessary to explode the idea that these forms of representation are in conflict or even that there is some deep sense in which the former *transcends* the latter.

---

[4] Even this is conceding too much. Is there really any intelligible sense in which scientific investigation could show, consistently with what we *mean* by 'red', 'sweet', 'shrill', that *all* our accepted judgements about the colour, taste and pitch of red objects, sweet foodstuffs and shrill noises are *false*? Occasional error is intelligible; complete error of the kind envisaged is not.

Some steps towards such an analysis will be suggested *en passant* in later chapters. For present purposes a few schematic remarks will suffice to arouse further suspicion.

First, it is true that when we see an object, photons (which are imperceptible) are absorbed by the photosensitive cells of the retina, causing changes to protein molecules, which consequently transmit an electrical impulse to the nerve fibre. But this fact does *not* show that we do not see ('objectively') coloured objects, let alone that we do not see them 'directly'. Nor does it show that what we perceive, when we look around us, are the *effects* of objects on us. For the changes to the retina, the activities of the optic nerve or 'visual' striate cortex, which are such effects of objects' reflecting light onto the retina, are *not* perceived, either by the eye or by the brain.

Secondly, the fact that it makes no sense to attribute colours to photons or sounds to sound-waves does not imply that what we see and hear is not (objectively, publicly) coloured or noisy. For although we would see nothing if not for the transmission of light (since one cannot see in the dark without special instruments) and hear nothing if not for the transmission of sound-waves (for one can hear nothing across a vacuum), the fact that the photons are not coloured and the sound-waves not noisy does not show that the colour and noise we perceive is *in us*. That thought seems to arise from the supposition that to perceive a perceptual quality the quality must be *transmitted* from object to percipient, and if it is not so transmitted, then it must be *caused in* the percipient. But it is no more necessary for my perceiving a red object that there be something red (a sensation!) 'in' me than it is necessary for my perceiving an explosion that something explode in me.

For, thirdly, it is a categorial confusion to think that seeing a red tomato (seeing that it is red, or seeing its colour) is the last link in the causal chain that begins with low-energy light of around 700 nm being reflected off the surface of the fruit and terminates with a sensation of colour in the brain. This misconception stems, *inter alia*, from a miscegenous crossing of the scientist's causal explanation of the physiology of perception with the normal description of a creature's perceiving an object. Because there is a causal transaction between the surface of the tomato and the retina of the observer, we are inclined to think that there must be reference to some such causal nexus implicit in the meaning of the sentence 'A saw the red tomato.'

We in effect project the causal relation between molecular surface, light, and retina onto A's seeing the fruit, concluding that the tomato causes a *visual sensation* in A's brain. But seeing the red tomato does not occur in the cerebral cortex. It occurs in the kitchen or green-grocer's![5] The only licit answers to the question 'Where did you see X?' or 'Where did the sighting of X occur?' specify either where I was when I saw X, or where X was when I spotted it. It is, as remarked in the previous chapter, not the brain but the person who sees, and his seeing is not a matter of having a visual sensation in the brain. In so far as there are any such things as visual sensations (a matter that will be pursued further below), they are not sensations in the brain. The only sensations which can be felt in the brain are sensations conse-quent, *inter alia,* upon pressure (the cortex can be cut without causing pain). These are typically *headaches.* And headaches are not sensations of colour, nor are colours sensations, let alone headaches.

Further suspicions may be aroused by noting what abuses of language occur in the very statement of the sensationalist thesis concerning the subjectivity or 'subjective aspect' imputed to second-ary qualities. First, it will have been noted that proponents of the thesis from Galileo onwards speak of perceptual qualities being *in* objects. Heat is said to be thought (wrongly) to be *in* the fire, the scent of the rose to be *in* the rose; we noted Mackie remonstrating that it is unnecessary to suppose that 'there are, in material objects, in the air or in the light, qualities which are at all like sounds as we hear sounds or colours as we see colours.' But colours are not *in* objects, and it is no part of our ordinary thought or suppositions that they are. Pigments may be, but not colours. Objects *are* coloured, *have* a colour or colours; the inside of an object (e.g. the lining of a drawer or box) may be coloured, but even that would be misdescribed by saying that there was a colour *in* the object. That style of thought and talk belongs to the fallacious *philosophical* doctrine of real accidents (see above, p. 21) rightly demolished by Descartes and Boyle. Of course, we speak correctly and harmlessly of there not being much heat in the dying embers of the fire, as we speak of there being little

---

[5] But not because when I see a tomato in the kitchen or greengrocer's my brain too is there! That contention multiplies the confusion, for it is as misleading as the claim that my watch was in London yesterday, when what is meant is that I was in London yesterday and wore my watch.

warmth in the watery winter sun. But no one would assume that such turns of phrase imply that there is heat *in* the fire in the sense in which there are logs in it; rather, to say that there is little heat in the embers is just to say that the rate of combustion has declined, and the embers are cooling down.

Secondly, it is wholly obscure what could be meant by such a remark as 'heat as we feel heat and coldness as we feel coldness are not present in the things themselves *in the same way* as their shape (or . . . their mass)' [my italics]. For what *is* the *way* shape or mass is *in* objects? The shape of an object is not *in* the object, and although objects *have* a shape, they do not have a shape in any *way*. Presumably what is meant is that 'objectively' things have a shape, i.e. they really do have a shape (and do not merely appear to have one). But really having a shape is not a way of having a shape, and merely seeming (deceptively) to have a certain shape is not a different way of having one. If 'the way in which objects have a shape or mass' signifies only that they really have shape or mass, then what appeared to be an argument is merely a dogmatic restatement of the claim that colour, but not shape, is, in some sense, 'subjective'.

Thirdly, the phrase 'colour (sound, heat) *as* we see (hear or feel) it' is misused.[6] How do we see red, feel heat, hear noise? With our eyes, hands and ears! But that is hardly what is meant. Of course, 'How do you hear that noise?' might mean 'What do you take that noise to be?', which might be answered by 'I heard it as a cry of fear'. But this too is not what is wanted. What, then, do we see red *as*? Do we see it *as* anything? Is this not a nonsense question? Not necessarily. One kind of answer might be of the synaesthetic kind, for example 'I see the red in that painting as a crescendo.' Alternatively, 'What do you see that colour as?' might mean 'What do you take it to be?', which could be answered by 'I see it as maroon' or 'I take it to be maroon'. (Notice the difference here between sounds and colours: 'What do you take that pitch to be?', not 'What do you take that noise to be?' is parallel to 'What do you take that colour to be?') But these questions only make sense in such rather special contexts, and none of the humdrum uses exemplified by the answers satisfy the requirements

---

[6] It is striking that these odd locutions breed hyphens – a sure symptom of a philosophical disorder; cf. Evans, ibid. p. 99.

of the philosopher who argues that there are not, in material objects, 'qualities which are at all like . . . colours as we see colours'.

Fourthly, it is noteworthy how our ordinary conception of secondary qualities as qualities of objects is misrepresented. For as presented in the sensationalist account, this conception is said to involve the belief that colours *exist* as *entities* in 'the outside world'. This naive belief is allegedly corrected by the scientific insight that colours (tones, tastes, smells) do not exist 'outside living minds', or exist only when someone is present to experience the appropriate sensation. But no one uncontaminated by philosophy would claim that colours exist as entities. Indeed the very claim that colours *exist* is opaque, and can surely mean no more than that there are coloured things or that colour words are meaningful. Hence the suggestion that colours do not exist outside 'living minds' is doubly absurd.

These cracks in the surface of the sensationalist conception of secondary qualities or of their alleged subjective aspect are symptomatic of deeper flaws. These lie in misapprehensions of the notions of a perceptual sense, of sensing and feeling, of sensation and perception. We noted the prominence in the seventeenth-century arguments of the putative analogy between having or being aware of a pain and its patent dissimilarity to its cause (a pin pricking, or knife cutting, the flesh) and perceiving or being aware of a colour, sound or smell and its alleged cause in objects. But is having a pain or feeling a pain really analogous to seeing the colour of an object or hearing the noise it makes? Equally prominent was the argument from *feeling* the heat of a fire and *its* assimilation to sensation. But should we not distinguish feeling heat from feeling hot? Writers in the venerable tradition we have been examining speak happily of sensations of pain, of colour or of sound, of visual and auditory sensations. A contemporary scientist writes that 'the sensations called green, yellow, pain, tickle, loud, hot, sick, fear and love are very different kinds of sensation and seldom if ever confused.'[7] It is true that we do not confuse green with a toothache or the pangs of dispriz'd love with a tickle. What is puzzling, however, is the suggestion that one might do so, i.e. that it is *intelligible*. Surely one can no more confuse these than one can confuse a railway engine with a railway company, or a

---

[7] R. L. Gregory, *Mind in Science* (Penguin Books, Harmondsworth, 1984), p. 510.

seat in the train with a right to a seat. One may indeed take something yellow to be green, but that is not to confuse two sensations (nor is it to fail to distinguish different wavelengths of light)[8] but rather to mistake the apparent colour of an object for its actual colour. Are all the expressions on the above list indeed names of *sensations?* Do they differ only in kind? Or are they, if sensations at all, sensations in quite different senses of the term?

If a wedge can be driven into these cracks, and pressure put upon it, we may discover the deeper sources of the surface flaws evident in the sensationalist conception. That can be done by an examination of the uses of such expressions as 'a sense', 'sensation' and the uses of sensation-names, as well as 'perception' and the uses of names of perceptual qualities. This grammatical investigation is of interest in its own right, and will shed light not only upon our immediate problems but also upon other matters that will concern us in the sequel.

2 The senses

The senses are faculties or capacities of certain kinds. We traditionally distinguish five *perceptual* senses.[9] The faculties of sense-perception, unlike such faculties as reason, memory or imagination, involve a perceptual organ or organs *with which* one perceives (whereas there is no organ of reason, memory or imagination; one does not reason, remember or imagine with a part of one's body). The concept of an organ of perception is that of a part of the body sensitive to a certain range of stimuli, employed in distinctive ways in discriminative behaviour. The ears are sensitive to sound, the nose to smells and the tongue to tastes; the eyes are sensitive to a multitude of things, given

---

[8] As Gregory suggests (ibid.); for one can only distinguish different wavelengths of light by perceiving readings on appropriate light-meters, not by perceiving the colours of objects.

[9] But tradition distinguished *seven* senses, as in 'to be frightened out of one's seven senses', apparently on the basis of the Apocrypha, where the residual non-perceptual senses are, remarkably, *speech* and *understanding*.

[10] Of course, one cannot think or do anything else without a brain, but it does not follow that one thinks with one's brain. The brain is not an organ of thought in the sense in which the eyes are the organs of sight, or in any other sense.

illumination or luminosity (light does not stand to the eye as sound to the ear or smell to the nose, although it is true that the eye is light-sensitive, and that in more senses than one). The organs of perception are used in exploratory behaviour, we orient our eyes (and head) in looking, follow a moving object with our eyes, bring them closer to a small object to discern it better, put them to the crack in the door to see through it. Similar orientation is characteristic of hearing (we cock our ears or cup them to hear better and put them closer to the source of sound) and smelling (we bring our nose closer to the odorous object to smell it better). Taste is somewhat different, for although we may lick a substance (or insert it in our mouth) to sample its taste, we do not thereby taste it *better*. Rather, such oral contact is a *sine qua non* of tasting. The sense of touch or feeling is anomalous in a different way. There is no unique organ of tactile perception, although with us the hands dominate. We can feel features of objects with most parts of our body (although we typically explore the feel of an object with our hands, cheek or lips), and the other perceptual organs are also tactually sensitive, for we feel the food in our mouth and its texture with our tongue, pressure on or grit in our eyes with our eyes, and our ears and nose are sensitive to cold and touch.

The organs of perception have both morphological and functional features. Deformation of a perceptual organ typically affects its functioning, and harmful deformation affects the exercise of the perceptual faculty which the organ subserves. The organ of perception may be good, poor or weak.[11] The goodness of a perceptual organ, for example the eyes, is distinct from the goodness of the faculty, although it is internally related to the optimal employment of the faculty. This distinction is often masked by the equivocal use of 'good eyes' and 'good eyesight' to refer now to the normality of the perceptual organ and now to the excellency of the discriminative skill in its employment. Nevertheless we should note that good eyes are not good at seeing, but the person with good eyes (i.e. non-defective organs of vision) may be good at spotting, discerning or descrying,

---

[11] See G. H. von Wright, *The Varieties of Goodness* (Routledge and Kegan Paul, London, 1963) pp. 51ff for an illuminating discussion of 'medical goodness'. On the concept of a perceptual sense, see A. J. P. Kenny, *Action, Emotion and the Will* (Routledge and Kegan Paul, London, 1963), ch. III.

and he who has good eyesight (i.e. visual discriminatory skill) is good at these tasks. Good perceptual organs are perceptual organs which perform their function normally, and the functioning of eyes or ears is tested by reference to standards of normalcy in seeing or hearing. The goodness of a perceptual organ is an innate endowment (although it does not follow that it can be used immediately at birth in the optimal exercise of the faculty). Weak or poor eyes may be innate or the result of illness, injury or ageing. It is curious that we do not talk of good *ears* but of good *hearing;* someone has *a* good ear (or nose) if he is good *at* hearing (or smelling) certain things – i.e. the evaluation is of use of the faculty. (But we do, of course, speak of a diseased ear.) Defects of eye and ear may be permanent or temporary, partially remediable by surgery or by artificial means such as spectacles or hearing aids. Such remedies enable a person to exercise the faculty in question better than he otherwise would be able to, given the defectiveness of the organ.

The perceptual organs are used in the exercise of the corresponding perceptual faculty. Hence the concept of the sense of sight is essentially connected with the concept of *looking* (and watching, observing, inspecting, scanning, surveying, glancing and peeping). Hearing is similarly associated with listening or harkening, smell with smelling, sniffing or scenting, and taste with savouring or tasting. The sense of touch is associated with *feeling*, but this is characteristically connected with a wide and disparate array of perceptual activities, for example fingering, handling, touching, stroking, groping, pressing, pulling, immersing, and lifting or weighing.

Possession of a sense-faculty is therefore manifest in behaviour. The sighted are identified by their competence in finding their way around without bumping into or falling over things, by their searching for and finding things by looking, by their following things with their eyes (and orienting their head and body to facilitate this) and by their responsiveness to optical stimuli such as lights, glimmers or flashes. The behaviour that manifests possession of a perceptual sense consists in relative efficiency in discernment, pursuit of certain goals and exploration of the environment. It is noteworthy that there is no unique form of behaviour that manifests perceiving innumerable specific objects of perception. How one reacts to seeing a door (or something green, moving, round, etc.), hearing a door shut, feeling the warmth of the fire, etc. depends upon the circumstances, one's desires and beliefs. One may see, hear, smell, taste or feel innumerable things without responding at all, and if one does respond, one's responses will typically vary in conformity with other factors. On the other hand, there are characteristic forms of behaviour associated with smelling a stench, tasting something bitter, hearing a sudden bang or feeling something very hot. This is no coincidence, since it manifests the fact that the perceptual faculties, especially taste and smell in the case of humans, are *also* hedonic faculties. The characteristic forms of behaviour associated with perception in such cases are also criteria for liking or (more markedly) disliking.

All faculties are tautologically faculties *for* something. The perceptual senses are faculties for acquisition of knowledge about what is *currently* perceptible in one's environment. To perceive is to apprehend, discern, observe, recognize or distinguish some current feature of one's environment by the use of one's sensory organs.[12] Hence the notion of a sense is essentially connected with cognition. It is striking that we once spoke not of the five *senses* but of the five *wits*, and hence too not only of common sense but also of common wit. Just as *percipere* (*per + capere*) is etymologically connected with the notion of grasping, taking hold of or apprehending through or by means of the senses, so too the Germanic *wit* is even more obviously connected with knowledge. The residue of this usage is still evident in the interchangeability of 'to come to one's senses/wits', 'to have one's wits/senses about one', or 'to be frightened out of one's senses/wits'. The nexus with cognition is grammatically marked, as noted in the previous chapter, by the fact that the generic *perceive* – as well as the residual 'to sense' (see below) – and the specific perceptual verbs 'see', 'hear', 'feel', 'smell' and 'taste' all take propositional and *Wh*-clauses as grammatical objects. One can be said not only to perceive X, to perceive that X is present, that X is F, but also that X is more F than Y, that X differs from Y in respect of F, and hence to perceive the difference (or similarity) between X and Y. In the primary use of *perceives that* and its particularizations, if A perceives that *p*, it follows that *p*. In this respect *perceives that,* and indeed *a* central use of *perceives*

---

[12] Although, of course, one can see *that* something *was* thus or *will be* otherwise.

(and its particularizations), is a success-verb (like 'recognize'). The mark of success is the possession of the relevant knowledge consequent upon perceiving.[13]

In as much as the perceptual senses are faculties for acquiring knowledge about one's environment by the use of one's organs of perception, it is only to be expected that these concepts be internally related to the notions of endeavour, success and failure. One can try to perceive and attempt to discern better. Hence voluntariness is associated with the exercise of the perceptual faculties (although much of what we perceive is not the result of trying, and most of our hearings, seeings, and smellings – unlike our tastings – are neither voluntary nor involuntary). One may look, listen, or grope for something or other, try to smell what is for dinner or taste which spices are in the dish. One may do so carefully or carelessly, deliberately or accidentally. But one may also see, hear or smell, glimpse, overhear or scent things one was not trying to observe, apprehend or discern. As one may try, so too there is success, failure and error. One may perceive, fail to perceive, or misperceive, for one may see M, fail to spot it despite looking, or see it but mistakenly take it to be N. The successful upshot of perceptual activities such as looking, listening, feeling for, is seeing, hearing or finding, descry-

---

[13] Note that the nexus with cognition is preserved (albeit in increasingly attenuated forms) in derivative concepts of a sense. We speak of a sense of time, speed or distance, signifying thereby a capacity for reliable *estimation* of these features. These skills obviously presuppose perception. A 'sixth sense', by contrast, is spoken of as a (putative) faculty, independent of any organ of sense, for (non-inferential) knowledge of what is not spatially or temporally present. An aesthetic sense (including a sense of colour, design, rhythm, style) is a discriminatory power connected essentially with the perceptible. It involves a sensitivity to perceptible features and their blends, as well as knowledge of what is fitting or appropriate in matters of taste. The notion of a moral sense (and the different but related notion of a sense of duty), however, is much more tenuously connected with the perceptible. One does not perceive what is right or wrong by the use of one's organs of perception, nor is there an organ of moral sense. (The conscience is not an *organ* of moral insight.) Nevertheless a quasi-cognitive affinity is retained in this concept in as much as the person with a sharp moral sense *knows* what must or may not be done, what is morally fitting, and acts accordingly. There is a further nexus with the notion of moral *sensibility,* in which the cognitive flavour of the moral sense is at least partly displaced by that of *feeling* or compassion. More attenuated notions of a sense are exhibited by our conception of a sense of humour, i.e. a capacity to apprehend the comic or incongruous; a *sense of balance,* however, has little cognitive association.

ing, espying, or more generally recognizing, discerning or distinguishing.

Since the senses are faculties in the exercise or use of which there is, in certain cases, success, failure or mistake, the network of associated concepts can be expected to incorporate strands appropriate to skills. One may be better or less good at perceiving such and such items, at discerning, discriminating or distinguishing this or that. As with many other innate faculties, one can be trained to use one's perceptual senses better for certain purposes, i.e. to detect or distinguish more through their exercise. Hence one can acquire a trained eye or ear, or a discriminating palate. Acquisition of such skills, which may be more or less specific in respect of visual, auditory or gustatory discrimination, is dependent upon the quality of one's innate endowment. But the possession of good eyes, for example, is no guarantor of specific competence in seeing, spotting or discriminating visibilia of one kind or another. The bespectacled copy-editor may be better at spotting misprints than the author with 20/20 vision, and the elderly game-tracker with ageing eyes may see the traces of a footprint where young bright eyes discern none. But, other things being equal, the better the natural endowment, the greater the potentiality for acquisition of such specific skills in the use of the faculty.

The temporary impairment of an organ of perception affects deleteriously the exercise of the perceptual faculty. One can taste or smell little when suffering from a heavy cold, and tactile perception is deficient when one's hands are numb with cold. Similarly, the efficiency of the senses is typically reduced by exposure to certain kinds of excessive stimulus. One cannot hear well after listening to the cacophony of a discothèque, see well after being dazzled, or make fine discriminations of taste after sampling too much.

Just as permanent or temporary impairment of an organ of perception reduces the efficiency of its exercise, so too variations in the environmental conditions affect one's ability to perceive. One can distinguish *absolute* from *relative* opportunity conditions for perception. In pitch dark a non-luminous object is not *visible* at all. Being illuminated is an absolute condition of visibility for such things. This is not a contingent feature, but built into our concept of the visible. Similarly, *not* being enclosed by an opaque container or covering is a logically necessary condition of visibility. However, an object may be visible *from* one vantage point but not from another. Even if well illuminated, an object is visible from a given vantage point only if it is not too far away, and if the light is poor, it may be visible only from close by. Similarly, an object may be visible from here, but not from over there where it is occluded by an intervening object. As Sam in *Pickwick Papers* comically puts it: 'Yes, I have a pair of eyes, and that's just it. If they was a pair of patent double million magnifyin' gas microscopes of hextra power, p'raps I might be able to see through a flight o' stairs and deal door: but being only eyes, you see, my wision's limited.' This 'limitation' is a fact of grammar: it is not a contingent truth that one cannot see something occluded by a wholly *opaque* solid object. We further distinguish *ordinal* opportunity conditions for perception. Optimal conditions for visibility maximize the clarity and distinctness with which one sees. Distance, camouflage, failing light, intervening dust, rain or fog reduce visibility. The character and pattern of opportunity conditions for the different senses is strikingly varied, highlighting how *different* are the conceptual structures of specific sense and correlative sensible qualities in each case. This, however, will not be further pursued for the moment.

Although we speak of the five *senses,* the cognate verbs are striking in as much as 'to sensate', originally synonymous with 'to perceive',[14] is wholly obsolete, and 'to sense' has suffered a diminution of range. It is now largely confined to peripheral perception or 'intuitive' apprehension, as in 'I could sense that someone was in the darkened room; how, I cannot say', 'I could sense the excitement (fear, tension) in the air' or 'I sensed that something was amiss'. Other cognate terms display connections not only with the perceptual, but also with reason and consciousness, the emotional and hedonic (as well as, of course, with the semantic dimension which can be ignored here). A person can be said to be a man of good sense or sensible if he is reasonable; he can be said to be as yet insensible if he has lost consciousness and not yet come to his senses. An object is sensible if it is perceptible; similarly a magnitude (weight, distance) or difference is sensible if it is large enough to be perceived. Experience is said to be sensible, as opposed to emotional or mystical, if it

---

[14] For example 'Each of them can distinctly sensate or see only those parts which are very near perpendicularly oppos'd to it' (Hooke, 1665) or 'experiments proved nothing but the simple sensating of certain crude colours by bees' (Parker, 1883).

pertains to the perceptual senses. Someone is said to be sensitive if he is readily affected by or responsive to something or other (and, by transference, instruments are said to be sensitive). Hence 'sensitivity' straddles the perceptual and emotional domains. 'Sensibility', as in *Sense and Sensibility,* is focused upon the emotional, particularly the more tender emotions, while 'sensual' and 'sensuous' are firmly connected with the hedonic – the pleasures of the senses.

While the verb 'to sense' shrank in its range, leaving its place occupied by 'to perceive', the nominalizations 'a sensation' and 'a perception' assumed very different significance. 'Sensation' has widespread currency, whereas 'a perception' as in 'a visual (auditory, etc.) perception' is poor coinage, being a term of art found largely in psychology and philosophical writings, where it is a source of extensive confusion. It is noteworthy that while both are grammatically count nouns (have plurals, take 'many' and 'several' rather than 'much',[15] and the indefinite article in the singular), nevertheless there are only rough criteria for counting sensations and barely any for counting perceptions. One can ask how many times I have seen St John's College or heard the 'Eroica' (although what *counts* as seeing or hearing something *n* times will vary from context to context), but one cannot sensibly ask how many visual or auditory perceptions of them I have had. There are tolerably clear criteria of identity for sensations, but not for perceptions. The pain I now have in my knee may be the same as the pain I (or you) had yesterday. But the question of whether my current visual perception of St John's is the same as the one I (or you) had last week is a question in search of a sense. One can ask only whether St John's looks the same as it did last week; or whether it looks the same to me (or you), i.e. strikes us as being unchanged; or whether I am viewing it from the same or a different vantage point, whether I discern what you did. The concepts of a sensation and a perception are *very* different. Yet it is a characteristic feature of the tradition of thought on the subject of perception from the seventeenth century onwards to assimilate them. To clarify the reasons for this and the errors generated, the concept of sensation must be examined more closely.

---

[15] 'There is not much sensation in my leg' is a different use. When there is little sensation in a limb, the sensations one feels in it are numbed or blunted.

3 Sensation

The noun 'a sensation' displays a bewildering diversity of use and multiplicity of divergent conceptual connections with other psychological concepts. Although originally simply a nominalization of 'to sense', its focal point shifted over the centuries as the range of 'to sense' shrank. It is no longer located in the same area as 'perception' but is rather centred on 'physical' sensations, a notion which itself is by no means uniform. Nevertheless, via the concept of *feeling* it is firmly connected with the concepts of tactile perception, bodily desire and the more violent emotions. These uses of 'sensation' differ, sometimes in small but subtle ways, sometimes more radically. Although there are obvious connections and analogies between them, *sensation* is not obviously a family-resemblance concept. For sensations of pain or nausea, of giddiness or lassitude, of hunger, of fear or gloom, of creaking joints, or floating or of the position of one's arm, of warmth or of slime, of pressure or resistance, and many others, are not self-evidently related as members of a family after the manner in which games, kinds of propositions or numbers are argued to be. One would not readily think of localized sensations, awareness of one's local or global physical condition, kinaesthetic awareness, dispositions of certain kinds, emotions and moods, tactile perception, etc. as being all different *kinds of sensations,* even though in each of these cases the expression 'sensation' has an application. It is perhaps preferable to conceive of somewhat different but *diffuse* concepts of sensation. It should, however, be stressed that nothing essential to the following argument turns on deciding one way or the other in this matter.

Paradigmatic sensations (i.e. what have traditionally been taken as paradigms of sensation), or *sensations proper* as I shall call them, are such things as aches, pains, tickles, tingles, twinges, nausea, heartburn, erotic sensations, itches and prickles. These are characterized by the following features:

First, sensations proper have a location – it always makes sense to ask where it tickles, what part of the body hurts, where the pain is located. The criterion for the location of a sensation is where the owner points, what part of the body he assuages, scratches, etc. This may be distinct from the locus of its cause, as in the case of 'reflected pains', and may, exceptionally, be outside the body, as in the case of 'phantom pains'.[16] Though pains are said to be in one's hand, foot or stomach, the representational *form* of location is misleading (when philosophizing). Such sensations are not *in* the body in the sense in which a pin or splinter may be, or even that in which a wound is. A pain may be deep within the body (as opposed to a surface pain) but cannot be deeply embedded in it nor can it be extracted from it – the waning of a pain may be described as the pain's going away, but when a pain goes away it does not go out. One may have a wound in the leg and hence a pain in the leg, but while one can bandage the wound, one cannot bandage the pain, and whereas the wound is visible in the leg, the pain can only be said to be visible in the face of the sufferer (although it is visibly his leg that hurts him). Note that the location of a pain is not a phenomenal quality of the sensation – it is not the *character* of the pain that enables one to say where it hurts.

Secondly, there is no organ of sensation. We do not feel pain *with* our hand, but *in* our hand. But there are sensations in our organs of perception: salt in the eye causes a smarting sensation, snuff causes a tickling sensation in the nose, and piping hot coffee burns one's tongue.

Thirdly, sensations have degrees of intensity, from the excruciatingly painful or intolerably itchy to the easily endurable minor twinge. Unlike perceptions, however, they do not have degrees of clarity. One does not have or feel a pain clearly or indistinctly in the sense in which one hears a cry clearly or indistinctly. Sensations have phenomenal qualities, marked by such predicates of pain as stinging, gnawing, smarting, nagging, throbbing, sharp, piercing, dull (derived from causal or analogical association). They have genuine duration, may be momentary or persistent; if persistent they may wax or wane over time. But they cease with loss of consciousness – pains do not persist unfelt during anaesthetic or sleep. Of course, the persistent cause of pain (the injury or illness) may cause disturbed or restless sleep, and we do say that the pain caused, for example, by a

---

[16] But it would be misleading to characterize the phantom pain as located in an object adjacent to the stump of the limb, for if the object is moved the pain does not move with it. Could we not imagine it being so, envisage feeling pain in the body of another person? Up to a point, perhaps; but beyond a certain point our concept of pain would crumble (how would a pain felt in London be manifest in a patient in Oxford?) and so too our concept of our own body.

post-nasal drip woke us up. It does *not*, however, follow that one felt the pain in ones' throat while one was asleep.

Fourthly, sensations proper belong to the category of the hedonic, i.e. we may call them 'pleasant' or 'unpleasant'. Most are painful or unpleasant – we have a much richer vocabulary for pains and unpleasant sensations than for pleasant ones. They disturb our well-being and optimal functioning, and their characterization is important for remedial reasons. Nevertheless, erotic sensations are typically enjoyed, and small children like being tickled.

Fifthly, sensations are had or felt, but not *perceived*. It only makes sense to talk of perceiving X if it makes sense for X to occur unperceived, or of misperceiving X. But there is no such thing as an unfelt pain or an unowned tickle, nor, as we shall elaborate below, does it make sense to suppose that one mistakenly takes oneself to have a sensation. One may err about the cause of a sensation one has, but not about its occurrence or location. It is noteworthy that in place of 'I have a head- (tooth-, stomach-) ache' one can say 'My head (tooth, stomach) hurts'; if I have a tickle in my throat, my throat tickles. No analogous transformation is licit in the case of perception where what is perceived is independent of the perception of it.

Sixthly, the owner of a sensation is he who *manifests* it in behaviour (although, of course, not all sensations are expressed). The criteria for having a given sensation consist in typical behaviour in certain circumstances. Pain is characteristically manifest in crying out, groaning or moaning, in assuaging the painful limb, in protecting it from further impact, in limping, etc. Tickles are manifest in laughter, and itches in scratching. These are *natural* forms of behavioural manifestation of sensations. Upon them are grafted learnt forms of linguistic behaviour that function as further criteria for ascription of sensation.

Ownership of sensations is unsharable: I cannot feel your pain, any more than you can have my toothache. These propositions are, however, misleading. 'I cannot feel your pain' looks like 'I cannot feel your pulse', but it is more akin to 'I cannot sneeze your sneezes'. The 'cannot' does not signify failure to do or inability to do something that can be done, rather it signifies logical (not empirical) imposs-ibility. One might say that 'cannot' here is not the negation of 'can' for it signifies *senselessness*, i.e. there is no such thing as having or feeling another person's sensation. For 'the pain I have' = 'the pain I feel' = 'my pain'. So if you feel a pain, *you* have it, not I – and what *I* feel is not yours but, tautologically, mine. It does not follow, however, that I cannot have the *same* sensation as you. If my sensation has the same phenomenal qualities and place as yours (i.e. is in a *corresponding* location), then it *is* the same sensation as yours – that is what is *called* 'having the same sensation'. And sameness of sensations as avowed by patients is an important datum in diagnosing the sick as suffering from the same disease.

Seventhly, there is no room for genuine error or doubt on behalf of the subject of a sensation.[17] A sincere avowal by a person that he has a pain located in such-and-such a place and having such-and-such a character is a logical criterion for its being so. 'I think I have a pain, but I'm not sure' or 'Maybe it tickles me, but I don't know' either express the indeterminacy of a sensation (hence not *ignorance*) or are nonsense. 'I think it's a headache, but it might be a stomach-ache' makes as little sense as taking a person's nursing his swollen jaw as a criterion of his having a stomach-ache. But it would be a grievous confusion to think that mistake and doubt are ruled out by knowledge and certainty – as if one's perception of one's pains were utterly infallible. As remarked, one does not perceive one's pains at all; and 'I know I have a pain' is either an emphatic way of saying 'I (really) *do* have a pain' or it is a nonsense. For it only makes sense to speak of knowing where it makes sense to speak of learning or coming to know, of answering the question '*How* do you know?', which may be by way of citing a source of knowledge or a ground of knowledge (i.e. a piece of evidence). The various modes of perception are sources of knowledge; 'I saw the penny' and 'I felt the penny' are answers to the question 'How do you know that there was a penny there?' (although they are not evidential grounds for my cognitive claim). But if someone says 'I have a toothache', the question 'How do you know?' must be rejected as senseless. It looks as if it can be answered on the model of citing a perceptual source of knowledge, viz. 'I feel it', but that is an illusion. To feel toothache is not distinct from

---

[17] This is a pivotal point in Wittgenstein's philosophical psychology. It is hotly contested and has not won widespread acceptance. Nevertheless it is, to my mind, a profound and widely ramifying insight. For a detailed examination of Wittgenstein's views, see P. M. S. Hacker, *Insight and Illusion, Themes in the Philosophy of Wittgenstein*, rev. ed. (Clarendon Press, Oxford, 1986), ch. X.

having toothache, and to feel or have a sensation is not to perceive a sensation. Hence there is no question of knowledge or ignorance of one's own current sensations, or of doubt, or error. Does this mean that one is *certain* of one's sensations? No. It would make sense to be certain that one has a pain only if it also made sense to doubt whether one does. Absence of doubt only makes room for certainty if doubt is *intelligible*.

Eighthly, not only does it make no sense to talk of knowing that one has a sensation but the general nexus of sensation to knowledge of or information about how things are is slender. One is tempted to say that sensations do not inform us how things are, that we do not learn that things are thus-and-so by having sensations, as we learn that sugar is sweet by tasting it. This is not quite right: when one burns oneself one not only has an acute pain, one also knows that one has touched something hot, and if one grazes oneself painfully, one knows that one has scraped against a rough surface. We shall revert to this matter below. One might say that sensations inform us about the state of our body. This is correct for some kinds of cases: the piercing pain of a burn or the smarting sensation of a graze indicate damage to one's skin. Obviously enough, toothache is typically associated with a defect in a tooth. On the other hand, animals or small children have toothache (or other sensations) without learning anything about their defective teeth (or other parts of their body); an itch gives one no information about the state of one's body, and it is an empirical discovery (inductive correlation) that heartburn is a symptom of indigestion and a sharp pain in the left of one's chest of angina pectoris. 'Having' or 'feeling' a sensation is not grammatically connected with propositional and *Wh*-clauses as verbs of perception are. To smell a stench in the kitchen is to perceive, by smelling, that there is a stench in the kitchen; to see what colour something is to see that it is such-and-such a colour. To feel a pain (tickle or itch), however, is to have one, not *per se* to perceive anything, even though one may, of course, feel *that* one has grazed or burnt oneself, and that is painful.

Finally, though one may, through disease or local anaesthetic, lose one's sensitivity to sensation, i.e. cease to have or feel sensations, to have sensations is not *per se* to exercise a faculty. Sensations, *unlike* perceptions, belong to the category of passivity, not in the sense that one cannot *bring it about* that one has a certain sensation, but in the sense that having sensations is an undergoing, whether endured, suffered or enjoyed. They are not voluntary, although they may be voluntarily self-inflicted or given. One cannot feel an itch intentionally or have a toothache carefully and deliberately. There is no skill in having sensations, and although people's pain-thresholds vary, the more sensitive are not better at feeling pains than others, and to lose all sensation in one's gums after an injection is not to be poor at feeling the pain of the drill, but to have no pain caused by the drill. Hence too there is no *learning* to have sharper or more *accurate* sensations. For sensations, being tenuously connected with knowledge and being quite different from perceptions, are not accurate or inaccurate, correct or incorrect. On the other hand one can learn to suppress one's behavioural manifestations of sensations, and people may become better at tolerating pain and preventing it from dominating their lives.

These are the central features characteristic of sensation proper. But if we move through the conceptual network, loosening reticulations here, tracing other connections and analogies there, differences, and in due course different concepts, emerge. Note first how a slightly different notion of sensation comes into view if we loosen the nexus with *location*. After having been on a merry-go-round, one feels giddy. Where? One is tempted to say 'In the head' (at any rate – not in the foot!). But that may be misleading. One does not feel giddy *in* the head in the sense in which one has a pain in the head. For one cannot transform 'I feel giddy' into 'My head giddies' on the model of 'I feel an itch' and 'My head itches' or 'I have a pain in my head' and 'My head hurts'; and even 'My head is giddy' sounds awry. (And 'My head is in a whirl' is largely, if not exclusively, figurative.) Nor can one give a clear location to giddiness *in the head,* as one can say that one has a headache in the temples or in the occipital region. This slight and subtle difference (which may be a peculiarity of English) seems to be associated with the fact that giddiness is a *general* disorientation *of the person,* not a disturbance to a part of his body, but a sensation manifest in inability to keep his balance, walk in a straight line, reach out unerringly to grasp what is wanted.

This holistic feature becomes more pronounced in the case of feeling tired, wide-awake, feverish or ill. One's limbs feel tired when one has certain sensations, typically aches, in them. But my legs can feel tired without me feeling tired, and I can feel tired without any part of my body feeling tired. For it suffices for me to feel tired that I *desire to rest* or sleep, and have a feeling of lassitude – which is not a sensation but a *disinclination to act*. Feeling ill displays a slightly different conceptual pattern. If I feel ill, I typically have various localized sensations such as nausea, aching joints, a sore throat, but whereas when I feel aches in my joints, my joints ache and when I feel nauseous, I have a feeling of nausea in my stomach, if I feel ill no part of me feels ill (as opposed to painful) nor do I feel ill *in* a given part of my body, although I may believe rightly or wrongly that some part is infected or awry. Unlike giddiness, feeling tired or ill are not themselves sensations, although they are bound up, in slightly different ways, with sensations. As one moves further into the range of concepts of overall condition of a person, the nexus with bodily sensation weakens, for example feeling refreshed, wide-awake, vigorous, well, contented, depressed, cheerful. The end of this spectrum lies firmly in the area of *mood* and is adjacent to concepts of emotions, attitudes and dispositions.

A somewhat different conception of sensation comes into view if the nexus between sensation and desire is strengthened. Pains are sensations one seeks to avoid or alleviate; one naturally wishes that they would abate. Itches are sensations one wishes to scratch and tickles stimulate a desire or inclination to laugh. Hunger, thirst and lust are spoken of as *physical* desires, and *also* as sensations. But note that while a sensation of pain is a painful sensation, a sensation of hunger is not a hungry sensation. A sensation of hunger is an 'empty feeling' in the stomach, a sensation of thirst involves a 'dry feeling' in the throat, and erotic sensations typically accompany lust. Hunger, thirst and lust, however, are directed at objects; these desires are not merely for the abating or amelioration of the characteristic accompanying sensations (as in the case of pains, itches and tickles), but are desires *for* food, drink or sexual intercourse. Being hungry, thirsty or lustful is not the same as wishing that one did not feel thus, and these are not normally accompanied by such a desire or wish in the manner in which pain normally involves the desire that it should cease. Note, however, the peculiarities of the nexus with sensations. One can want a drink without having any sensations of thirst, and one's throat may be dry without one's feeling thirsty (as when one is acutely afraid). Further, one may be hungry, thirsty or lustful without desiring any *specific* food, drink or woman; or one may crave for caviar, thirst for champagne, or lust after Bardot. But though there are typical sensations of hunger, thirst and lust, there are no specific champagne-desiring sensations in one's throat, caviar-craving sensations in one's stomach or lusting-after-Bardot sensations in one's loins. The concepts of desire and sensation are interwoven here in a way different from the weave characteristic of sensations proper and also from that of less 'physical' desires.

The strengthening of the nexus between sensation and cognition is evident in our concepts of bodily feelings which involve an explicit awareness of one's localized bodily condition. One can, after running, feel the pounding of one's heart; as one ages, one can feel the creaking of one's joints; after overeating, one can feel one's distended belly; and in exerting physical effort, one can feel the straining and relaxing of one's muscles. These feelings are *essentially* sensation-involving (hence unlike hunger, thirst and lust) and the relevant sensations are localized. One feels one's joints creak in one's joints, one's heart thumping in one's chest, and the sensation of surfeit in one's belly. They are not, however, instances of tactile perception, for one does not feel what one feels either *on* one's skin (as one feels a spider on one's neck) or indeed *with* any organ. Of course, one can – one can feel (tactually perceive) one's heart pounding with one's hand, hear one's joints creak or feel them doing so with one's fingertips, and one can see one's distended belly. Bodily feelings are informative in a manner in which sensations proper are not, even in those cases where the sensation is indicative of a physical condition or malfunctioning. To feel a pain, tickle or itch is not to feel a spatial object, an event or a state; rather, what is felt is, in the sense explained, 'private' and 'unshareable'. To have a toothache is to feel a toothache, but it is not to feel the defectiveness of the tooth – that would be to feel the cavity with one's tongue. By contrast, when one feels one's pounding heart, creaking joints, tensed muscles or cramp, one feels that one's heart is pounding, that one's joints creak, that one's muscles are tense or in a spasm. And others can confirm visually, auditorily or tactually what one feels. The condition felt can obtain whether one feels it or not, for one's joints may creak without one noticing it, and one's distended belly does not cease to be so when one falls asleep and no longer feels it. What is felt is a physical condition or event which is not 'private' or 'consciousness-dependent'. There is room for error, as when one thinks one has a knot in one's neck (for one's neck feels tense) even though the muscles are relaxed, and also persistent illusion, as in the case of a lump on one's lip which characteristically feels larger than it is. Hence it makes sense here, but not in the case of sensations proper, to talk of knowledge. One cannot intelligibly say 'I know I am in pain because I feel it', but one can say 'I know my heart is pounding because I feel it'. Bodily feelings are sensation-involving forms of awareness or consciousness of one's localized bodily condition. Unlike perception, they involve no organ with which one apprehends thus the condition of one's body, and they do not give one information about one's environment. Since no perceptual organ is involved in such bodily feelings, the nexus with the voluntary is attenuated – one can but concentrate one's attention.[18] The gap between error and illusion is vanishingly small – in the case of mistake one cannot 'feel again', since one does not, in *that* sense, feel. They lie intermediate between sensation and perception.

There is an affinity as well as a difference between localized bodily feelings and what is sometimes (slightly misleadingly) called 'kin-aesthetic sensation'. We can normally say where our limbs are, describe their disposition, and specify how our body is oriented. Unlike bodily sensations, however, such positional awareness is not, or not typically, grounded in specific sensations. I do not feel that my fingers are bent because I have a feeling-of-being-bent in my fingers. It may well be that one cannot say how one's limbs are disposed when they are locally anaesthetized and senseless, but it does not follow that when they are not anaesthetized one's judgements are based on disposition-indicative sensations.

We speak of sensations of fear, terror, distress or acute anxiety, excitement or nervousness. The reasons are obvious: these violent emotions and intense moods involve complex patterns of circumstance, an appropriate object in the case of emotions (together with a distinctive pattern of beliefs), characteristic desire and action, and sensations typically manifest in symptomatic behaviour. When frightened one's pulse races, when moved to grief or pity one may

---

[18] This is also true of certain kinds of tactile perception, e.g. feeling an insect on one's neck. But here one is apprised of something in one's environment impinging on one's body, not merely of the condition of (part of) one's body. (Of course, one can feel *for* the insect with one's hand.)

have 'a lump in one's throat', and when excited or nervous one may have 'butterflies in the stomach'. It is noteworthy how peculiar are the characterizations of these sensations that are part of the syndrome of an emotion or mood; aches, pains, itches and tickles are not, in their literal sense, characteristic of emotions, although by *extension* we talk of twinges of remorse, pangs of jealousy, and of itching with excitement (yet *these* twinges, pangs and itches have no location!). Yet emotions are not sensations. Though they may be accompanied by typical localizable sensations, as in the case of fear or pity, the emotion itself is not localizable. Unlike bodily feelings, they do not inform us of the state of our body (although one may have palpitations, sweat and tremble with fear and be aware of it); they are 'directed', involving beliefs and desires about their objects; and there are reasons and justifications for them. It makes sense to tell someone that he has no reason to feel fear, but not that he has no reason to feel a toothache, only that there is no (physical) cause. The nexus between the concepts of sensation, attitude and emotion is perspicuous in the use of 'sensational', 'creating a sensation' and 'sensationalize', i.e. creating astonishment and strong, crude, emotional responses and attitudes.

The concepts of sensation are located at a point of intersection of strands of numerous other psychological concepts – awareness of bodily condition, physical desires, overall condition of a person, kinaesthetic or positional awareness, emotion, mood and disposition. As the notion of sensation approximates more closely to one rather than another of these, so the meaning of 'sensation' shifts, sometimes only slightly, sometimes markedly. It is tempting to try to impose a systematic order, to determine how many different meanings 'sensation' has. This should be resisted:

Mere description is so difficult because one believes that one needs to fill out the facts in order to understand them. It is as if one saw a screen with scattered colour-patches, and said: the way they are here, they are unintelligible; they only make sense when one completes them into a shape – whereas I want to say: Here *is* the whole. (If you complete it, you falsify it.)[19]

---

[19] L. Wittgenstein, *Remarks on the Philosophy of Psychology*, vol. I, ed. G. E. M. Anscombe and G. H. von Wright, trs. G. E. M. Anscombe (Blackwell, Oxford, 1980), § 257.

Attempting to draw sharp boundary lines between essentially diffuse concepts can only distort matters, unless the boundary is drawn relative to a specific purpose in a particular context.

A feature not yet examined, but manifest in everything thus far said, is the connection between *sensation* and the even more extensive and heterogeneous notion of *feeling*.

4 Sensation and feeling

'Feeling' has manifested expansionist tendencies over the centuries. It covers much the same range as 'sensation', but also various forms of perception, emotion, disposition, awareness and opinion in ways *not* characteristic of 'sensation'. Etymologically connected (via the Germanic *folm* and *folma*) with the *hand,* one focal range of its present use is that of exploratory perception by means of the limbs. A variety of locutions highlights different aspects of such activities that parallel, and are as manifold as, looking, peering, peeking, etc. in the case of vision. One may *feel about* one in the dark to locate oneself relative to objects in one's environment or to locate objects around one. One *feels for* the keyhole with the key, and fumbles for the key in one's pocket. One *feels one's way* along a corridor, groping along in the dark. One *feels out* the contours of an object by running one's fingers around it, and one may feel the ground, test or try it out, with one's foot or indeed with one's walking stick.

The successful upshot of these exploratory activities is that one finds one's way, finds the object one was groping for, finds out how things are disposed, whether the ground is firm, what one is touching, etc. Feeling in this sense is a form of perception, which, though usually called the sense of touch or tactile perception, is in fact *also* exercised other than by touching, as when we feel the warmth of the fire from a distance or the wind blowing from that ⟋ direction. (It is striking that originally the perceptual use of 'feeling' was much broader, for one could until the nineteenth century speak of feeling (i.e. perceiving) smells and tastes as in 'Com nere son and kys me, that I may feyle the smelle of the' (1460) or 'To feel how the ale dost taste' (1575).) We can distinguish feeling an object and its tactile qualities by touching and manipulating it with our limbs (primarily hands) or other parts of our body, as when we feel an X or the Fness of the X by handling, fingering, stroking, pushing, pulling, kneading, or poking it, from feeling the effect of an X's touching one, as when we feel a blow, the pressure of an X pushing against us, the graze or tickle of an X moving along the surface of our body.

It was noted, in the above discussion of sensation, that the various modes of sensation all lend themselves to characterization in the idiom of feeling. If one's limb is rendered insensible through anaesthetic or cold, one has no feeling in it. Sensations proper are said to be feelings as are sensations that border on perception, as when one feels the palpitations of one's heart or the swelling of one's lip. So too are unlocalized sensations such as feeling giddy, and generalized bodily conditions, such as feeling tired, ill or feverish. Physical desires associated with sensations (of hunger, thirst or lust) are similarly said to be felt.

The wide range of emotions, emotional attitudes and receptivity, moods and inclinations is also subsumed under feeling. Feeling angry or jealous are emotions, feeling depressed or cheerful are moods; feeling pleased, curious or interested are attitudes; and one who feels sympathy or compassion evinces his feelings *for* another. Our emotional susceptibility is manifest in our acutely feeling the loss of what we cherish, and a form of sensitivity in our feeling for language or music. And our inclinations are evident when we do what we *feel like* doing.

Feeling is also bound up with opining and with awareness or sensing. To feel that it would be better to do thus–and–so, or that things are getting out of hand is to think or opine thus. To feel (or feel conscious of) the tensions in the room is to sense or be aware of the brewing scene. Those who have once felt their power are unlikely to forget it, for they have become aware of what they can effect.

The network is vast (we have not touched on feeling oneself again or feeling up to the task) but it would be erroneous to think it disorderly or confused (as opposed to confusing). The categorial differences between the different feelings are precisely the different kinds of grammatical combinatorial possibilities and impossibilities, implications, compatibilities and incompatibilities which the various uses of 'feel' display with other parts of speech and specific expressions. The manifold distinct uses of 'feel' are (tautologically) determined by different rules of use, different conditions of application of the relevant expression. For the behavioural criteria (actions, reactions, verbal behaviour, grimace, demeanour, etc.) which justify ascribing a feeling in one sense or another are altogether distinct, and the circumstances in which various forms of behaviour count as criteria for feeling this or that are equally multifarious.

Our concern is with the perceptual uses of 'feel'. We have already noted that there is no *single* organ of tactile perception, although the exploratory senses of 'feel' are obviously associated especially with movable parts of the body, viz. the limbs and tongue. Like sight, but unlike smell, taste and hearing, feeling has no proper object, not in the Aristotelian sense, but in the sense that if A hears X he necessarily hears a sound and if A smells X he necessarily smells an odour, whereas if A feels X there is no corresponding feature he necessarily feels. The categorial range of what can be felt includes objects, events (as when one feels a stick snap, the ground give way), processes (the vibration or warming up of an engine), states (the icy state of the road) and dispositions (the elasticity of a stick, the slipperiness of a surface).

The focal point for tangible characteristics is that of a space-occupant which we feel by touch. We are embodied creatures moving about in a world of physical objects. We can feel solid objects and liquids (with respect to which we can feel their relative viscosity – whether they are 'thick' or 'thin' – by stirring them with finger or implement, or wading through them). Concentrating on solid objects, note that we can feel properties pertaining to their space-occupancy, namely their shape, height, and size – and dimensions pertinent to these, viz. whether they are (relatively) thick or thin, long or short, narrow or broad. So too we can feel features of their boundaries or edges, viz. whether they are pointed, sharp or dull, their location and their orientation. And we can feel whether they are solid or hollow. The sense of touch is exercised by pressure and manipulation, hence we can feel whether an object is compressible or not, whether it is plastic or has a relatively permanent shape, whether it is bendable (rigid or flexible), breakable (tough or brittle) and whether it is elastic or inelastic, i.e. whether it is stretchable, and if so whether it returns to its original dimensions after stretching or not. By pushing, pulling and tugging we can feel not only these properties of the materiality of the object, but also whether it is movable or immovable and hence too whether it fits into another object and whether the fit is loose or tight. We can similarly feel whether an object, independently of us, is moving or at rest, sometimes by feeling it move, sometimes by feeling the vibrations it causes around it, sometimes by feeling its vibrations as it moves. By fingering an object or surface, rubbing against it or walking on it we can feel its textural qualities, whether it is smooth or rough, slippery, granular, soft or sticky. We can similarly feel its cohesive properties, viz. whether it is solid, as opposed to crumbling, cracked and hence fissile. By trying to lift an object, or by weighing it in our hand, we can feel whether it is heavy or light, and by touching it we can feel whether it is wet, damp or dry. Similarly we can feel, not necessarily by touching an object, whether it is hot, warm, cool or cold. And we can feel the number of objects of a (limited) collection of tangibilia.

Lest one be mesmerized by such physical objects and these (relative or absolute) tangible properties, one should bear in mind that one can feel holes (in one's tooth as well as in one's shoe), bumps (in the road as one drives over them), distances between objects or points; one can feel the sun on one's brow and the wind on one's cheek, the stifling humidity of the air on a torrid day and the frosty bite of a winter's morning. One can feel the strength of the wind as it blusters about one, its direction (with one's wet finger) and the speed and power of the car as one accelerates down the motorway, that it is going round a bend or into a skid.

Like other perceptual verbs, 'feel', in its perceptual use, takes propositional and *Wh*-clauses. As one sees *with* one's eyes and smells *with* one's nose, so too one feels *with* one's hands, fingers, etc. Yet unlike the other senses, not only is there no specific organ of touch, but also one feels things *on* part of one's body, as one feels the (warmth of the) sun on one's brow, the (wetness of the) rain on one's face, (the movement of) an insect on one's hand, and (the weight or pressure of) a rucksack on one's back. Hence there is a *passive* aspect to such kinds of tactual perception which gives them a striking affinity to sensations (see below). One can look listen, or smell *again*, from closer, but one cannot in *that* sense *feel again* in such cases. The part of the body *on* which one feels such things is also the part which is sensitive to what one feels, hence feeling something on one's hand is unlike seeing or smelling something on one's hand. (But it would be misleading to say that one felt an insect crawling on one's hand with one's hand.) Whereas one can see through transparent glass but not feel anything through it, one can feel a solid object through or beneath a cloth covering but cannot see it. Like the other senses, touch or feeling is a trainable skill. Some people are better than others at feeling the relative warmth of the bathwater for the baby, when the child's clothes are damp or dry, whether its pulse is normal or if it is feverish. There is success, failure and mistake in tactile as in other forms of perception, as well as illusion. Disparity between actual feature and how it strikes one is marked in the case of vision by projecting the verb 'to look' upon what is seen and contrasting how *it* looks with how it actually is. Similarly with 'to feel': the bridge may feel unsafe but not be so, the water may feel cold (if one has been sunbathing) but be warm, and if one moves a marble over one's crossed fingers it feels (note that here the pronoun is a dummy) *as if* there are two marbles. Over a restricted range we speak of the look of an object (see below, pp. 121ff), and in a likewise restricted manner we talk of *the feel* of the velvet, of the steering (of the car), of (the condition of) the bridge. (Yet just as the sky at sunset looks red, but we don't speak of it having a red look, so too the boiling kettle feels hot, but we don't say that it has a hot feel.) Like the other senses, one may feel something attentively, carefully and deliberately or inattentively, carelessly or accidentally.

It is immensely tempting to associate the sense of touch very closely with sensation proper, to think that when we perceive tactile qualities of objects we do so by way of having *sensations* characteristic of or caused by the objects thus qualified. Hence we are inclined to think of tactile perception as a matter of having tactile-quality-indicative sensations. (It is noteworthy that in seventeenth-century pictorial representations of 'The Five Senses', the sense of touch, i.e. feeling, is often represented by a person who has hurt himself and is feeling a pain!) On this conception we are aware of, or perhaps even *identify*, the particular character of a sensation, and *infer* from the features of the sensation that the object touched has such-and-such tactile qualities. Many considerations induce this thought. There is no organ of sensation, and no *specific* organ of touch; one can feel (tactilely perceive) *with* almost any part of the body, and one can have sensations *in* almost any part of the body. Some kinds of tactile perception, like sensation, are essentially passive and lack the exploratory potentialities of sight, hearing or smell. We do have sensations in the organs we employ to feel objects, and often have these sensations as a result of touching, for example we burn our fingertips when we feel whether the kettle has been on, and get a nasty sting when we touch a nettle. Sensations belong to the category of the hedonic; feeling the soft texture of velvet or fur is pleasant, it gives one a pleasant sensation of softness; feeling the slimy surface of a jellyfish is revolting and can be agonizing. The very language of tactile quality and of sensation seem inextricably interwoven: we speak of wet, slimy sensations; it makes sense to talk of a dry sensation as well as hot and cold sensations (as when we speak of feeling a hot flush or a cold shudder). A limb that is numb with cold is said to be insensible – one can feel nothing *with* it.

Nevertheless, the temptation should be subjected to close scrutiny. We can feel the shape of an object, whether it is round or square, but not by having round or square sensations, rather by feeling the contours of the object. Of course, to do so one must feel the edges of the object with one's fingertips but so to feel is to feel *that* one's fingers are in contact with the edges and *that* they are moving along an unbroken edge – hence a matter of tactile perception. But when one feels a plate one does not have a sensation of roundness but rather it (the plate) feels round. (One might say that one has a sensation *of something* round, but that is equivalent to saying that the object in question feels round.) To feel that an object is thick or thin is not to have thick or thin sensations, let alone to feel thin (as after prolonged illness). It is, to be sure, dependent upon kinaesthetic awareness, (for example of distance between thumb and index finger), but not *inferred* therefrom.

Similar features are evident in the case of perception of qualities associated with pressure, viz. feeling the compressibility, rigidity, plasticity or elasticity of objects or substances. For when one feels that a rod is rigid, a lump of matter is plastic, or a cord is elastic one does not have a sensation of rigidity, plasticity or elasticity in one's fingertips, hands or arms. Perceiving these features involves manipulation or attempted manipulation, viz. pushing, bending, pressing or pulling. Hence feeling that something is rigid, plastic or elastic *may be* accompanied by sensations. But these will primarily be bodily feelings, such as muscular strain, and kinaesthetic awareness; only exceptionally is one likely to feel aches, tickles or prickles. It may well be the case that one could not feel these qualities of objects if one's limbs were insensible (through anaesthetic) and rendered one *incapable* of feeling these sensations. It does not, however, follow that one *must* have felt such sensations (only that one must be able to have them), let alone that one's perception of the quality is *derived* from a sensation or sensations had.

Does this argument imply that feeling tactile qualities is uniformly a matter of perceiving the tactile qualities of objects, which may or may not be *accompanied* by sensations, and that it is a mere coincidence that when one's hands are numb or otherwise insensible (e.g as a result of a local anaesthetic), one cannot feel the texture and surface qualities of things one touches, strokes or rubs? If so, the argument is implausible, because the implication is unacceptable. Does it make sense to suppose that one could feel that a knife is sharp even though one cannot feel that its point, when one presses one's finger against it, hurts one? Of course, when one feels (perceives) its point prick one, one does not have a pointed sensation. Rather one has the sensation of something pricking one, which may be painful. We recoil from the prick, for it hurts, and we perceive that the object is sharp and pointed. But we do not perceive the sharpness of the point independently of the sensation of a prick. The sensations one has when one tactually perceives are neither a datum from which one infers the tactile quality one apprehends, nor are they coincidental accompaniments of such perception. Rather the *concepts* here intermingle. That is not explained by reference to the mere co-ordination of the passive and active powers, which is coincidental and only implies an overlap in the instantiation of distinct concepts. Rather is it explained by reference to an overlapping of the criteria for having certain sensations with the criteria for tactually perceiving. Thus, for example, the behavioural expression of pricking one's finger painfully is, in the appropriate context, also a criterion that one has felt that the point of the knife is sharp. So too the utterance 'Ow, it's sharp' gives verbal expression both to pain and to perceptual knowledge painfully accquired.

Similarly, our tactile perception of textures and surface qualities displays what might be called a suffusion of perception and sensation. If one passes one's finger over glass, sandpaper, or velvet, they feel smooth, rough, and soft respectively. One has a sensation of something smooth, rough or pleasantly soft. Of course, 'a sensation of softness' looks like 'a sensation of pain'. But this is misleading: the softness is felt *with* the fingertips, not *in* the fingertips (unlike the sensation of pain caused by touching the hot kettle). If one feels a pain in one's fingertips, one's fingertips hurt or are painful, but if one feels a sensation of softness with one's fingertips, one's fingertips are not soft. Yet it would be equally misleading to jettison the term 'sensation' in such contexts and conceive of our perception of the softness of velvet as independent of, or merely coincidentally accompanied by sensations of softness. To talk here, as we do, of a sensation of softness *is* to talk of perceiving the quality of the velvet – its soft feel, which is pleasant. What is enjoyed is *stroking* the velvet, which one would not take pleasure in if one's fingers were insensible. Perception and sensation are here fused, and any attempt to drive a wedge between them, to view the former as *inferred* from the latter, or the latter as a mere *accompaniment* of the former, misrepresents our concepts.

Stickiness is different again. We speak of a sticky feeling and a sticky sensation; a surface feels sticky to the hand when one's fingers stick (however slightly) to it, and one feels a (slight) resistance to detachment. One's fingers themselves feel sticky when they are felt to stick to each other or to surfaces one touches. Stickiness is an adhesive power of surfaces, and one feels the stickiness of a surface by touching it to discern whether it sticks to one's fingers. Here bodily feelings are essentially involved, although feeling one's skin slightly pulled is not the same as feeling the stickiness of the surface, nor is the latter inferred from the former. One finds out whether a surface is tacky by touching it and feeling *that* it is tacky, not by inferring that it is tacky from the sensation of a slight tug on one's skin. One perceives an adhesive power by actualizing it through contact.

Perception of qualities in the wet/dry scale is not a matter of tactilely perceiving a potentiality, even though it is true that if one feels that something is wet by touching it, the limb with which one touches it will become (at least slightly) wet. When thirsty one sometimes has a dry sensation in one's throat or mouth (although it is not uniformly marked by lack of saliva). But when one feels whether the laundry is dry, one does not find it to be so by having a dry sensation. One's hands or body may feel wet when one feels water on them, or dry – when one does not (but we also talk of our skin's being dry when it is lacking in natural oils). But we do talk of a sensation of *being* wet or dry, again a merging of perception and sensation. We say that touching a dead fish gives one a repulsive wet sensation, but that too is equivalent to a repulsive feeling of wetness.

What is perceived is the slimy feel of the fish, but *touching* it is unpleasant and we recoil with disgust.

The weave of concepts of sensation and tactile perception is dense and confusing. Sometimes tactile perception is accompanied by bodily feelings, although what is perceived is not inferred from the judgement that one has such-and-such feelings. In other cases, the boundaries between perceiving and having sensations blur. Further difficulties are undoubtedly generated by thermal qualities and our perception of them. It is, one suspects, no coincidence that they played so prominent a role in the seventeenth-century argument. It is to this that we shall now revert, bringing to bear some of the lessons learnt in the course of these lengthy perambulations through the logical geography of sense, sensation and feeling.

3

Sensations, Secondary
Qualities and Appearances to
Normal Observers

1 Sensation and perception

In chapter 1 it was noted that Galileo, observing that perception
involves the impact of particles or waves upon our sensory organs,
assimilated secondary qualities to sensations. A feather passed over
the nostrils causes a tickle, which is a sensation of the conscious
creature, not a property of the feather. By analogy, sound is a
sensation caused by vibrations of the eardrum produced by sound-
waves in the air, heat a sensation caused by rapid motions of particles
adjacent to the skin, and so on. Descartes followed suit, emphasizing
that the painful sensation of a strap pressing harshly into our flesh or a
sword cutting it is not a property of the strap or of the sword and its
motion, and that nothing exists in the strap or sword that *resembles*
the pain it causes. By analogy, the secondary qualities are sensations
caused by objects which are not themselves qualified by any properties resembling these sensations. Boyle repeated the argument from
pain, and so did Locke. Wedded, as they were, to a representational
conception of perception, they held that the application of predicates
of primary qualities to ideas and to objects alike was to be explained
in terms of a resemblance, whereas in the case of predicates of
secondary qualities their application to objects is metonymical: '*Flame*
is denominated *Hot* and *Light: Snow White* and *Cold;* and *Manna
White* and *Sweet,* from the *Ideas* they produce in us', but 'there is
nothing like our *Ideas,* existing in the Bodies themselves'. Locke

placed emphasis on an argument equating the perception of intense heat with suffering a sensation of pain:

he, that will consider, that *the same Fire,* that at one distance *produces* in us the Sensation of *Warmth,* does at a nearer approach, produce in us the far different Sensation of *Pain,* ought to bethink himself, what Reason he has to say, that his *Idea* of *Warmth,* which was produced in him by the Fire, is actually *in the Fire;* and his *Idea* of *Pain,* which the same Fire produced in him the same way, is *not* in the *Fire.* Why is Whiteness and Coldness in Snow, and Pain not, when it produces the one and the other *Idea* in us; and can do neither, but by the Bulk, Figure, Number, and Motion of its solid Parts? (II–viii–16)

Berkeley seized upon this argument and made it and variations upon it the centrepiece of his *First Dialogue between Hylas and Philonous.* Intense heat, he insisted, is not distinct from acute pain, and since pains exist only in the mind, so too must heat. Similarly, moderate degrees of warmth are a pleasure, but pleasure 'cannot exist without the mind', hence warmth too must be a sensation 'in the mind'. Furthermore, if feeling degrees of heat and cold were the perception of objective properties of objects, it would not be possible for the same object to occasion a feeling of hot and cold simultaneously, since that would imply that the same object was both hot and cold. But, as Locke had noted, lukewarm water feels cold when one immerses a hot hand and hot when one immerses a cold one.

Certainly we do not say that a pin or blade has a pain, but rather that they may cause a pain by pricking or cutting a sentient creature. It is, however, misleading to characterize this by the claim that nothing exists in the pin or sword that resembles the pain caused. For what would it be if something *did* exist in the pin that resembled the painful prick it occasions, i.e. what is it that is held *not* to be the case? It would, presumably, be for the pin to feel a similarly painful prick, for the pin to suffer a pain in its point or in the pinhead! But there is no such thing as a pin having a pain in its head – this is a nonsensical combination of words, not a characterization of something which happens not to be the case.

It is equally misguided to suppose that when we see or feel the shape or size of an object, its location or motion (which may be audible too), predicates of shape, size, location or motion are applied both in characterizing our perception and in characterizing the object we perceive because there is a *resemblance* between the perception and what is perceived. When I see or feel the circular shape of a coin I do not have a round sight or feeling. I may be said to have a round impression, but a round impression is an impression *of* something round and is not itself round (or any other shape) and is not seen or felt. To see the penny on the table or to feel it in one's pocket is not to see one 'idea' atop another or to have one feeling on another feeling, and to feel the penny to be larger than the ha'penny is not to have two feelings, one larger than the other. Of course, something may feel larger than it is (a cavity in one's tooth) or look oval when it is round. Yet in such cases there are not two items differently propertied, but only one misperceived or appearing to be other than it is.

It is just as mistaken to suppose that 'white', 'sweet', 'cold' and other predicates of secondary qualities are applied to objects metonymically 'from the ideas they produce in us'. On the contrary, as will be argued in detail later, these properties are defined by reference to public paradigms or samples and are applied literally, not metonymically, to objects. Perception of thermal qualities, duly misconceived, is *one* source of the temptation to think otherwise.

Note in the first place that thermal qualities should not be equated with temperature. Having a certain temperature is a linear scalar property. Thermal properties are not, for things may be neither hot nor cold. Nor do thermal properties correspond ordinally to temperature, for heat-conductive materials are characteristically colder than poor conductors at the same temperature, as one can perceive by feeling a piece of metal and a piece of cloth on a chilly day. The introduction of the concept of temperature placed powerful subjectivizing pressure on the concepts of thermal qualities.[1] It is notorious that humidity intensifies the cold or heat of the weather: a rise in humidity will make the day much colder or insufferably sultry despite constancy of temperature. 'It is much colder today than yesterday', we say as we shiver, and may be surprised to find the temperature unaltered. We are then inclined to rephrase our remark: 'Well, it feels much colder', implying that nevertheless it is not. But if

---

[1] But it is noteworthy that the classical arguments supporting the subjectivity of thermal qualities *predate* the introduction of the metric concepts of temperature and the invention of thermometers.

that *is* the implication, then the use of the expressions 'cold' and 'colder' has shifted, since temperature is now being employed as a criterion for whether the day is colder than yesterday. That is perfectly legitimate, but it is no less legitimate to retort: 'It does not just feel colder, it *is* colder, although the temperature has not dropped.' Here heat and cold are not judged by temperature or measured by thermometer, but by thermal perception.[2] In this common sense of thermal predicates, they are explained by reference to paradigms which are perceived by touch: '*This*', we say, 'is cold', and give someone a piece of ice to hold; and, of course, the *this* is not a sensation. '*This* is colder than *that*', we explain, giving someone a piece of metal and a piece of wood to touch on a chilly day, or a chilled drink from the fridge and one from the tap. We do not learn the use of thermal predicates by learning to employ a thermometer but rather employ thermal predicates in mastering the use of thermometers; and we do not correct someone who says of a given surface that it is neither hot nor cold by saying, 'It can't be, it must have *some* temperature!'

Of course, our concepts of thermal qualities are employed, like other perceptual concepts, against a background of facts about us. Were our body temperature lower or higher by a significant degree, our current paradigms would be differently used, and we might judge snow to be warm or boiling water to be tepid. But then, of course, 'warm' and 'tepid' would have a different meaning. That we have *shared* thermal concepts depends on our having shared *reactions* to warmth and cold and on our having a common bodily temperature – if they varied significantly from person to person we would not have a thermal vocabulary, for there would be neither agreement in definitions of thermal predicates, since we would not agree on the defining samples, nor would there be agreement in judgements. Our capacity to make accurate judgements of heat and cold depends on our hands (or cheeks) not being hot or cold. The tepid water of the swimming-pool feels cold after sunbathing and may feel warm after

---

[2] But it is immensely misleading to suggest, as J. J. C. Smart does, that thermal perception 'is less anthropocentric than our colour sense because the human being is much more like an (inefficient) thermometer than he is like an (inefficient) spectrometer' (*Philosophy and Scientific Realism* (Routledge and Kegan Paul, London, 1963), p. 85.)

five minutes' immersion, although it is neither cold nor warm. But *pace* Locke and Berkeley, there is no contradiction here.

Secondly, we distinguish feeling heat from feeling hot and feeling the chill of the evening from feeling chilly.[3] Feeling hot, warm, cold or chilly are indeed sensations. They may be local or global: one's hands or feet may feel hot (or cold) without one otherwise feeling hot, and a swollen finger feels hot without the owner feeling hot; but one may also feel hot *tout court:* a generalized bodily condition. Thermal sensations, whether local or global, have a typical behavioural expression. If one feels hot one typically perspires, loosens or removes one's clothing, and fans oneself. If one feels cold, one shivers, one's teeth chatter, and one seeks for more covering. If one's limbs feel cold, one chafes them to restore circulation, claps one's hands or stamps one's feet. If they feel hot one cools them, perhaps by trailing them in the river as one lies in a punt on a summer's day. Note, however, that thermal sensations are more akin to bodily feelings than to 'sensations proper'. When one's feet feel cold one does not have a cold sensation *in* them and when one feels hot one does not have hot sensations in every part of one's body. (When 'hot sensation' and 'cold sensation' do not signify a sensation *of* heat or cold, i.e. perceiving heat and cold, they are typically, though not only, used to signify emotional tone, as when one has a sudden cold sensation of doom or fear, and shivers.) As with bodily feelings, but unlike typical sensations proper, in having thermal sensations one can be said to become informed of characteristics of one's body and its parts, viz. the thermal condition, and may in certain cases be deceived. One may feel cold even though one is not, as when one has a raging fever; and after playing snowballs one's hands feel very hot even though they are very cold and may be *perceived* to be so when one puts them to one's cheek. There are, however, thermal sensations which approximate more to sensations proper, for example the pleasantly warm sensation one has when one drinks a double scotch.

Thirdly, perception of thermal qualities need not be, and often is not, accompanied by feeling thermal sensations. I may feel the heat of the fire or the cold draught by the window without feeling hot or

---

[3] Also 'feeling *the* heat (cold)', which signifies susceptibility or sensitivity to climate.

cold (locally or globally) as long as I do not remain near the fire or in the draught. The piping hot coffee is perceived to be too hot with the tongue, although the tongue does not feel hot (but hurts) even when it is scalded. One feels the heat of the fire *with* one's hands or face, but one does not feel hot *with* anything (save embarrassment). And when one's hands feel hot, they no more feel hot with themselves than if they feel swollen, they feel swollen with themselves. This is characteristic of the distinction between perception and bodily feeling.

As one warms up before the fire, one does not think that the pleasantly warm feeling of one's limbs is in the fire. But one does think, and one is right to think, that the warmth one feels *with* one's outstretched hands is the warmth *of* (although not *in*) the fire. Locke and Berkeley erred in failing to distinguish the perception of heat from feeling hot, and confused themselves by deploying the expression 'sensation of warmth' indifferently to signify feeling warm and feeling warmth. Approaching a fire, one *perceives* the heat of the fire, feels its heat with one's hand. But the feeling of heat, the perceiving of the heat of the fire, is not 'transformed imperceptibly' into a feeling of pain, as Locke and Berkeley argued. There is no such thing as 'transforming' a perception into a sensation. Rather, as one approaches closer, still perceiving the heat of the fire, one's hand will start to hurt. Of course, Berkeley disputed this:

Philonous	Upon putting your hand near the fire, do you perceive one simple uniform sensation, or two distinct sensations?
Hylas	But one simple sensation.
Philonous	Is not the heat immediately perceived?
Hylas	It is.
Philonous	And the pain?
Hylas	True.
Philonous	Seeing therefore they are both immediately perceived and at the same time, and the fire affects you only with one simple, or uncompounded idea, it follows that this same simple idea is both the intense heat immediately perceived, and the pain; and consequently, that the intense heat immediately perceived, is nothing distinct from a particular sort of pain.[4]

[4] Berkeley, *Three Dialogues between Hylas and Philonous*, in T. E. Jessop (ed.), *The Works of George Berkeley*, vol. 2 (Nelson, London and Edinburgh, 1949), p. 178.

This is surely confused. If one puts one's hand too close to the fire one may feel the intense heat and feel the pain of burning oneself. But the former is perceived and not had, and the latter is had but not perceived. The pain had 'cannot exist without the mind', but only in the sense that insensible things cannot be said to have (or to be free of) pains. The pain had is not in the mind, but in the hand; the only pains 'in the mind' are the pangs of anguish, grief, and other forms of 'mental' suffering. (Philosophers should make more of the fact that we speak of *physical* pain!) The pain suffered and the heat perceived are not two sensations nor are they one and the same sensation, but rather one sensation undergone and one perceptual quality apprehended. The sensation resembles nothing in the flames, and the heat felt does not *resemble* the heat of the fire – it *is* the heat of the fire. If one comes too close to the fire, one's perceiving of the heat is painful, but this is mischaracterized by claiming that the sensation of heat becomes a sensation of pain. What is, of course, true is that one's capacity to perceive heat and one's susceptibility to the pain caused by excessive heat are co-ordinate and the criteria for their instantiation, in certain cases, merge. Hence when one accidentally touches something very hot, one withdraws with a cry of pain. 'That's hot!', one may exclaim; but also 'It hurts!' or 'Ow! I've burnt myself!'. The experience of thus burning oneself displays that blending of sensation and tactile perception noted above, which makes it wholly misguided either to assimilate the perception of a hot object to a sensation (as Berkeley did) or to hold that one has a heat-indicative sensation from which one infers that one has touched a hot object.

So much for the classical arguments. The moderns, particularly scientists who embedded the seventeenth-century misconceptions in their empirical theories, speak of visual (auditory, etc.) sensations as involved in perception. Art theorists, encumbered by the same tradition, talk of the wonderful sensation of swirling colours that a canvas by a great colourist gives one. Does this make sense? And if so, what sense? We observed previously that all the organs of perception are also organs subject to sensation, and that in various senses of the term. One can have sensations *in* organs of perception, as when one's eyes itch, one has a tickle in one's nose, or an earache. These are sensations proper. One's nose may feel swollen and one's ears can feel cold. These are bodily feelings. And one can feel grit in one's eye, as one can feel something pressing on one's nose, and one can feel one's broken tooth or the texture of food with one's tongue. These are cases of tactile perception. But, of course, none of these sensations are specific correlatives of the perceptual faculty in question.

What, if anything, are visual sensations? The uses of 'sensation' are multifarious, but one thread that runs through all is their affiliation with 'feeling'. If the expression 'visual sensation' is to have any genuine currency, we should expect visual sensations to be felt *in* the eyes, yet also to have an essential affinity with *visibilia* (rather than *tangibilia*). Only one thing comes close to fitting the bill, namely the sensation of being dazzled. The eyes are our uniquely light-sensitive organs, and the sensation of being dazzled is produced by exposure to a sudden glare. We say indifferently, 'I was dazzled' or 'My eyes were dazzled' but not, curiously, 'I felt dazzled'. Nor do we say, 'I was dazzled in my eyes',[5] let alone 'I felt dazzled in my eyes'. So the nexus with 'feeling', and 'feeling . . . in . . .' is not what one would expect. Why 'sensation' at all then? Perhaps because the sensation of being dazzled, like paradigmatic sensations, has characteristic forms of behavioural expression, viz. looking away, blinking and shielding the eyes, as well as assuaging the sensation by rubbing them. Though one is not dazzled in the eyes, the nexus with location is preserved in as much as it is the eyes that are dazzled, and it is they that are assuaged by rubbing; and the tie-up with the hedonic is manifest in the fact that being dazzled is typically unpleasant and sometimes painful.

Are there analogues for the other senses? For hearing obviously the sensation of being deafened by a loud noise is similar. We speak of being deafened by the din or one one's ears being deafened, but, again, not of feeling deafened either in or with one's ears. Being deafened is for most people unpleasant, and one typically blocks one's ears when exposed to a deafening noise.

In the case of the other senses there seem to be no *verbal* analogues of 'to be dazzled' or 'to be deafened', but there are analogues, more or less remote, of being dazzled or deafened. In the case of taste, sampling a strong curry is perhaps the gustatory analogue of a dazzling glare. It reduces or obliterates one's perception of the tastes of the dish, temporarily impairs one's sense of taste, is (for most

---

[5] This does not seem to be merely because of pleonasm, as in 'I felt a headache in my head'.

people) unpleasant, and has characteristic forms of behavioural manifestation. Something similar applies, perhaps a little more tenuously, to smell. Overwhelming smells are unpleasant and typically reduce one's olfactory sensitivity, and substances such as ammonia are not merely painful to smell but also have a numbing effect upon one's sense of smell. It should, however, be noted that these are but *analogues;* nothing in the dimensions of hearing, smell or taste corresponds to light in the dimension of sight. Hence nothing corresponds precisely to being dazzled by a blaze of light. It is more difficult to find even a good analogue in the case of touch, and this is no coincidence. Like sight, but unlike taste, smell or hearing, tactile perception has no proper object. However, unlike sight, touch has no unique perceptual organ and involves nothing akin to light or illumination. It is true that one's tactile sensitivity is diminished by cold, but that is a thin analogue of being dazzled or deafened.

If these, in particular being dazzled or deafened, are the paradigms of non-tactile perception-associated sensations, i.e. visual and auditory ones, it is obvious that they are not what philosophers and scientists have in mind. For far from sensations of being dazzled or deafened being the essential aspects or accompaniments of visual and auditory perception, they are abnormal, and *impair* seeing and hearing.

Does it follow that it is mistaken to speak, as scientists, art-theorists and philosophers do, of visual sensations? The answer must surely be equivocal: it depends what they mean or intend to convey. When the art critic writes of the wonderful sensation of colour conveyed by a great Chagall canvas, he may mean nothing more than that it is wonderful to behold, that it impresses one as a veritable symphony of colour. And that is innocuous enough. On the other hand, when philosophers and scientists talk of visual sensations of redness, they are more obviously enmeshed in conceptual confusions of venerable ancestry. 'A has a visual sensation of redness' might be a garbled way of saying 'A sees something red' or 'Such-and-such looks red to A' or 'Such-and-such strikes A as being red'. But if it does not mean what these sentences mean, or if it means something further – as it typically is intended to – then it is incoherent. We should place pressure on the concept of sensation deployed. Is the visual sensation of redness *felt?* No, for one does not feel red, let alone have a red feeling either in or with the eye. Nor does one feel a sensation of redness in the brain, let alone in the mind. Does the visual sensation of redness have a characteristic behavioural expression, does one scratch it or assuage it? No, for there is no specific 'seeing-something-red' behaviour that is an expression of the putative sensation. Is it akin to bodily feelings such as the sensations of cramp, or of having overeaten? No, for a visual sensation of redness is not a form of awareness of a bodily condition, save in cases where one sees that one's skin is sunburnt – but there the sensations involved are not visual, and what is visual is not a matter of having a sensation but of seeing one's ruddy skin. Is it akin to thermal sensation? I may feel hot, have the sensation of being hot, or my foot may feel hot. But when I observe the colour of a ripe tomato and allegedly have a sensation of red, I do not have a sensation of being red, I do not feel red, nor does any part of me – I see the red tomato. Is it like feeling heat? Yes – I feel the heat of the fire with my hands and see the colour of the tomato with my eyes. But I do not feel the sensation of red with my eyes, nor do I *see* a sensation of red.

Philosophers and scientists will remonstrate. For not only is it claimed that seeing coloured objects (and seeing their colour) is a matter of having visual sensations, but it is further contended that the colours seen are themselves sensations. This, as should by now be obvious, is a further quagmire of confusion. Its contours and muddy depths will be plotted in the next section.

2   Sensations and secondary qualities

The sensationalist conception of secondary qualities represents colours, sounds, smells, tastes, thermal and various other tactile qualities as being sensations caused 'in us' by sensory stimulation. Of course, it is conceded, we *say* that roses are red, sugar sweet, and ice cold, but that merely reveals our naivety in confusing appearance with reality and our scientific ignorance in *projecting* upon objects features which properly characterize only our sensations. The survey of the concept of sensation in the previous chapter provides the material for demonstrating that this sensationalist thesis itself is conceptually awry, that far from penetrating the veil of appearances it is enmeshed in the web of philosophical illusion. This verdict can be sustained by comparing the concept of sensation with concepts of secondary qualities. As is customary, colour will occupy stage-centre in the following discussion, but since the conceptual differences between the various perceptual qualities are great and rarely noticed,[6] other *dramatis personae* will be brought upon the stage.

Secondary qualities are not sensations in the head, as headaches are, nor are they in the mind as ideas (but not sensations) are. Of course, only sentient creatures can (tautologically) perceive them, and different creatures have different perceptual discriminatory capacities – a fact which can readily lead to philosophical confusion via such questions as 'What does the world look like to a mouse?' (see below, pp. 159ff). But most sentient creatures (animals) do not have minds, although they have sensations, and what they perceive in respect of perceptual qualities, just as what humans (who do have minds) thus perceive, is not mental. To perceive the colour, smell, taste or sound of an object is not to *have* a sensation and what is perceived *is* not a sensation.

It is paradigmatically objects and stuffs which can be said to be this or that colour; but also shafts or pools of light, flames, shadows and similar ephemera. (Note, however, that events cannot have colours, although they may be exciting and colourful or dull and colourless). Objects that have colours or are a certain colour do not make colours, although they may make coloured flashes of light (mixing stuffs, of course, makes different colours, but that is a matter of making coloured paints, dyes, etc.)[7] Sounds are quite different. We must distinguish here between sounds (noises) that are *made* and sound-qualities that are had. People, animals, instruments and objects make sounds by doing something or having something done to them. Hence also events, actions, processes or activities make a noise. It is the sounds thus made that have the aural qualities of being mellow, silvery, gentle or melodic. But not everything that makes a sound *has* a sound of this or that quality, since sound-qualities are attributable to objects only if they typically, by nature or design, make sounds of that quality. Cordelia had a gentle voice, and a cello has a rich and

---

[6] A shining exception is J. O. Urmson's 'The objects of the five senses', *Proceedings of the British Academy,* LIV (1968), pp. 117–31, to which the following discussion is indebted.

[7] Blending light of various wavelengths is also said to make such and such colours – in yet a different sense.

mellow sound, but a pile of bricks, though it makes a clatter when dropped, does not have a sound; and to say that something has a certain sound is not to say that it is making a sound, but rather that if it makes one, then the sound it makes will typically be of that character. Smells, like sounds, are made, and like colours, are had. Something can have a smell without making a smell, and make a smell without having one. Objects and stuffs have smells, and through action, make smells. Hence events, processes and actions make smells. An object or stuff that makes a smell when undergoing a process of transformation, for example combustion, is commonly said to have, in so far as it is thus changing, the smell it then makes – hence *burning* rubber both has and makes a distinctive smell. Tastes, on the other hand, are had, not made, although mixing a spice into a dish will make the dish taste thus-and-so. Tastes are properties of objects and stuffs, not of events, processes or actions, although one can taste *that* the meat is going bad or the cheese getting overripe. (Tactile qualities, discussed in the previous chapter, will be neglected here.)

These are grammatical observations, not empirical ones. They concern what it *makes sense* to say. It makes sense to attribute a colour to an object (but not to an event) and such a judgement may be true or false. As previously noted, to claim that an object is not coloured or has no colour is to assert that it is colourless,[8] but then it makes *sense* to say that it is coloured. To say that something made no sound is to assert that it was silent, but then it is intelligible to say that it made a noise, even though false. Hence the defender of the sensationalist thesis must claim not that it is false that geraniums are red and delphiniums blue, but that it is senseless to assert this. The scientist may argue that, when a tree falls on a deserted heath, 'We can assume that the fall would cause vibrations in the air. They would exist, to be sure. But there would be no sound because sound, by definition, implies the sensation evoked in a living being by such vibrations.'[9] Such a scientist must be committed to the view that it is nonsensical to predicate auditory predicates such as 'yelp', 'clank' or 'noisy' of creatures, objects or events. Yet it is surely misconceived to

[8] In certain contexts this will signify that it lacks chromatic colour and is black, white or grey. In other contexts it will signify being transparent and without colour.
[9] I. Rock, *Perception* (Scientific American Books, New York, 1984), p. 4.

hold that the statement that geraniums are red or that the door is creaking is on a par with the claim that natural numbers are green and raucous. The option remains, of course, of arguing that attributing colour or sound to things has a quite different meaning from that which we 'pre-scientifically' think it does, that it is really to attribute to things powers or dispositions to affect us in such-and-such ways. This suggestion will be examined in chapter 4.

A scientist may remonstrate indignantly at this point and his objection deserves a digression. We have been appealing to the ordinary grammar of names of secondary qualities to convict the scientist of traversing the bounds of sense. But ordinary grammar, he may object, simply embodies the metaphysics of the stone age and the scientific naivety of common sense. Our grammar of secondary qualities rests on a false picture; the ordinary canons of sense and nonsense misrepresent the nature of colour, sound, smell etc. Indeed ordinary grammar here is *systematically* wrong, and hence too systematically misleading. It would be absurd, the scientist will argue, to take ordinary grammar to be the final court of appeal. Somebody who, ignorant of the advances of science, misconceived the nature of colours, sounds, smells, etc. *would be expected* to treat secondary qualities and primary ones alike as objective properties of things. The weight of grammatical evidence for this way of speaking simply attests to the *consistency* with which grammar has been moulded to error. And do we not have an obvious example of this in other departments of discourse? For does our talk of the sun's *rising* and *setting* not embody the false geocentric theory of the solar system?

The objection rests on multiple misunderstandings, some of which will be unravelled only in later chapters. No grammar is answerable to the facts, neither the grammar of ordinary, non-technical parlance, nor the grammar of technical terms in advanced sciences. It is *propositions,* expressed in a given grammar, that are answerable to the facts – for truth and falsehood. Grammar, however, consists of *rules,* rules for the use of words – and these are not, in the same sense, true or false at all. (To say of a grammatical proposition that it is true is just to say that it *is* a proposition of our grammar, a norm of representation. It is not to say anything about how things happen to be in reality.) But do the *rules* of grammar not presuppose a theory? Do they not presuppose an array of facts certified by a theory? And if these presuppositions are false is the grammar not defective? No –

these questions rest on misunderstandings. Our talk of sunrise and sunset, for example, does not presuppose a geocentric theory as a condition of sense. To say that the sun *rises* in the east is just to say that it is first visible in the morning on the eastern horizon; to say that it *sets* in the west is just to say that it is last to be seen before nightfall on the western horizon; and if one says that the sun has *risen* higher in the sky that just means that it was visible earlier at so-and-so many degrees and later at greater altitude. The use of the verbs 'rise' and 'set' no more commits one to geocentrism than the use of the preposition 'above' (in 'Planes fly high above the earth') commits one to the claim that the earth is flat. *Grammar* has nothing to say on whether the sun circles the earth or the earth spins on its axis. The rules of grammar presuppose no theory, nor do they presuppose the truth of an array of empirical statements. They *can* be said to presuppose certain facts, but only in the sense in which, for example, the rules of tennis presuppose such facts as the persistence of a constant gravitational field of approximately 1g. If certain facts were different then the rules would become *useless*. But just as the theory of gravitation is no part of the rules of tennis, so too no theory of colour, sound or thermal qualities is part of, or presupposed by, the grammar of colour, sound or thermal predicates. The rules of grammar determine what makes sense, but not what is true or false. There can be no appeal from the tribunal of grammar to the facts or theories discovered by science. *Any* appeal to the facts presupposes a grammar, a distinction or distinctions between sense and nonsense. For the *statement* of facts or theories is effected in a given language or segment of language with a certain grammar. If it is the same grammar as ordinary discourse, it cannot confirm its 'correctness', since it presupposes these very distinctions between sense and nonsense that are in question. If it is a distinct (technical) grammar, it determines different *concepts,* and so talks of something different.

With this (partial) clarification behind us, we can return to our main theme. Do colours have a location? Not as objects or sensations do. It is tempting to hold that colours are akin to objects in so far as two colours, like two objects, cannot be in the same place at the same time. Hence it could be argued that 'That which corresponds in reality to the function "( )PT"[10] leaves room only for one entity – in

[10] 'PT' signifies a spatio-temporal point in the visual field and the function takes colours as arguments.

the same sense, in fact, in which we say that there is room for one person only in a chair.'[11] So it will seem in order to hold that 'colours possess impenetrability'.[12] On the other hand, one might be struck by the dissimilarity between colours and objects and by the kinship of colour concepts to concepts of stuffs. For one might contend that the colour red can be at many places at the same time, just as water may be scattered in various drops, puddles or pools in different places. Hence the same colour, unlike the same *piece* or collection of matter but like matter of a given kind, 'may be in many places at once' and, one might add, a colour and a piece of matter may *occupy* the same place.[13]

This is confused, and the analogy with objects and stuffs is misleading. Colours, unlike objects and quantities of stuff, are not *occupants* of space, and their mutual exclusiveness is not that of *space-occupants*. They are neither penetrable nor impenetrable. Nothing can be red and green all over simultaneously, but not because there is *room* for only one colour. Red and green are mutually exclusive *properties,* as are being one metre long and being two metres long. A one-metre-long plank cannot also be two metres long, but not because its one-metre length prevents the *property* of being two metres long from occupying the same space. Similarly, it is misleading to say that red can be at many different places at the same time, since all that can signify is that many distinct items in various places may be red, just as they may all be one metre long. But no one would say that the length one metre can be at different places at the same time! Apart from illuminations, for example flashes, glows, glimmers and light itself, only what is extended can be coloured (and that is why events cannot be coloured or not coloured, for while they typically need space to take place and occur at a place, they do not occupy a space or fill a space as objects and quantities of stuff do.)[14]

[11] L. Wittgenstein, 'Some remarks on logical form', *Proceedings of the Aristotelian Society,* suppl. vol. IX (1929), p. 169. Wittgenstein shortly afterwards changed his mind about the explanation of colour-exclusion and was the first to give, in his subsequent writings, the correct explanation of this puzzle.
[12] B. Russell, *The Principles of Mathematics* (Cambridge University Press, Cambridge, 1903), p. 467.
[13] Ibid.
[14] For more on the relation of events to space, see P. M. S. Hacker, 'Events and objects in space and time', *Mind* XCI, (1982) pp. 1–19.

The relation of colour to space is parasitic on the spatiality of the items that are coloured (or upon the light shed). The colour red, unlike patches of red, is not *at* any place, *a fortiori* not at many different places at the same time, unlike water or sand. Different objects or quantities of material variously located may be red, as indeed may some of their parts or insides, surfaces or depths. One can, of course, point at the colour of something, but to point at its colour is to point at the object (quantity, heap, pile, puddle, etc. of stuff, or flash, glimmer, gleam, etc.) which is that colour.

Sounds are quite different. The location of a sound is typically, though not uniformly (see below), the location of that which is making the sound. 'Where is that noise *coming from*? is the typical question the answer to which normally gives the location of the sound. The rustling noise coming from over there ↗ is a rustling noise *in* the undergrowth. If a garden party in the quad makes a hubbub, then there is a hubbub in the quad. Sounds, however, are not three-dimensional objects, for they are not objects and have no height, length or breadth.[15] Unlike colours, but like light, they may fill a space, as when we say that the sound of the orchestra filled the concert hall (and that the hall was flooded with light), but they do not fill a space as a pint of beer may fill a tankard, for unlike quantities of liquid, they do not take up space. While an object cannot be red and green all over simultaneously, it can emit a variety of distinct noises simultaneously, and the room may be full of the different sounds of the various instruments of the orchestra, for different sounds do not *exclude* each other, though one may mask or drown the other. What corresponds in the domain of sound to exclusion in the domain of colour is the pitch or timbre *of a sound* excluding another pitch or timbre *of that sound*. The tone-colours (in a given dimension) of a sound are mutually exclusive. A *patch* of colour has boundaries, which may be well- or ill-defined, but it would be misleading to say that sounds have ill-defined boundaries − like mist. For that which has spatial boundaries, for example a cricket pitch or a lake, one can step into or be inside. What is here thought of as the boundary of a sound is the audibility-range or audibility-limits of a sound (and we do indeed say that we walk to a point *within hearing* of a source of

[15] Here I disagree with Urmson, 'The objects of the five senses', p. 120.

sound). It is noteworthy that as one walks *towards* a constant noise one can hear it *better*. 'It is louder here', we say as we get closer, knowing that the volume has *not* changed. Increase in audibility may result from increasing proximity or from change in sound produced. To point at a noise is to point at the place from which a sound is coming (which is usually the locus of what is making the noise) but not necessarily to point at that which is making the noise, for in the case of objects moving at high velocity these may be distinct. Note that one can point out, draw attention to, a noise without pointing at or indeed knowing its source; however, one cannot point at, but only point out the tonal qualities of a sound.

The concepts of the location and spatiality of secondary qualities (taste, smell and tactual qualities can be left to the reader at this point) are altogether unlike the concept of the location of sensations. The criterion for the location of A's pains, itches or tickles is his indicative behaviour or avowal. But whether the back of the chair is dark brown or faded, where a noise is coming from, whether there is a smell in the cupboard, and what it is in the salad that gives it its distinctive flavour, we determine by looking, listening, smelling and tasting. The behaviour of the perceiver is a criterion for whether *he has perceived* what is thus perceptible and whether he has located it correctly. But whether *this here* is red, whether the noise comes from *there* or whether there is a smell in the kitchen is not determined by a perceiver assuaging, scratching or rubbing a part of his body. One can point at coloured objects and their coloured parts, and a bystander can look and see the coloured item for himself (as he can hear the sound coming from the nursery or smell the scent wafting from the hyacinths). But if I point at my toothache, others cannot feel my pain in my tooth (for it makes no *sense*) although they may be able to see *that* I am in pain and where it hurts me. Sensations are felt in one's body, but colours, smells and sounds are not *in* one's body in that sense at all, but are rather properties of or made by bodies (including one's own), stuffs, or events and processess in the world around us.

Similar divergences are evident in respect of motion. Here there are distinctive differences between the various perceptual qualities.

---

[16] But smells are different from both.

Coloured flashes may shoot across the sky, glows may spread along the horizon and coloured shadows or reflections may move, but colours do not. The foliage may change in the autumn, but the summer green does not migrate elsewhere, and though the autumn reds and browns spread from the edges of the leaves inwards, this does not mean that the red or brown colour moves, but that the periphery *becomes* red or brown before the rest of the leaf. Similarly, we say, pointing at a piece of cloth, pot or painting, that the red has spread or run, but that means that the dye, glaze or paint has done so. The taste of an object cannot be said to move or not to move, even though a clove of garlic may infuse a whole dish with its taste. But the smell of dinner may waft from the kitchen to other parts of the house and linger there long after the dinner has been consumed – hence one may open the window to let the smell out, as one may close it to keep the heat in. The movement of sound is different again, and must not be confused with the movement of sound waves. We speak most commonly of sounds moving when we talk of the objects making the sound moving, as when we say that the sound of marching soldiers died away in the distance as the parade moved out of sight. Here the movement of the sound *is* the movement of its source. Quite different from this is the manner in which we describe echoes, which we individuate and count, as reverberating along the walls of a canyon and bouncing from one side to another. Here we conceive of, and *perceive* the sound itself moving, even though what made it does not (and indeed may no longer exist or be occuring – as in the case of an object's exploding). Between these two kinds of case lies the description of the sound of rapidly moving objects that emit sound, such as jet aeroplanes. Here we perceive the aircraft moving silently across the sky at great speed, and then hear the sound it makes moving *behind* it.

It might be objected that sounds *always* move, although proximate sounds move too fast to be perceived as moving. Is this not obvious, even pre-scientifically, from the fact that if a loud explosion occurs, a person A one mile away will hear it before B who is two miles away? And do we not say in such cases that the sound of the explosion took longer to reach B than to reach A? But if it took longer *to reach* B than A, it must travel from its source, i.e. *move!* We must take care here not to confuse sounds with sound-waves. If we say that the *sound* moves from the locus of the explosion E to point *a* and then to point *b*, then we must, absurdly, require A to deny that he heard a sound *over there* ↗ (pointing at the afterglow of the explosion), and, if the noise is not of an explosion but rather the continuous sound of a machine in the distance, A must still insist that the noise is *here*, where he is standing. But this too will be wrong, for the sound must be said to be, in the case of the explosion (for a split second) not merely *here*, but everywhere on the circumference of the radius from E to *a*. Yet this is precisely to confuse a sound with a sound-wave. We do not conceive of the sound of the explosion as being at many different places at the same time, but rather as being *audible from* many different places at the same time. We conceive of sounds more or less 'under the aspect' of an *object*, not of a wave. The continuous unchanging sound of a machine in the distance is *one* sound, even though a multitude of sound-waves are continuously transmitted through the air in a vibration field consisting of concentric spheres of moving wave fronts. To say that it takes time for the sound of the explosion (or machine) to reach A, and a longer time for it to reach B, just *means* that it takes time for the sound to *become audible* at *a* (or anywhere else on the circumference of the circle with radius E*a*), and takes longer for it to become audible at *b*. But this does not mean that the *sound* (as opposed to the sound waves) has moved – that would be the case only if the machine making a continuous noise (for example a train) moved and its sound *could be heard* to move. If I say 'There's a rustling in the grass' and you reply 'I can't hear anything', I might answer 'It has *stopped* now' but not 'It has gone (away)'! Do we not say that sounds are carried on the wind, and if they can be *carried* surely they can *move*? No – for what looks like a claim about auditory motion is simply a claim about audibility: a sound which is inaudible upwind is typically audible downwind – that is what it *means* to say that a sound is carried by the wind (and hence is unlike a leaf's being carried by the wind)! The *representational form* of some propositions about audibility is dynamic, but the form must not be confused with the content. *In so far as* we attribute location to sound, we do not identify its location with the position or positions from which it can be heard. The hubbub in the Hall on Commem-night may wake the neighbours down the road, but that does not mean that the hubbub was in their bedrooms, only that it was audible from there. And *in so far as* we conceive of sounds moving, the movement of a sound is either the audible movement of what makes it (as in the case of the parade) or the perceptible movement of the sound as opposed to its source, as in the case of echoes, rolling thunder, or the sound of a jet aircraft being dragged across the sky.

It might be objected that this is merely pre-scientific nonsense, an elementary but primitive theory of sound, long superseded by the advance of science.[17] But this is confused. What we have been adumbrating is not a *theory* of sounds but the *concept* of sounds, indeed the concept we all employ in talking about the multitudinous variety of noises around us. The distinction between sounds as characterized above and sound-waves as described by physics is not a matter of the difference between primitive science and sophisticated science, but rather of the difference between the *grammar* of sound, which is no theory, and the physics of sound, which is no grammar. Moreover, the grammar of sound does not, indeed cannot, conflict with physical discoveries about sound, for *what it makes sense to say* cannot *conflict* with what is true or false.

Back to sensations: can *they* be said to move? Yes, but not across the sky or out of the window, rather only in the sense in which a sharp pain may shoot up one's arm, or the pain of an inflammation may spread as the inflammation spreads, i.e. a greater (or different) area of the infected organ may *become* painful. But when I, suffering from a headache, go to lie down, my headache does not move from study to bedroom, but remains where it was, namely in my temples. (A sensation, in this respect, is like the colour of a chair, which does not move when the chair is moved, and unlike the sound of the battalion that moves away with the marching soldiers.)

Sensations are felt or had, not made – though some may be inflicted or given. Since we conceive of substances and their properties in the representational form of ownership, we talk of objects *having* a red colour, sweet taste or fragrant smell (but of their *being*, not having, red or sweet). But whereas a person who has a pain feels a pain, an object that has a colour (for example, is red), or a person who has (but is not) a red complexion, does not feel it. Objects that are or have a certain colour do not make a colour, (although, as noted above, a

---

[17] Something like this misconception runs through Evans' discussion of our concepts of material objects (G. Evans, 'Things without the mind', in Z. van Straaten (ed.), *Philosophical Subjects, Essays presented to P. F. Strawson* (Clarendon Press, Oxford, 1980), pp. 95ff).

mixture of ingredients may, and events may make coloured flashes or glows). Sounds, as was observed, are both made and had, although to have a sound of a certain kind is not to make one, and that something makes a type of sound does not imply that it has one. Objects have smells, i.e. give off smells, without anything being done to them, although they may make a smell through some change to them (their rotting, being crushed or burnt), hence not only objects and stuffs, but also processes can smell. It is, however, noteworthy that we conceive of events as *making* smells, but not as *having* smells. One can smell the acrid scent of a gunshot, but one cannot smell the gun fire. In this respect events are unlike processes (for one can smell fermentation, decay or burning) and smells are unlike sounds (for one can hear events happen). Perhaps the reason is that the smell made by an event (for example gunshot), unlike the noise it makes, typically lingers on. Hence one cannot smell the event occur as one can hear it occur, for the temporal duration of the smell does not correspond sufficiently well with the temporality of the event which makes it. Processes, however, go on in time, and the continuity of the smell they make corresponds rather better with the enduring process (although of course, it may endure after cessation of the process). Sensations, however, are very different. I do not see, hear, smell or taste my sensations, I feel sensations, but not, as was observed in the last chapter, as tactile qualities are typically felt. For to feel a sensation is to have one, and it is felt in one's organs not with one's organs. Note, however, that it is wrong to say 'I feel *my* sensations' – that would make sense only if it also made sense to say 'I feel your sensations'. I cannot feel (there is no such thing as feeling) the sensations of others (but I can see or hear *that* they are in pain, see the pain in their face or hear it in their voice). Hence I cannot be said to feel *my* sensations.

If one ceases to feel a pain, itch or tickle, then the sensation has passed. But although if one shuts one's eyes and blocks one's nose or ears, one will not see, smell or hear objects in one's vicinity, they do not lose their colours, cease to smell or fall silent when one no longer perceives them. Ceasing to see or hear something is not to render it invisible or inaudible, let alone to make it colourless or silent. If my leg hurts less than it did before, then the pain has diminished, but if my perceptual impression of a scene or sound changes, it does not follow that the colours or sounds have changed at all. We distinguish here, as we do not in the case of our feeling sensations, between appearance and reality, and that in *various* ways (see below chapter 6). Thus, for example, adjacent to a green object red things look redder and brighter than they are (a matter of objective circumstance); rather differently, after eating sweets, oranges taste more sour than they are (a matter of subjective affection). But though the pain of an injury tends to be worse at night than during the day, it is not felt to be more painful than it is.

Discrimination of perceptual qualities, as observed in the last chapter, involves skill, feeling sensations does not. Those with a trained eye or ear, or with a discriminating palate, can better distinguish, compare, match and contrast the corresponding qualities than others. Observational conditions and subjective conditions affect discriminatory performance. Doubt, error and ignorance, and hence too knowledge, certainty, finding out, checking again all make sense in the case of seeing what colour something is, what taste or scent it has, though these epistemic verbs have no application in the case of one's own sensations. Of course, they do in the case of the sensations of *others*. Sensation-expressions manifest the distinctive first/third person asymmetry characteristic of most psychological concepts (for example, it makes sense to know or doubt, to be certain or mistaken whether *another* is in pain, but not so in one's own case). But concepts of perceptual qualities are not psychological concepts and display no such asymmetry.

Concepts of secondary qualities are explained by reference to paradigmatic samples. 'That ↗' we say, pointing at a patch of purple, 'is purple'; 'This,' we explain, striking a key on the piano, 'is B-flat.' Such explanations constitute rules for the use of the name explained. 'Purple' is correctly predicated of any object which is that ↗ colour. The object pointed at, the sound made, or smell picked out thus is given the role of a standard of correctness, a sample or pattern, for the application of the term explained. And the utterance is a definition, not a description. The ostensive definition of purple could be paraphrased as 'That ↗ colour is purple' or 'The colour of that ↗ piece of fabric is purple', but not as 'That ↗ piece of fabric is purple', for if the latter is a description of an object as being a certain colour, it presupposes the meaning of a colour name. Note that to say of some other object that it is purple is not to say that it *resembles* the colour of the sample, but rather that it *is* the colour of the sample. (To be such-and-such a colour, as indeed to be one metre long, is not to possess a *relational* property.) In the case of subtle shades of colour we typically employ colour charts in judging whether an object is this or that shade. Sensations, by contrast, are not explained by reference to samples or paradigms, for there is no such thing as a sample of pain which can be employed as a standard against which to judge correct or incorrect applications of sensation-words.[18] We do not judge another person to be in pain, feel an itch or tickle by comparing his sensation with a standard sample, since this is senseless. To compare a feature F of an object with a sample of F, both feature and sample must be perceptible, but there is no such thing as feeling another's pains, itches or tickles, and there are no samples of sensations that can (logically) fulfil the role of standards for the correct use of sensation-words.

Of course, it is easy to generate the illusion that in one's own case one judges that (or would justify the claim that) one's sensation is a pain, tickle or itch by comparing it with a *mental* sample of the relevant sensation which is 'stored in one's memory'. But even if this made sense, it could explain nothing. For one must call up the *right* sensation from one's 'storehouse of ideas', and that requires that there be a criterion of correctness for whether *this* 'idea' is an idea of pain or of something else. Yet that is precisely what the sample *itself* was meant to supply. Similarly, deliberately calling up the *memory* sample of pain rather than of some other sensation requires that one knows what 'pain' means; yet calling up *this* sample was meant to be what knowing the meaning of 'pain' consists in, not to presuppose it.[19] Finally, this tale is a charade, since in order for an image one calls to mind to be used as a *sample,* there must be a *method of comparison* for the putative sample, an established way in the practice of using sensation-names of 'laying the sample alongside reality' for match or mismatch which determines what is to *count* as being the same or different. But there is no such thing.

In fact we judge that another person is in pain or feels a tickle or itch on the grounds of his pain-behaviour, his laughter and wriggling in response to tickling, his scratching his itching skin. The

---

[18] This point lies at the heart of Wittgenstein's private language argument in *Philosophical Investigations* (Blackwell, Oxford, 1953), §§ 243–315.
[19] Ibid., § 265.

behavioural expressions of sensations constitute the criteria for ascribing sensations to a person, and no sample is or could be involved. In one's own case, one's avowal that one has a certain sensation is groundless, as are one's groans and cries. Avowals of sensations are a learnt extension of the natural expressive behaviour that manifests one's sensations, and they too are criteria for ascribing sensations to a person.

Perceptual qualities are not ascribed to objects on the basis of any criteria. The *perception* of secondary qualities by a person, like the perception of primary qualities, has criteria in the behaviour of the perceiver in appropriate circumstances. But the discriminatory behaviour that provides grounds for saying of a person that he has perceived this or that is not typically *expressive,* hence not at all like manifestations of sensation. There is no specific expressive behaviour, no typical facial grimace or gesture that manifests seeing red or blue, hearing this or that sound, although there *is* in the case of tasting something very bitter, smelling a stench, being dazzled or deafened. Not surprisingly, these latter approximate to sensations. The utterances 'I see green' or 'I hear a tinkling sound' are not learnt extensions of natural green-seeing or tinkling-sound-hearing behaviour, but rather additional articulations grafted on to learnt verbal behaviour, viz. 'The chair is green' or 'There's a tinkling sound'.

Every aspect of the grammar of sensations on the one hand and of secondary qualities on the other (and of the having of sensations and the perceiving of secondary qualities) reveals on scrutiny deep and extensive logical differences. The assimilation of secondary qualities to sensations is a *categorial* confusion.

3   The reductive thesis

The sensationalist thesis that things in the world around us cannot be said to have colours, since colours are sensations and only sentient beings have them is a hard doctrine to swallow. Even those sympathetic to the Galilean tradition were sensitive to this – after all we talk of things being coloured and this is surely not *nonsense*. In an endeavour to reduce the philosophical pressure at this point without sacrificing the alleged scientific insight into the real nature of things, philosophers, especially in this century, have sought to remould the original claims in the form of novel explanations of the meanings of colour words and other names of secondary qualities. Thus Russell argued: 'When, in ordinary life, we speak of *the* colour of the table, we only mean the sort of colour which it will seem to have to a normal spectator from an ordinary point of view under usual conditions of light.'[20] Here Russell came close to the reductive thesis that to *be* such-and-such a colour is to look thus-and-so to normal observers under normal conditions. But Russell did not take that step: a bad argument in support of a paradox typically captured his imagination. He insisted that other colour appearances under different conditions 'have just as good a right to be considered real', and hence, to avoid favouritism, 'we are compelled to deny that in itself, the table has any one particular colour.' This argument is weak, since the apparent colour of the table in abnormal lighting conditions really *is* its apparent colour under those conditions. But if by 'is such-and-such a colour' we *mean* 'appears thus-and-so under normal lighting conditions to a normal observer', then how a thing appears under abnormal lighting conditions does not have any right to be considered the real colour of the object.

The step towards the reductive thesis was taken by numerous philosophers after Russell. His admirer A. J. Ayer argued that 'what is ordinarily meant by saying, for example, that the table is really brown is that it looks brown to normal observers under standard conditions.'[21] This account has gained in popularity in recent years. 'All it can amount to for something to be red,' it was recently argued, 'is that it be such that if looked at in the normal conditions, it will appear red.'[22] And again, 'for an object to be red is for it to present a certain kind of sensory appearance to perceivers.'[23] Different variations upon this theme are possible and divergent refinements have been attempted. The thesis that will be examined here is that to be red

---

[20] B. Russell, *The Problems of Philosophy* (Oxford University Press, London, 1967), p. 2. Russell was not the first to make this move.
[21] A. J. Ayer, *The Central Questions of Philosophy* (Weidenfeld and Nicolson, London, 1973), p. 83, where the above criticism of Russell is also made. A similar view was voiced earlier by W. Kneale, 'Sensation and the physical world', *Philosophical Quarterly*, 1951, p. 121.
[22] Evans, 'Things without the mind', p. 98.
[23] C. McGinn, *The Subjective View* (Clarendon Press, Oxford, 1983), p. 5.

(to be or have any secondary quality) is to look red (to sound, smell, taste or feel thus-or-so) to a normal human observer under normal conditions.

The prima facie merit of this reductive thesis in relation to the sensationalist conception (and its dispositional counterpart) from which it springs resembles the apparent advance of linguistic phenomenalism over classical idealism. Proponents of such reductivism need no longer claim that objects are not really red, fragrant or noisy – just as the phenomenalist need not claim that chairs and tables cease to exist when they are not observed. Rubies and geraniums really are red, but that just means that they look red, present an appearance of red, to a normal human being in daylight, just as chairs and tables really do exist when unobserved, but that merely means that if someone were to observe them he would have such and such sensory impressions. The gain in subtlety is purchased at the expense of drawing the knot in our understanding of these concepts tighter and tighter.

The contention that to be red is to look red to a normal observer under normal conditions is immediately baffling. If 'red' *means* 'looks red to a normal observer under normal conditions', then 'to look red to a normal observer . . .' means the same as 'to look look red to a normal observer under normal conditions to a normal observer under normal conditions'. This not only generates a vicious regress, but is also plain gibberish. The reductivist will sidestep this objection. To be sure, 'red' does not mean 'looks red to a normal observer under normal conditions', but 'is red' means 'looks red to a normal observer under normal conditions'. This sidestep avoids gibberish, although it fails to budget for nominal uses of colour words, for example 'Red is my favourite colour.' Moreover, little enlightenment is obtained from the explanation. For if, in our philosophical fever, we need an explanation of what 'is red' means that will stop our head from whirling, we will hardly be enlightened by being told that it means 'looks red to a normal observer in normal conditions'. For, first, 'red' occurs in the explanans and, secondly, we need an explanation of what counts as normal conditions and as a normal observer. The latter point will be deferred for a moment (p. 127).

One might respond to the first objection in various ways. One might deny that the equation is *stricto sensu* an explanation of meaning. Alternatively, one might deny that 'looking red' can be decomposed into 'looking' plus 'red'. These merit separate scrutiny.

The first riposte runs as follows: 'to be red' does not *mean* 'to look red', but this is what the truth of sentences ascribing secondary qualities *consists in*.[24] This is merely to retreat from fallacy into obscurity. What does the phrase 'consist in' signify here? One suggestion made is as follows: being red consists in looking red in as much as an object is red *because* it looks red, whereas in the case of a primary quality such as squareness, this relationship is inverted: an object looks square because it is square.

The suggestion that red objects are red because they look red is awry. Blood is red because it contains haemoglobin, and my shirt is red because I have been picking mulberries. The question 'Why is this red?' is answered in such ways, not by 'Because it looks red' (although 'Because they look salient like that' might be an intelligible and correct answer to 'Why are British postboxes red?'). In certain circumstances one might ask 'Why do you think that such-and-such is red?' and the answer might be: 'Because I looked at it', i.e. that is how I found out or came to think this. I did not ask anyone or infer its colour from any evidence – I just looked. (In some, rather special, circumstances of possible doubt, I might expand my answer with 'and it looked red'.) But this does not explain why the object *is* red, but only why I think it is, namely I judge it to be red not inductively or on hearsay, but *because I saw it.*

The reductivist typically holds that appearances are necessarily *someone's experiences* or appearances *to someone* (thus papering over the difficulties of equating secondary qualities with sensations). If he holds that red things are red because they look red, it would seem to follow on this account that a given object is red because it looks red to me or to you or to any other normal observer under normal conditions. Yet surely things may be red even though no one has ever or will ever look at them. At this point the phenomenalist's gambit becomes attractive, viz. that red things are red because they *would* look red to normal observers under normal conditions. But this puts

---

[24] Cf. Evans, 'Things without the mind', p. 98n., where he argues that the dispositional character of secondary qualities is not a matter of the *meaning* of sentences containing names of secondary qualities, but is 'that in which their truth *consists*'. Similarly McGinn argues that 'what we should claim is that being red *consists in* looking red' (*The Subjective View*, p. 6).

the cart before the horse: it is because rubies are red, whether observed or unobserved, that they would look red in daylight to the normal-sighted if the rubies were observed, as a fragrant rose would smell fragrant to a normal perceiver if he smelled it. Moreover, something looks red (smells fragrant) *to* a person if, on looking at it (smelling it) he takes (or would, other things being equal, take) it to be red. But to be red (or fragrant) neither is, nor means, nor consists in being taken to be red (or fragrant) by most people most of the time. Finally, on this account, how could one explain what it is *to take something to be red*? When one takes something to be red, what is it that one takes it to be? It is, tautologically, *red* that one takes it to be. But *that* is precisely what the reductivist is trying to explain away.

The second riposte to the above objection that the reductive thesis is useless since it employs the word 'red' in explaining what it is for something to be red is to insist that the concept of red is not a constituent of the concept of looking-red (hyphenated). *Looking-red* is a unitary predicate, not the product of the predicate-forming operator on predicates: 'looking', operating on 'red' (and, by parity of reasoning, smelling-fragrant, sounding-melodic, tasting-sweet). Reductivists are prone to conceive of looking-red, sounding-shrill, etc. as subjective, psychological states or conditions of a perceiver that are caused by the light-reflective or sound-wave generating propensities of objects, events, etc. Something appears red, it is held, only if there is a perceiver to whom it appears thus. An object can no more look red when no one is looking than a knife can be causing pain when no one is suffering. So it is argued that

the philosophers who claim to find intelligible an objective but non-dispositional colour property try to conceive of an object's possessing such a property in the absence of any observer by imagining a red object which no one sees – a feat of the imagination which is impeded if part of the imagined story is that the object exists in a pitch-black cellar.[25]

And this, it is suggested, is absurd.

This is a curious argument to put to 'the philosophers'. For, *pace* Berkeley, there is nothing problematic about conceiving of, or imagining, unobserved red objects, whether they are conceived to be

[25] Evans, 'Things without the mind', p. 100.

in daylight or in the dark. To conceive is not the same as to imagine; to imagine is not necessarily to indulge in mental imagery; to have a mental image of an object is not to see an object. So one *can conceive* of unobserved coloured objects without imagining them, one *can imagine* them without picturing them to oneself, and to picture them to oneself is not to observe anything coloured. Of course, a picture (or photograph) of a pitch-black cellar containing a red apple will not differ from a picture of a pitch-black cellar containing a green apple (or even no apple); but to conceive of a red apple in a pitch-black cellar is not the same as to conceive of a green one there. And to imagine Little Red Riding Hood looking for a red apple in a pitch-black cellar and finding one is not the same as imagining her looking for a green apple and finding one. How can this misplaced argument even *seem* to have an impact? Only through question-begging!

Objectivists, the reductive theorist remonstrates, 'have tried to make sense of the idea of a property of redness which is both an abiding property of the object, both perceived and unperceived, and yet "exactly as we experience redness to be".'[26] The latter scare-quoted expression he equates with the hypenated 'redness-as-we-see-it' and, having drawn this red herring across the trail, objects that one cannot follow the scent. This, he proclaims, is an absurd attempt to make sense of the exemplification of a property of experience in the absence of any experience. It is *as* absurd as to conceive of the occurrence of pains without any sufferers. The absurdity of the objectivists' conception is evident, he concludes, when the objectivist is challenged to answer the question: 'Is X red in the dark?' For the objectivist cannot say 'Yes', since it is wholly obscure how a 'colour-as-we-see-it' can exist when we cannot see it. And he cannot say 'No' on pain of relinquishing or at least gravely compromising his understanding of colours as objective properties of things.

This argument only appears to work by thrusting upon the objectivist the very reductive thesis which he rejects and by assuming the truth of the dispositional account of colours (and other secondary qualities) 'as they are in the objects' which he questions. For it is misconceived to think that 'redness is a property of experience' in the

[26] Ibid., p. 98.

sense in which sensations might (opaquely) be said to be. It is a property of objects, stuffs, flashes or glimmers, not of experiences. Red is the colour we see when we look at rubies or vermilion, not a property of *seeing* but of *what is seen*. Of course, the philosopher may say that redness is an abiding property of the object, perceived or unperceived, 'exactly as we experience red to be', as long as he understands the latter misbegotten phrase to signify no more than that we see the (objective) red colour of the object in question. 'Red-as-we-see-it' or 'Red-as-we-experience-it', if it means anything, simply means red (as 'one metre-as-we-measure-it' presumably means one metre). For how *do* we experience redness to be? We might reply 'Like that ↗'. But do we then point at the ruby, or at our sense-impression? It is confused to conceive of 'looking red to X' as an *experience* of X akin to X's pain, and even more misguided to impute to the objectivist the view that colour concepts are understood in virtue of 'concentrating upon one's experience of colour'.[27] The first error conflates the concept of a sensation with that of an impression (viz. what colour something strikes one as being). The second is an empiricist fiction wholly alien to a correct conception of colour (or other secondary qualities); for it is not concentrating on seeing a red patch that constitutes coming to know what 'red' means, it is rather coming to know how to use the word 'red' in accord with an ostensive definition incorporating a sample. For this, to be sure, one must be able to see, and to discriminate, a sample of red from samples of other colours.

A further gambit might be essayed. Forewarned of the perils of being forced back onto a private ostensive definition, the reductivist may explain that looking red is inherently an 'intentional property'. 'Experiences are distinguished by their representational content,' it might be claimed, 'so naturally we shall need to use predicates of the external world in specifying them.'[28] What 'predicates of the external world'? Dispositional ones such as 'being red'. To be red, it is argued, is to have a disposition to cause an observer to have a 'sensory experience' which is characterized as 'looking-red'. This is an experience with an intentional content, which is specified by the predicate of the external world 'red'.

---

[27] *loc. cit.*
[28] McGinn, *The Subjective View*, p. 7.

This is not coherent. Having deprive 'being red' of the trousers, 'looking red' must wear them on pain of mutual exposure. If 'is red' means the same as 'has a disposition to cause a sensory experience of looking red', then this alleged sensory experience cannot be characterized as 'looking as (having the intentional content of) things with a disposition to cause a sensory experience of looking red'. For that is evidently circular. There can be no intelligible characterization of the alleged 'intentional content' of the 'sensory experience' of something's looking red to one save by reference to the simple concept, explained by reference to a (visible) sample, of being red!

It might further be argued that to grasp the concept of red it is necessary to know *what it is* for something to look red.[29] But this is deeply misleading, for it can be variously understood. On the one hand, if it signifies that only someone who, by *looking* at an object, is able to distinguish between its being red and its being some other colour, can be said to know what 'red' means, then it is a correct and innocuous claim. The colour-blind, who cannot distinguish red from green and grey, cannot employ defining samples of these colours *as* defining samples, i.e. as standards for the correct application of these expressions. There is no point in giving someone known to be thus colour-blind a pair of samples of red and green, and telling him to distinguish those objects in his vicinity that are this ↗ colour (red) from those which are that ↗ colour (green), for he lacks the requisite discriminatory capacities which are presupposed by our normal colour grammar (see below, pp. 148ff). On the other hand, it is not innocuous but erroneous to suggest that one must master the concept of *looking red* prior to grasping the concept of *being red*. As Wittgenstein pointed out: 'To begin by teaching someone "That looks red" makes no sense. For he must say that spontaneously once he has learnt what "red" means, i.e. has learnt the technique of using the word.'[30] For if someone has mastered the use of 'That looks red' or indeed 'That looks red to me', he must also be capable of answering the question 'And what is red like?' or 'And what does something look like when it looks red?' And that question is answered by saying 'Like *this* ↗', pointing to a correct paradigm or

---

[29] Ibid., p. 8.
[30] L. Wittgenstein, *Zettel* (Blackwell, Oxford, 1967), § 418.

sample of red.[31] One no more starts teaching a child to say 'It looks red to me' from the first than one starts by teaching it to say 'That's probably a so-and-so' before it has learnt the use of 'That's a so-and-so'. This is not, of course, because the child is not sufficiently sophisticated to understand the rather refined distinction between seeming and being, but because the concept of such a distinction is erected upon, presupposes the mastery of, the concept of *being,* for example, red.

Confusion is multiplied by the further suggestion that there is a contrast, in *this* respect, between colour concepts and shape concepts. Having suggested wrongly that to grasp the concept of red it is necessary to know what it is to look red, a misguided philosopher may go on to claim that, by contrast, to grasp the concept of being square 'it is not constitutively necessary to know how square things look or feel, since what it is to be square does not involve any such relation to experience.'[32] This is doubly wrong. First, there is no contrast here between 'red' and 'square' in respect of the logical priority of 'being red' or 'being square' over 'looking red' or 'looking (or feeling) square'. Secondly, the formulation 'it is not necessary to know how square things look or feel' suggests erroneously that if a person explains 'square' as 'being a four-sided equilateral with a 90° angle', then he has mastered the concept of being square *even though* he calls the spheres, circles and triangles which he sees and feels 'square', and cannot identify a square shape when he sees or feels one.

Nevertheless, it might be said, surely 'the ultimate criterion for whether an object has a certain colour or taste (etc.) is how it looks or tastes to perceivers; whereas this is not how we think of qualities like shape and size.'[33] This is gravely misleading. It is true that I determine whether an object is red or a foodstuff sweet by looking at the one and tasting the other. But that the one looks red to me and the other tastes sweet to me is not a *criterion* for the first being red and the second sweet. For that it looks red to me or tastes sweet to me is not my *evidence* for its being so. Looking and tasting are *ways of finding out* what colour or taste thngs have (and asking other people is a different way); they are not ways of finding out something else, viz. how

---

[31] Ibid., § 420.
[32] McGinn, *The Subjective View,* p. 8.
[33] Ibid.

things look or taste to one, which is *evidence* from which one can infer what colour or taste they are. This might be conceded; nevertheless, is not the fact that strawberries look red to most people the ultimate criterion for their colour? No; it is wholly misleading to suggest that there is any such thing as a criterion, let alone an ultimate criterion, for whether *this* object is red. There is a way of finding out, namely by looking. Of course, one may ask others too, for we are eyes to each other. But finding a dozen people to whom this tomato looks red, as it does to me, is not adding to my *evidence* for its redness – I can *see* that it is red; rather is it collecting witnesses to its redness!

Are shape and size any different? Do we find out what shape and size something is other than by looking and feeling? Is there, in these cases, 'an ultimate criterion', perhaps even one that is 'experience-independent'?[34] There are cases and cases. We can and do find out the shapes and sizes of things by looking: that tree has the shape of an oak and the farther one has the shape of a poplar, but this one – being a yew-tree in a formal garden – has been clipped into the shape of an urn. As Smith junior walks with his father one can see that he is taller than his parent; and that this coin is the same size as that can be seen or felt by placing one on top of the other and seeing that each perfectly occludes the other or feeling, with one's fingers, that their edges coincide. Of course, we are relatively poor at distinguishing the precise, absolute as opposed to relative *dimensions* of an object without *measuring* it. But it would be absurd to suppose that measurement is 'experience-independent', for we must lay down the ruler alongside the measured object and see that *this* graduating mark coincides with the edge of the object. Similarly, not even an expert can discern whether every line in a Wierix copy of a Dürer print is exactly the same shape as in the original, so we employ a Hinman collator and then we *see* whether the shapes coincide precisely. It is true that we do not measure colours (but only colour intensities), but it should be borne in mind that we are just as poor at determining fine shades of colours as we are at estimating exact sizes of objects. Here we employ books of colour samples which, like a ruler, we lay alongside objects to determine whether they are this or that shade. But note that neither being the length of the one-metre rule nor being the colour of

[34] Ibid., p. 11.

the sample is a *criterion* for being a metre long or for being peach-blossom pink, they are what it *is* to be this long or to be that colour.

It is, however, important not to confuse the fact that general agreement in judgements over whether an object has a certain colour or taste is a condition of mutual understanding of such judgements with the misguided thought that such consensus is a criterion for things being thus-and-so. It is equally important to note that this condition of communication by means of language is a general one. If our measurements fell into chaos, we would not understand the concepts concerned. It was Wittgenstein who drew attention to the requirement not only for agreement in definitions, but also in judgements, but one ought to remember that he explained what he meant here by reference to *measurement:*

If language is to be a means of communication there must be agreement not only in definitions but also (queer as this may sound) in judgements. This seems to abolish logic, but does not do so. – It is one thing to describe methods of measurement, and another to obtain and state results of measurement. But what we call 'measuring' is partly determined by a certain constancy in results of measurement.[35]

In this respect colour and taste do *not* differ from shape or size: in neither case is consensus a *criterion,* and in both cases general agreement is a framework condition for the common employment of the concepts involved, not a ground for their application.

4 Being and seeming: the different modalities

The reductive thesis is typically tailor-made for colours. To be red, it is argued, means, consists in or amounts to looking red to normal observers in normal conditions. But this formula is intended to be generalizable. The extensive grammatical differences between the various secondary qualities should alert one here: can the formula be readily generalized? Is 'looking red' or 'looking red to A' precisely

---

[35] Wittgenstein, *Philosophical Investigations,* § 242.

parallel to 'tasting sweet' or 'tasting sweet to A'? Are looks analogous to tastes, sounds or smells? And what of feels?

It is important to bear in mind the previously noted fact that sounds, smells and tastes are proper objects of the corresponding senses, but that neither sight nor touch has a proper object in this sense. Also that sounds, and to a lesser degree smells, are conceived in a representational form *akin* to that of objects. Bangs, thumps and yelps are sounds; stenches, scents and aromas are smells. (Tastes differ, being properties of objects and foodstuffs. That which is sweet or salty does not make a taste, though it may impart a taste to *other* edibles.) There are no such things as feels made by an object in the sense in which sounds and smells are made. We do, over a narrow range of tangibilia, speak of the feel of an object: materials are said to have a soft or silky feel, i.e. are soft or silky to the touch. But the nominalization here is weak (the plural is barely used at all); we do not count feels even in the highly context-dependent manner and limited extent to which we count sounds and sometimes smells.

There is no denying that things have looks; but not as they have smells or tastes, let alone as they make sounds or have *a* sound of a certain character. A person may have a tired look about him, a child may have good looks, and a building a decrepit, Mannerist or Baroque look. Here we are concerned with facial expressions, demeanour or characteristic visible behaviour, or complex visible features. But colours are *not* looks. Roses are red and fragrant, they have a fragrant smell, but they do not have a red look any more than the way to Tipperary has a long look. To be red is to have a *colour,* not a look. This grammatical difference merits scrutiny.

We say of flowers that they are sweet-smelling, of quinine that it is a bitter-tasting stuff, and of a person that he has a harsh-sounding voice. The perceptual expressions 'tasting', 'smelling', 'sounding' do not signify here experiences of observers – a rose does not cease to be sweet-smelling when no one is smelling it. Rather, these hyphenated locutions are quasi-pleonastic, serving merely to emphasize or clarify the sensory modality of the quality in question. A sweet-smelling flower is a flower which is, in respect of its smell, sweet, as a sweet-tasting substance is one which, as far as its taste is concerned, is sweet. These perceptual qualities do not alter if no one happens to perceive them, any more than a square-*shaped* object ceases to be square if no one perceives it. We do say of substances that they are, for example, red-looking, particularly in the context of talking about stuffs. Sulphur is a yellow-looking crystalline substance, whereas vermilion is red-looking. In this use, to say of something that it is red-looking is to say that it is red in colouring. But 'looks' is not parallel to 'tastes' or 'smells', for something that is sweet-tasting is, as far as its taste is concerned, sweet. However a red-looking stuff is, as far as its *colour* is concerned, red – not: as far as its *looks* are concerned, red. A red-looking substance does not have a red look.

Of course, an object may look red for a while, as the Parthenon in the rays of the dying sun, without being a red-looking object. Red light may give certain things a ruddy appearance (though white light does not make things look whitish!) Here, perhaps, is one source of the confused idea that being red *consists* in looking red. For it might indeed be said that being red consists in being red-looking, i.e. red in colouring, as being sweet consists in being sweet-tasting. But it cannot be said that being red consists in looking red. For something, for example the Parthenon, may look red without being red and vice versa. (And adding the rider 'to normal observers in normal conditions' merely compounds the error, as will be shown below.)

To say that sugar is sweet is to say that it has a sweet taste or tastes sweet. These are equivalent statements. For roses to be fragrant is for them to have a fragrant smell or to smell fragrant. But since smells are emitted or made, and can persist after that which emitted them no longer exists, fragrance is a characteristic of the smell and *hence* (typically) of the odorous object in a way that is not paralleled in the case of colours. This is even more marked, as noted above, with respect to sounds, since objects do not have noises but make them, and for an object to have a certain kind of sound is for the sound it typically emits to have that feature. Colours are, in this respect, more akin to tastes than to sounds or smells. Although objects may make flashes or emit glows of a certain colour, an object that makes a red flash is not therefore red. Colours are *primarily* properties of objects, not of something objects make or give off. Nevertheless, even if it is conceded that to say that a rose is red is to say that it has a red colour, not a red look, might one not still insist that for a rose to be red just is for it to look red, as things that are bitter or fragrant taste bitter and smell fragrant?

That would be misleading. Smells, tastes and sounds are characterized both intrinisically and extrinsically. 'Fragrant', 'fetid', 'balmy' are intrinsic characterizations of smells; 'smelling of . . .' or smelling like . . .' are extrinsic characterizations. If something smells fragrant, i.e. has a fragrant smell, then it *is* fragrant. If something smells of or like fish, i.e. has a fish-like or fishy smell, it may *not* be a fish for all that. In the case of the intrinsic characterization, the smell *is* a fragrant smell, hence the object is fragrant, since to be fragrant just is to have that sort of smell. In the case of the extrinsic characterization, the smell is *of* fish (petrol, smoke), but the object which has the fishy smell or smell of petrol may not *be* what it smells *of*. Here the wedge between the real and the merely apparent is driven between the smell which the object really has and the character of the object in relation to the extrinsic characterization of the smell. Similarly with tastes: if A tastes sweet (or sour, salty, bitter, etc.) it is sweet and has a sweet taste. But it may taste *of* or *like* pineapple without being a pineapple, although it really does have a pineapple flavour. (Sounds involve greater complexity, but we can similarly distinguish intrinsic characterizations, such as shrill, melodious or mellow, from extrinsic ones such as sounding cracked, sounding as if it needs oil, sounding like such-and-such an object.)

What now of the relation between is . . . and looks . . . ? Putting aside equivalences or virtual equivalences (is elegant/looks elegant), which will be discussed in chapter 6, it is obvious that there is typically a potential gap between how things are and their visible appearance. Age, health and wealth, for example, have typical manifestations. A lively look, good complexion, springy walk (all discernible by looking) are symptoms of good health. But one may look healthy, yet be ill. And millionaires may look like tramps. To look well or ill, young or old, rich or poor is to have the looks or appearance typical of someone of the relevant category. But being well or ill, young or old, rich or poor are not perceptual properties; they are properties that correlate fairly well with perceptible (visual) features. To look young is to have an array of visible features that the young typically have. Hence the judgement that A looks young can be supported by citing grounds consisting of those features. Hence too, A's looking young, *ceteris paribus,* is a ground for judging A to be young.

This pattern of relations is not, however, repeated in the case of colour. First, colour characterizations are typically intrinsic. But unlike the intrinsic characterizations of smells and tastes, where smelling fragrant is being fragrant and tasting sweet is being sweet, looking red is *not* being red. For something may look red but be white (though illuminated by a red torch) or even colourless (though reflecting red light, as a window often does at sunset). In such a case the object is not red, does not have a red colour (unlike the item that smells fragrant and so has a fragrant smell) and does not have a red look (unlike the object that smells of fish and though not a fish has a fishy smell). Secondly, to look red is not parallel to looking young, well or rich. To look red is not to have an array of visible features distinct from colour which things that are red typically have. Hence the judgement that A looks red cannot be supported by citing grounds consisting of such a constitutive array. Hence A's looking red is *not* typically a *ground* for the judgement that A is red.[36] For there are no features which constitute looking red that can be *correlated* with being red. And that perhaps further explains why we have little if any use for the transformation of 'looks red' into 'has a red look', unlike *both* 'smells fragrant' (= 'has a fragrant smell') – where there is no possibility of a gap between how it smells (fragrant) and the smell it has (a fragrant smell), and 'looks healthy' (= 'has a healthy look') – where a healthy look is evidence for being healthy.

Having clarified these differences between colours and such proper objects of the senses as smells and tastes, and between 'looks thus-and-so' and 'smells', 'tastes' and 'sounds', we may return to our original question. The reductivist offers us the formula 'to be red is to look red to normal observers under normal conditions', suggesting that it can be generalized over all the secondary qualities. Hence, it is implied, to be sweet (fragrant, shrill) is to taste sweet (smell fragrant, sound shrill) to a normal perceiver under normal conditions. But this is entirely misleading. Of course to be sweet is to taste sweet, i.e. a foodstuff which is sweet is a sweet-tasting substance. And something which is fragrant tautologically smells fragrant, i.e. has a fragrant smell. But, as we have argued, what parallels these tautologies in the case of colours is the proposition that an object which is red is red-looking, i.e. has a red colour which is discernible by looking, not that it has a red look.

---

[36] Not typically, but in certain circumstances it may be. If we are in a room lit by a certain colour-distorting light, we might claim that the fact that A looks red is, in these circumstances, evidence that it is red, since this lighting does *not* affect the appearance of red objects, but only of blue and yellow ones.

To be sweet, as sugar is, is one thing, to be perceived to be sweet is another; roses are fragrant whether smelled or not, and they are red whether seen or unseen. To be sure, a normal person with unimpaired sense of smell can, if there is no wind blowing, smell the fragrance of the rose, i.e. he is *able* to perceive olfactorily what is perceptible as far as smell is concerned. So too a normal sighted person in ordinary light will be able to see what colour the rose is – he may (but need not) see its colour, i.e. see that it is red. But he cannot be said to see its red looks. Hence the licit transformation of 'is sweet (fragrant)' into 'tastes sweet (smells fragrant)' is unlike that of 'is red' into 'looks red', but is rather akin to that of 'is red' into 'is red in colour'.

It is misguided to think that we can explain what it is for something to be sweet or fragrant by embedding these expressions in the phrases 'to taste sweet (or to smell fragrant) to A'. On the contrary. Rather do we explain what 'fragrant' means by the use of a sample (a rose, say) which is smelled, and further explain that being fragrant, acrid, etc. are what we call smells. Similarly we explain what 'red' means by reference to a sample, and further explain that being red or green or blue, etc. is what we call having a colour. What then of 'looks red', which is *not* parallel to smells fragrant?

Should one explain it thus: to look red is to look as a thing that *is* red looks in normal light to the normal-sighted?[37] Unlike the reductivist strategy, this gives conceptual priority to *being red,* which is surely right. Nevertheless, it seems unhelpful. For how does a thing which *is* red look in normal light to a normal observer? If our arm is thus twisted, we will no doubt say that it looks red to him. But that means no more than that it strikes him, on looking at it, as being red. And to be sure, in normal light, red things can be seen, by the normal-sighted, to be red. (That is part of what it *means* to be normal-sighted.) Yet this is not obviously a perspicuous explanation of what it is *merely* to look red.

It is most natural to explain what it is for something to look red by pointing in optimal (though not necessarily normal) lighting conditions at something which is red and saying 'Like that'. But that presupposes a grasp of the possibility of a gap between how a thing

---

[37] As suggested by G. E. M. Anscombe, 'The intentionality of sensation', in R. J. Butler (ed.), *Analytical Philosophy,* second series (Blackwell, Oxford, 1965), p.172.

looks and how it is. Hence we might best explain what it is (merely) to look red by reference to examples of objects clearly established as *not* being red. We might shine a red torch onto a white board saying 'That ↗ looks red, but of course it is not'. We learn the use of this articulation *in certain circumstances,* which we can (if articulate) then describe. A crucial feature of the explanation is that the indicated object is not red but *only looks* so. The concept of being red obviously wears the trousers, and it is incoherent to suppose that we could introduce the concept of (only) looking red prior to the concept of being red. Having explained the concept in these circumstances (but not *by reference* to these circumstances), one may further add that things which look red but are not sometimes look *as if* they are red (though not always). On this basis one may construct the *further* joint 'looks red *to me*'.[38] For something looks red to me if, on looking at it, I take it (or would, other things being equal, have taken it) to be red. And I may then find out that it *only* looks red but is not, or that it is indeed as it strikes me as being.

Note the asymmetry here between colours and smells or tastes. One cannot say 'This smells fragrant but is not fragrant' or 'This tastes sweet but is not sweet', since to be fragrant is to smell fragrant and to be sweet is to taste sweet. But one can say 'This smells of sulphur but is not sulphur' or 'This tastes of pineapple but is not pineapple'. And one can drive the wedge between the real and apparent at a different point: viz. 'This tastes sweet to me, but it is not sweet' (I have just been eating lemons), and this *does* parallel 'This looks red to me but it is not'. Yet note that in the case of colours there is a *tripartite* distinction, namely between being red (as geraniums are), looking red (as the Parthenon does at sunset), and looking red to a person (who peers through a piece of red glass at a white surface). In the case of smells and tastes intrinsically characterized there is only a bipartite distinction, and if they are extrinsically characterized the tripartite distinction differs from the parallel tripartite distinction characteristic of colours (since there is no 'having a red look' corresponding to 'having a fishy smell').

[38] Wittgenstein, *Zettel,* §§ 422ff.

5 Normal conditions and normal observers

It was suggested above that the rider which the reductivist adds to his formulation, viz. 'to normal observers under normal observational conditions' is misconceived. It is clearly true that to the typically colour-blind person red things do not look red, but are indistinguishable from green and grey; and under abnormal observational conditions, such as green illumination, red things look black. This qualification is surely indisputable! It is not the truth of this truism that red things look red to the normal-sighted in daylight that is in question, but its import and elucidatory value. Far from the concept of a normal observer in normal conditions being the handle to grasp in explaining what it is for an object to have a given secondary quality, it is the concepts of objective discernible secondary qualities that provide the handle with which to grasp the concepts of a normal observer and of normal observational conditions.

A normal observer, in respect of chromatic vision, is a person who can, merely by looking, perceive the colours that objects have. Standard tests for colour-blindness involve matching things that are red, green and grey or yellow, blue and grey. Normal chromatic vision is determined (roughly) by whether the subject can see that these ↗ objects (or distribution of coloured dots on a background of differently coloured dots) are red and hence different in colour from those ↗ which are green, etc. To the typically colour-blind, red things look indistinguishable from things of similar brightness that are green or grey. Far from the concept of red being explained as signifying that which looks red to a normal observer under normal conditions, it is the concept of a normal observer that is explained as a person to whom things which *are* red (green, blue, etc.) look red (green, blue, etc.), i.e. a person who can see how things are in respect of colours, who can discriminate, on the basis of looking, between differently coloured (but otherwise similar) things. (This point will be explored in detail in the next chapter.)

With respect to normal observational conditions, we must distinguish two different kinds of question. First, what determines such-and-such conditions as normal? By reference to what features do we *count* these conditions, but not others, as normal ones? Secondly, given a normal observer, what determines the normality of the subjective conditions under which he exercises those capacities? These questions concern the *concept* of normality in these contexts.

The reductivist may argue that in characterizing an object as being such-and-such a colour, we select from among its manifold appearances the colour which it looks to a normal observer under conditions we take to be standard.[39] But if the above argument is correct, this must be awry, for the concept of a normal (colour) observer presupposes the concepts of colours and cannot be invoked to explain them. Likewise the concept of looking such-and-such a colour to a person presupposes the concept of being such-and-such a colour.

This attempt to explain perceptual concepts such as colour names, names of tastes and smells, etc. in terms of the concepts of normal observers and normal perceptual conditions wrongly builds the stable background of the use of these expressions into the rules for their use (the explanations of their meaning). Perceptual concepts (of colours, sounds, tastes – but also of lengths and weights) are introduced *in the context* of conditions which may be denominated 'normal', but not *in terms of the concept* of normal conditions. Normal observational conditions are no more constituents of perceptual concepts than the constant gravitational field of the earth is part of the rules of tennis. But only in something like these conditions, against this background, do the rules have a point, can the game be played as we play it. It is in the context of fairly stable sunlight, fairly constant surface structures, that we introduce our colour vocabulary and typically use it. (And were this background wildly unstable, our colour grammar would be as useless as tennis equipment on the moon.) Once introduced, the concept of normal observational conditions can then be explained as those conditions under which things which are red (sweet, fragrant, etc.) are visibly (perceptibly) red (sweet, fragrant); i.e. those conditions under which the actual perceptual quality of something can be discerned by looking (tasting, smelling, etc.)

There are, however, further complications. As far as colour is concerned, daylight illumination is a primary normal condition of observation. But there is nothing *abnormal* about seeing a tomato by candlelight or neon light, and indeed seeing that it is red. Nor is it impossible to discern the colours of *any* objects under abnormal conditions; some colours can be seen perfectly well under ultra-violet

---

[39] Ayer, *The Central Questions of Philosophy*, p. 77.

lamps, but others cannot. Hence ultra-violet illumination may well be termed 'abnormal', whereas candlelight might more properly be termed 'non-optimal'; the former makes some things look other than they are, the latter makes some things look indistinct. Note that even in normal lighting conditions, we might rightly claim that the conditions under which we looked at, and perhaps were asked to judge, the colour of an object, were abnormal, as when a red object is placed on a green background. In strong direct sunlight, from certain angles, a shiny or moiré surface will gleam and glint deceptively, and it may be that only by shielding it from direct light can one discern its colour at a glance.

Determination of the concept of normality with respect to the exercise of one's perceptual capacities is, in general terms, clear. Accurate colour discrimination is impossible after staring at bright light or gazing at brightly illuminated red. Careful taste discernment is impossible immediately after tasting something very sweet or very sour. Detecting thermal qualities correctly requires that one's hands should not have been exposed just beforehand to extremely hot or cold environments. And so on. These conditions of an observer are picked out as non-normal, or perhaps better as non-optimal, precisely because they are found to be conditions under which competent observers typically err in their perceptual judgements (or refrain from making perceptual judgements and offer only expressions of their sensory impressions). In such circumstances, how things look, taste, sound or feel *to* such an observer is not, typically, how they actually look, taste, sound or feel. Nor is it how things are in respect of colour, taste, sound or warmth.

4

Secondary Qualities, Dispositions and Related Conundrums

1 The dispositional thesis

Dispositional analyses of secondary qualities are, I have suggested, a typical counterpart to sensationalism. At the cost of ambiguity in names of secondary qualities, viz. sometimes signifying qualities 'as-we-perceive-them' and sometimes signifying those qualities 'as-they-are-in-the-objects', the dispositionalist conception defuses the subjectivizing thrust of sensationalism without losing its alleged insight. 'Of course objects really are coloured, noisy or odorous,' the Dispositionalist soothes the ruffled feathers of common sense, 'but that merely means that objects have the power or disposition to cause sensations of colour, noise or smell in us in appropriate circumstances.'

It is noteworthy that the temptation to conceive thus of secondary qualities is far older than the scientific revolution of the seventeenth century. It was not scientific discoveries or empirical theories that led to these intellectual aberrations. The roots of the confusion lie in the grammars of our languages, in the representational *forms* of perception and perceptual qualities. Scientific theorizing, the conceptual structure of which was misunderstood by the scientists themselves, greatly encouraged an antecedent confusion. This is well exemplified by a venerable misconception about taste.

Aristotle, followed by Aquinas, argued that things untasted were sweet only *potentially*. To be sweet, he claimed, is simply to have the *power* to taste sweet to a tasting animal. This is surely wrong: it confuses the potentiality of perceiving with the idea that what is perceived is a potentiality. One cannot perceive how sweet an apple is unless one tastes it, to do which one must take a bite (there is no 'tasting at a distance'),[1] just as one cannot see the colour of a rose without opening one's eyes. But what one perceives by the sense of taste is the sweetness of the apple – not a potential but an actual quality. Something is potentially sweet if it *can be* sweet but is not, or will – given further conditions – become sweet. So unripe Coxes on the tree are potentially sweet, but unripe Bramleys are not. On the other hand, sugar is *not* potentially sweet in the bowl becoming actually sweet only in one's mouth. It *is* sweet, and if one tastes it, one will perceive that it is. The potentialities of sugar are not actualized in one's mouth, but rather its actual property, its taste, is *perceived* when the sugar is in one's mouth.

The seventeenth-century scientific revolution and its philosophical underpinnings made dispositionalism about secondary qualities immensely attractive. Developments in optics, rudimentary physiology and the conjectural corpuscularian theory of matter constituted an irresistible field of force, propelling scientists and philosophers alike into one form or another of representational idealism. Descartes argued that

we have every reason to conclude that the properties in external objects to which we apply the terms light, colour, smell, taste, sound, heat and cold – as well as other tactile qualities and even what are called 'substantial forms' – are, so far as we can see, simply various dispositions in those objects [in the shapes, sizes, positions and movements of their parts] which make them able to set up various kinds of motions in our nerves [which are required to produce all the various sensations in our soul].[2]

This is not yet the dispositional analysis, since Descartes equates the secondary qualities with their conjectured 'structural basis', viz. the disposition, i.e. *arrangement,* and motion of the constituent corpuscles

---

[1] But with respect to gill-breathing sea-dwellers, does it make sense to distinguish smell from taste? Do sharks *smell* blood from a distance or do they *taste* it?
[2] Descartes, *Principles of Philosophy* CSM 1 p. 285 (AT VIII A, 322–3); the square-bracketed phrases occur in the French translation but not in the Latin original.

of an object. As noted in chapter 1, Boyle followed a similar line. Locke, however, seems to have identified secondary qualities with the *powers* of objects to produce sensations in us, and Newton's optics urged that colours 'in the object are nothing but a disposition to reflect this or that sort of ray'. The precise interpretation of Locke may be (and has been) disputed; but it is crystal clear that Reid defended a dispositionalist analysis of secondary qualities 'as they are in the objects' coupled with a sensationalist analysis of secondary qualities 'as we perceive them'. It is equally evident that contemporary scientists have inherited a similar conception from von Helmholtz, who embedded it in the conceptual framework of his research into neuro-physiological psychology, and that he himself conceived of these 'insights' as transmitted by Herbart and Kant from Locke.

Helmholtz appears to have thought that all properties are dispositions to produce effects on other things.[3] Chemical properties such as being acidic or alkaline are in fact dispositions to produce certain effects on other chemical substances. But the capacity of bodies to induce sensations in us through their effects on our organs of sense is different, he argued, for their effects are essentially mental. In all such cases, however, we conceive of relative dispositions as properties when we disregard their circumstance- and patient-relativity. We say that a substance has the *property* of being soluble, when we implicitly mean that it is prone to dissolve in water at such-and-such a temperature. When we conceive of weight as a property we implicitly speak of the attraction of a body to the earth. So too with respect to secondary qualities: 'we may correctly call a substance "blue", understanding as a tacit assumption that we are only speaking of its action upon a *normal eye*.'[4] It is misleading in scientific discussion, Helmholtz argued, to conceal the relativity of such powers or dispositions:

When we speak of the properties of bodies with reference to other bodies in the external world, we do not neglect to name also the body with respect to

[3] H. von Helmholtz, 'The recent progresss of the theory of vision', *Preussischen Jahrbücher*, 1868, repr. in translation in R. M. and R. P. Warren (eds) *Helmholtz on Perception, its Physiology and Development* (Wiley, New York, 1986), pp. 101–2. (Subsequent references: WW)
[4] Ibid.

which the property exists. Thus we say that lead is soluble in nitric acid, but not in sulphuric acid. Were we to say simply that lead is soluble, we should notice at once that the statement is incomplete, and the question would have to be asked immediately, soluble in what? But when we say that vermilion is red, it is implicitly understood that it is red for our eyes and for other people's eyes supposed to be made like ours. We think this does not need to be mentioned, and so we neglect to do so, and can be misled into thinking that red is a property belonging to vermilion or to the light reflected from it, entirely independently of our organs of sense. The statement that the waves of light reflected from vermilion have a certain length is something different. That is true entirely without reference to the special nature of our eyes.[5]

This conception, or variants of it, dominate sophisticated scientific thought to this day. After a period of quiescence during which idealism and phenomenalism flourished, dispositionalism has come back into fashion among philosophers. 'Secondary qualities,' it is argued, 'are dispositional, which is just to say that secondary quality attributions are equivalent to counterfactual conditionals.'[6] 'For an object to have such a property is for it to be such that, if certain sensitive beings were suitably situated they would be affected with certain experiences.'[7] And again, 'A secondary quality is a property the ascription of which to an object is not adequately understood except as true, if it is true, in virtue of the object's disposition to present a certain sort of perceptual appearance . . . This account . . . is faithful to one key Lockean doctrine, namely the identification of secondary qualities with "powers to produce various sensations in us".'[8] Further examples could be multiplied to confirm the popularity currently enjoyed among philosophers by the altogether remarkable view that the world around us is not, *in the sense in which we all*

[5] Helmholtz, *Physiological Optics* (1866), repr. in translation in WW, pp. 190–1.
[6] J. Bennett, *Locke, Berkeley, Hume; Central Themes* (Clarendon Press, Oxford, 1971), p. 104. Bennett is here expounding Locke in modern dress, but does later endorse a version of the doctrine.
[7] G. Evans, 'Things without the mind', in Z. van Straaten (ed.), *Philosophical Subjects, Essays presented to P. F. Strawson* (Clarendon Press, Oxford, 1980), p. 94.
[8] J. McDowell, 'Values and secondary qualities', in T. Honderich (ed.), *Morality and Objectivity, a Tribute to J. L. Mackie* (Routledge and Kegan Paul, London, 1985), pp. 111–12.

normally and unreflectively take it to be, multi-coloured, noisy and smelly.

It may seem to the scientifically-minded philosopher that to deny the dispositional account of secondary qualities is a kind of intellectual Luddism. To do so in the name of 'what we all normally and unreflectively' take the world to be seems positively philistine. I shall try to show that it is this very response, rooted as it is in an uncritical and naive picture of the conceptual structure of scientific explanation, that is crude and philistine. As was previously observed, this critical defence of what we ordinarily take the world to be like in respect of perceptual qualities is not a defence of opinions but a clarification of concepts. Scientific theorizing is as subject to conceptual confusion and illusion as any other branch of human reflection. The philosopher cannot fulfil his role by applying for membership in the scientific community of ideas. His task is to evaluate the conceptual coherence of the activities of the scientific community – from the outside.

2   Pro and contra

Various arguments support the dispositionalist account. A preliminary array will be examined here; others will be scrutinized later.

The argument from illegitimate objectification

The first argument to be considered derives from Locke's assimilation of perception of colours and other secondary qualities to sensation. Material objects 'produce in us those different Sensations, which we have from the Colours and Smells of bodies', Locke suggested, but it is no more inconceivable 'that God should annex such *ideas* to such motions, with which they have no similitude; than that He should annex the *idea* of Pain to the motion of a piece of Steel dividing our Flesh, with which that *idea* hath no resemblance.'[9] We do not project pain onto the objects that cause pain, but there is, in

---

[9] Locke, *An Essay Concerning Human Understanding*, II–viii–13; cf. Boyle, *The Origin of Forms and Qualities according to the Corpuscular Philosophy*, in *Works*, vol. II (London, 1744) p. 466.

Locke's view, no more reason to suppose that the idea or sensation of red resembles something in the tomato than there is to suppose that the idea or sensation of pain resembles something in the knife. The fallacies involved in assimilating perception of colours (let alone colours themselves) to sensation have been clarified in previous chapters. Far from noticing them, however, contemporary philosophers have warmly endorsed this assimilation,[10] and have argued that our 'pre-philosophical' conception of colour (and other secondary qualities) involves illegitimate *projection* of an essentially subjective mental item upon the world.

It is striking that this misconception of the categorial differences between perceiving the colour of an object and having a sensation has been harnessed to a misconstrual of an argument propounded by Wittgenstein. Someone who tries to make sense of colour, not as a disposition of an object to cause 'experiences in us', but as an objective property of an object (whether seen or unseen, in daylight or in the dark) is, it is alleged, committed to an incoherence. For such an objectivist is attempting 'to make sense of an exemplification of a property of *experience* in the absence of any experience'.[11] He is in effect projecting a 'property of experience' onto the world in the belief that it is a property of objects. But this, it is held, makes no sense; and Wittgenstein is invoked to prove this:

Wittgenstein once imagined a world in which there were places which affected everyone painfully, so that pains were located at places in the way we locate smells. Suppose this fantasy came true. Would it then make sense to give a non-dispositional account of what it is for there to be a pain at such and such a spot; to suppose a 'pain as we feel it' existing in the absence of any observer? What can the latter form of words mean save that something awful is going on there, and how can that be, when there is no one who is hurt?[12]

---

[10] See, for example, J. L. Mackie, *Problems from Locke* (Clarendon Press, Oxford, 1976) pp. 21ff, especially p. 36; also E. Prior, *Dispositions* (Aberdeen University Press, Aberdeen, 1985), pp. 106–7.

[11] Evans, 'Things without the mind', p. 98.

[12] Ibid; cf. McGinn, *The Subjective View* (Clarendon Press, Oxford, 1983), p. 9 and fn. 5 thereto in which he quotes Wittgenstein's *Philosophical Investigations* (Blackwell, Oxford 1953) § 312, to establish the same point. 'Clearly,' he concludes, 'grasp of the property of . . . "paininess", as possessed by certain surfaces, would depend upon grasp of "pain" as a predicate of sensations, and thus requires knowledge of how pain feels.'

There is considerable question-begging and irony in this.

The question-begging is the assumption that the relevant passage in the *Philosophical Investigations* can be employed to sustain this projectivist account of secondary qualities. This is doubtful, for Wittgenstein's concern in that passage is to make clear the fact that there is no such thing as a *private* exhibition *of the private*. I can publicly exhibit the difference between a broken and an unbroken tooth, as I can demonstrate the distinction between a tree blown over in a storm and one that has withstood the storm.[13] It seems that I can give *myself* a private exhibition of pain, and *hence* exhibit to myself the difference between pain-behaviour with pain and pain-behaviour without pain. But, he argues, this private exhibition is an illusion. One might object that the case of the tooth (or tree) is *not* different from that of pain, for the visual experience in the one case corresponds to the sensation of pain in the other. But, of course, there is no such thing as a private exhibition of a visual experience either, just as there is no such thing as a private exhibition of pain, although there is such a thing as exhibiting pain and as exhibiting a visual experience. But there is a difference here, since a visual experience is a species of perception (or misperception) whereas a sensation of pain is not. We can imagine circumstances, however, in which pain might be regarded as a form of perception – a kind of tactile perception. That would be the case if objects (plants, stones) had regions on their surfaces that caused us pain on touch, so that we could detect the area with our fingertips. If these pain-patches, as we might call them, were importantly indicative of *other* features of objects, it would be altogether natural to conceive of feeling the pain-patch as a form of tactile perception (which was itself painful). It is, to be sure, no part of Wittgenstein's imaginary tale that the envisaged pain-patches *feel* pain or that when we (painfully) perceive the pain-patches we project our pain onto the object that has the pain-patch. But equally, it is no part of his story to suggest that colours have the same dispositional status as the imagined pain-patches. On the contrary, whereas the concept of pain is determined in terms of behavioural criteria, colour concepts are explained in terms of public ostensive definitions by

---

[13] The examples here are Wittgenstein's. The tooth example is the one in the final text of *Investigations*, § 311, the uprooted tree example occurs in the early draft of the MS 165, p. 173.

reference to *public samples*[14] Even in the case of the envisaged pain-patches one could not explain what 'pain' means by reference to a pain-patch *as a sample of pain!* Rather, one would explain what 'pain-patch' means by getting someone to touch a sample pain-patch.

The irony is that Wittgenstein apparently employed this very example to establish precisely the opposite point from that imputed to him.[15] One *can* delineate the functioning of the word 'pain' as a name of a secondary quality *as conceived by Locke and other dispositionalists* – that is what the tale of pain-patches makes clear. But one cannot reverse the operation by sketching the functioning of 'red', 'fragrant', 'melodious', 'sweet' on the model of dispositions to cause such-and-such sensations. If we were to talk of 'painy' or 'painful' patches (as indeed we talk of 'stinging nettles' or 'burning (hot) sand'),[16] then 'painy' or 'painful' would signify a dispositional property (like 'nauseating'). But this is precisely what does *not* apply to colours, smells, tastes, sounds, etc. When we say that the plant is a stinging nettle, we would not dream of inferring that the plant is in pain, although when a child who has grasped the nettle cries that his hand is stinging, we console him. By contrast, when we say that the plant is green and sour to taste, it is the *plant* that is green and sour, not something *other* than the plant. The *intelligibility* of this is no empirical *opinion* that might be gainsaid by science, but a matter of grammar, i.e. colours and tastes are predicable of items of which predicates of extension and shape are predicable. Nor does someone who says that a plant is (objectively!) green illegitimately *project* upon the plant a property of his visual experience, as someone would who

---

[14] It is noteworthy that in the first two drafts of *Investigations*, §§ 311–13, (viz. MS 165, p. 178 and MS 124, p. 290) § 313 was *followed* by the remarks now located at *Investigations* §§ 273ff that are concerned with clarifying the fact that colour names are *not* names of sensations or impressions, that they do not name or refer to something 'private' (an experience).

[15] The point is made by G. E. M. Anscombe's anecdote of an episode in one of Wittgenstein's classes in 1944. See G. E. M. Anscombe, *Metaphysics and the Philosophy of Mind, Collected Papers*, vol. II (Blackwell, Oxford, 1981), pp. viii–ix.

[16] Why do we not do this? To a very limited degree we do, as in the above examples of nettles and sand. The reasons we do not extend this style of representation further are clear enough. Virtually anything *can* cause pain in appropriate circumstances, but relatively few things uniformly cause pain on touch in whatsoever condition they be. Moreover, that something has caused one pain is typically relatively uninformative about the sortal character of the object and hence plays an insignificant role in identification of objects. Finally, when one ceases to touch the 'painy' object, the pain, alas, does not typically cease.

thought that a pain-patch on a plant meant that the plant was suffering. For seeing the green plant is not green, and tasting it is not sour. Acts of perception, so called, are not candidates for being green and sour. Colours are, *inter alia*, what we see; they are properties of objects of perception not properties of perception. The dispositionalist here *assumes* that colours 'as we see them' (as he puts it) are 'properties of experience'. But that was meant to be the conclusion of his argument, not a premise of it. Hence his argument does not establish that ascription of colours, conceived non-dispositionally, involves any illegitimate objectification or projection of something 'subjective'.

It is noteworthy that the very phrase 'properties of experience' is employed here in a highly misleading manner. 'Experience' in this context seems to be equivalent to 'perception' or perhaps 'perception and sensation'. 'Perception' in turn amounts to no more than 'perceivings', i.e. particular seeings, hearings, tastings, etc. What might one *call* 'a property of smelling this, feeling that or seeing the other'? Smelling this rose can be said to be enjoyable; feeling an object can be instructive, informative or interesting; seeing a sunset might be memorable or evocative. Such properties can, in appropriate contexts, be said to be properties *of* particular seeings, feelings or smellings. But nothing other than confusion can stem from talking of what is seen, smelled or felt, for example the scent of the rose, the warmth of the stove or the golden afterglow of the sunset, as *properties* of perceiving them. (Similarly, being fervent or passionate can be said to be a property of my believing that *p,* but that my belief is the belief that *p* cannot be said to be a *property* of my believing, save at the cost of generating confusion.)

It is worth pausing a moment to query what *would* be an illegitimate objectification. Perhaps the following approximates to the idea, but without the desired power to illustrate the subjectivity of secondary qualities. If one looks at the Ponzo illusion, the lower horizontal looks shorter than the higher one, although they are in fact of equal length. If we were to argue that since they look unequal therefore there must be something we see which *is* unequal, *that* is an inference involving illegitimate reification or objectification. To be sure, the appearance of unequal length is perfectly 'objective' in the sense of being perfectly *public* – anyone can see it. But there is no pair of unequal length lines.

The argument from causal idleness

It was previously observed that it is misguided to infer from the fact that science explains what physical processes occur when we perceive a coloured object by reference to the disposition of the object to reflect light of certain wavelengths, that science therefore shows that the object is not really coloured as we think it to be, but merely has a certain microstructure which explains its reflective powers. This misconception involves a further argument sometimes invoked by dispositional analyses, namely that colours (and other secondary qualities) are explanatorily idle. It is thus argued that, for the objectivist, 'There is no evidence that the secondary qualities *so conceived* make any contribution to what G. F. Stout called "the executive order of nature" . . . it is difficult to see how we could ever become aware of causally idle properties of physical objects. In particular, our perceptions would be the same whether or not the properties existed.'[17] Secondary qualities are conceived to be explanatorily idle in two ways.[18] First, they are not involved in explaining the causal interactions of objects with each other; secondly, they do not, while primary qualities do, explain our perception of them. So it is simply superfluous to postulate them in addition to the dispositional properties, grounded in the microstructure of objects, that science has discovered![19] This argument both begs the question and is manifestly false.

It begs the question in so far as one argues that 'The interactions between objects proceed independently of the experiences of perceivers, and these are definitive of secondary qualities'.[20] It is manifestly false, since secondary qualities are not explanatorily idle. We correctly explain why my hut is cool in the summer while yours is hot by reference to the fact that yours is black and mine is white. For black objects absorb light and warm up in the sun to a far greater degree than white ones. That *this* fact is *further* explained in terms of

[17] D. M. Armstrong, 'Perception, sense data and causality', in G. F. Macdonald (ed.), *Perception and Identity: Essays presented to A. J. Ayer* (Macmillan, London and Basingstoke, 1979), p. 91.
[18] McGinn, *The Subjective View*, p. 14.
[19] Mackie, *Problems from Locke*, p. 17.
[20] McGinn, *The Subjective View*, p. 15.

the molecular or sub-atomic structures of the white and black surfaces does not in any way show that the fact that a surface is black does not explain why it warms up (heats water effectively in a sunheater, etc.), let alone show that such things are not really black. Indeed, if it did, then by parity of reasoning, the fact that objects are solid, liquid or gaseous would also, *mirabile dictu,* be explanatorily idle, since these properties too are explained in terms of molecular structures. But an explanation of the molecular structures of solids, liquids and gasses does not demonstrate that things are not really solid, liquid, or gaseous at all. Thus, for example, the liquidity, size and shape of a raindrop may explain the contours of a wet patch on a piece of blotting paper. The fact that the liquidity of a drop of water is explained by reference to the arrangement of its constituent molecules, and that the size and shape of a raindrop is explained in terms of molecular surface tension (velocity and air resistance) does not in any way show liquidity, size or shape to be explanatorily idle. Far from being explanatorily idle, colours explain the light-reflective properties of objects. It is, for example, precisely because this object is red that adjacent white objects set at an appropriate angle to it will have pink shadows cast upon them. Again, this fact is further explained by reference to microstuctures. But to explain is not to explain away!

Does it not follow, one might object, that on this account the warming up of the hut is causally overdetermined – one cause being the hut's being black, and the other being the fact that it has such-and-such a molecular surface with such-and-such properties and dispositions to react to light radiation? And is not that absurd? Would it then not be better to argue either that (i) being coloured just *is* having such surface molecular properties, or (ii) colours are explanatorily idle (and, arguably, 'subjective' or 'phenomenal'), since the fundamental explanation is the advanced scientific one? This is misconceived. Being simultaneously warmed up by the sun and heated by a stove would be a case of causally overdetermined warmth. But what we have here is *not* a case of genuine causal over-determination at all. For it is not that the hut heats up because it is black, and *in addition* it heats up because its molecular surface responds thus-and-so to electro-magnetic radiation. Rather, the latter explanation *explains why* the former causal connection holds. Nevertheless, it might be said, it is *more fundamental!* In one sense, certainly:

the theoretical explanation explains the observational one, but not vice versa. But in another sense, not so: for refutation of the theoretical explanation would not refute the observational one, whereas refutation of the observational one would limit the explanatory scope of the theoretical explanation. And it would be absurd to suppose that the theoretical explanation displaces or renders invalid the observational one, and equally misguided to think that we *always* want or need the theoretical explanation in answer to our questions.

Colours are by no means unique among secondary qualities in this respect. It would be equally fallacious to claim that heat and cold are explanatorily idle. The fact that it has proved illuminating to explain things' being hot or cold in terms of molecular motion, and fruitful to operate with the distinct scalar concept of temperature, does not *invalidate* causal explanations of natural phenomena in terms of heat and cold. Rather it enables us to give futher explanations of why such causal correlations obtain, for example why hot water dissolves more salt per cubic centimetre than cold water, why there is condensation on the inside of cold windows, why people die of hypothermia.

Finally, if explanatory idleness is an empirical matter to be settled by experience (and it is difficult to see how it could be anything but that), then it is an empirical matter whether such-and-such a quality is a primary quality or a secondary one. Does this mean that, according to the dispositionalist's view, it is a contingent matter whether colours, for example, are secondary qualities? Is he suggesting that although as things are colours are explanatorily idle (and shapes are not), we could readily imagine what it would be for colours to be explanatorily active (and shapes idle)? The thought is far from clear, *inter alia* because colours are not explanatorily idle anyway. But this point apart, we should surely demand of the defender of this view that he give us an account of what it would be, according to his conception, for colours to be explanatorily active (and shapes of objects idle)? We should further stress that on this conception it seems that a quality might once have been explanatorily active, but later become idle. But this seems to be a confused description of an aspect of the development of different modes of explanation in science, rather than a lucid description of the objective character of objects and features in the world.

One might be inclined to respond that this is awry. It is inconceivable, the philosopher may claim, that an entity like colour play a causal role in interaction between objects. To this the reply is threefold. First, if it is inconceiveable that an entity like colour play a causal role, it is equally inconceiveable that an entity like shape do so. A patch of reflected light on a surface (for example from a torch) has a shape. Is the shape causally efficacious? Can shapes without objects interact with objects? Hence, secondly, the argument turns on a conceptual confusion. Neither colours nor shapes are *entities* of any kind. To say that colours play a causal role in explaining heat absorption or light reflection is to say that objects *having* such-and-such colours absorb heat or reflect light thus because they have such colours. If they were differently coloured they would absorb less heat and reflect light differently. So too, to claim that shapes are *not* explanatorily idle is to say that objects which have such-and-such shapes interact in such-and-such ways because they have those shapes. Thirdly, to say that it is inconceiveable that the fact that an object is of a certain colour should play an empirically explanatory role is to say that there is an internal relation between the concept of being coloured and the concept of playing a role in an empirical explanation, i.e. a relation of incompatibility. But that just means that it is a feature of our norms of representation, namely a convention or rule for the use of words than an expression of the form '*p* because A is black' is not to be called 'an empirical explanation' or 'a causal explanation'. But we have no such convention. No incoherence is involved in, nor are the bounds of sense traversed by, saying that this hut heats up excessively in the sun because it is painted black (and that if it were white it would not heat up excessively).

The supposition that science neither does nor needs to 'postulate' the objective existence of colours, since they allegedly play no role in scientific theory, is not merely false, since they play a perfectly respectable role in scientific explanation, but also multiply confused. First, it assumes that ascent in the hierarchy of the general conceptual scheme of physics invalidates the lower-level explanations. But this is wrong – explanation of interaction at the level of quanta does not show to be *false* explanations at the ionic, molecular or even mechanical levels. At most it shows such explanations to be, for certain limited theoretical purposes, superfluous. But that this is so (to the limited extent that it is), far from demonstrating the subjectivity or mind-dependence of the qualities that are cited in low-level explanations, presupposes their objectivity. For the very identification of the kinds of properties that occur at the higher levels of the hierarchy of explanations goes via the mundane perceptual properties. Furthermore, the assumption of a simple hierarchy of explanation rather than an interpenetration of different levels of explanations which varies in accord with the explanandum is unjustified. That conception of the unity of science and uniformity of scientific explanation is indefensible.[21] Once that philosophical prejudice is shed, it is obvious that the supposition that colour (for example) plays no role in the classificatory, diagnostic and *explanatory* activities of the sciences (especially the biological sciences) is simply false. And, finally, note that even if it were true that low-level explanations in terms of perceptual qualities were, in some deep sense, rendered explanatorily superfluous by the onward march of physics, that would in no way show that there is some sense in which these qualities are not really objective qualities of objects.

Secondly, it is senseless to talk of *postulating* the existence of colours (or other secondary qualities). For one can postulate the existence of objects or properties only if something *could* count as confirming their existence (and something else as confuting it), i.e. it must make *sense* to talk of them as existing. Hence scientists may postulate the existence of Vulcan and Uranus, and subsequently confirm the latter postulate and confute the former. But, of course, on the dispositionalist thesis it does not make sense to postulate the existence of colours *qua* objective properties as opposed to objective dispositions. There is no room in this account for an explanation of what would count as confirming the 'postulate' that objective colour properties exist. Dispositionalists are propounding a misguided claim about *meaning* under the guise of an empirical thesis about the *de facto* nature of reality. To be sure, on the objectivist conception likewise it makes precious little sense to 'postulate' the existence of objective colours, nor does the objectivist indulge in such postulatings. For the 'non-existence' of objective colours would amount to the world's containing no coloured objects. But it is by no means obvious that it is intelligible to *postulate* that the world does not consist only of transparent colourless objects or invisible ones.

---

[21] For powerful arguments against the naive conception of the unity of science, see J. Dupré, 'The disunity of science', *Mind*, XCII (1983).

Finally, is it the case that secondary qualities in general and colours in particular play no role in explaining our perception of them? How this question is to be answered depends upon what counts as 'explaining our perception of them'. If the fact that the apple is spherical is held to explain why, when one looks at it in daylight from a couple of feet away, one sees a spherical apple (sees that it is spherical), then the fact that it is green explains to just the same extent why one typically sees a green apple (sees that it is green) in these circumstances. One may well feel qualms about this pattern of putative explanation. (Why a normal-sighted person did *not* see something clearly visible and salient may need explaining, but not why he *did* see it. Of course, one may ask why A saw or noticed X, and the answer might be: because it was salient.) Such qualms turn on the coherence of the *philosophical* causal theory of perception. This will not be discussed in this book. It is, however, clear that whatever the rights and wrongs of this account of the concept of perceiving, it provides no grounds for differentiating secondary qualities from primary ones over and above the independent grounds given by *other* considerations about the subjectivity or dispositional character of secondary qualities.

It might, much more plausibly and uncontentiously, be argued that an explanation of perception consists in the *physiological* causal account of changes (in the case of vision, for example) in the retinae and consequent electro-chemical changes in the optic nerves and 'visual' striate cortex.[22] But then it is false that the colour of an object plays no role in explaining why such-and-such changes occur to the cones of the retina and to the appropriate cells of the cortex. It is just *because* X is red that it brings about *these* neural effects. For red objects reflect light of such-and-such wavelength causing changes of such-and-such a kind, while yellow objects reflect light of shorter wavelength producing different neural changes. It can therefore be concluded that the argument from explanatory idleness carries no weight.

---

[22] This is not to say that typical scientific explanations are not fraught with conceptual confusions, but only that the explanatory enterprise of tracing such neural causal sequences is uncontentious and intelligible.

The argument from the experiential component of concepts of secondary qualities

As noted previously, it is sometimes argued that colour as conceived by the objectivist ('colour-as-we-see-it') is really a property of experience. An aspect of this misconception that merits further scrutiny is that concepts of 'sensory properties', i.e. of 'colour-as-we-see-it' or 'smell-as-we-smell-it', etc. are *distilled out of experiences.*[23] This view is an almost unavoidable corollary of the dispositional thesis. For if secondary qualities are dispositions or powers of objects to cause sensory experience in us, then they are known to us only through their actualization, i.e. through *having* the experience which the secondary quality is a disposition to cause. Accordingly, we know what it is for something to be red or taste sweet only in so far as we have the experience of something looking red to us or tasting sweet to us. 'But if grasping colour concepts requires knowledge of certain kinds of experience, and if . . . this knowledge is available only to one who enjoys those kinds of experience, then grasp of colour concepts will depend upon the kind of acquaintance with sensory experiences which we have only from the first-person perspective . . . A man born blind cannot appreciate what it is for something to be red because he lacks the subjective experiences analytic of being red. Secondary qualities are thus subjective in the way sensations are'.[24] Hence the dispositionalist conception is bound up with the sensationalist one.

Is it intelligible to suppose that a concept, no matter of what kind, can be 'distilled out of an experience'? The analogous thesis for sensations, for example pain, is that the concept of pain is distilled out of one's headaches, neuralgias and cramps, so that a condition for

[23] Evans, 'Things without the mind', pp. 95ff, where he argues that concepts of primary qualities such as hardness are *theoretical,* resting upon implicit knowledge of primitive mechanics. 'The point is . . . that it is not possible to distil the concept of hardness solely out of the experiences produced by deformation of the skin which is brought into contact with a hard object, for it is not possible to distil out of such an experience the theory into which the concept fits' (p. 96). By implication concepts of secondary qualities (as-we-perceive-them) are 'distilled out of experiences'. The supposition that concepts of primary qualities are in this sense theoretical is thoroughly confused, erroneously conflating the 'geometry' of primary qualities with physics.
[24] McGinn, *The Subjective View,* pp. 8–9.

possessing the concept of pain is that one has suffered pain. A whole galaxy of errors clusters around this venerable empiricist illusion, errors which Wittgenstein identified and exposed in detail. This conception presupposes that the concept of pain can be explained by private ostensive definition; for what else could 'distilling the concept of pain out of experiences' signify other than forming for oneself a private paradigm of pain distilled out of one's past experiences of pain? But there is no such thing as a private sample of pain, and the concept of pain is not given by reference to a sample of pain, public or private. The doctrine assumes that someone, who uses the word 'pain' correctly, says truly of others that they are in pain when they are, and truthfully of himself that he is not, *must* have suffered pains in the past. Is that an empirical claim? Or is it logically necessary? Presumably the latter, since if it is empirical there must be evidence for it, and it *could* be otherwise. But if it is logically necessary, then we would have to deny that a person who *uses* the word 'pain' correctly, but who has never suffered a pain, knows what the word means!

We are no doubt tempted to say that such a person does not know what pain is *like*.[25] But what is it to know what pain is like? Does the yelping dog whose paw has been trodden on know what pain is like? No, for whatever 'knowing what pain is like' means, it does not mean the same as 'being in pain'. Is it to have 'knowledge of certain kinds of experience'? But what does that mean? If I have a toothache, do I *have knowledge* of a toothache? Am I *acquainted* with toothache? Do I *know* nausea or cramp? These are slightly curious, quasi-poetic expressions. They are either philosophical nonsense, or they signify no more than having had the sensation. One can indeed say 'I have known fear' or 'I am acquainted with grief', but this simply means that I have been afraid and have grieved. So too for knowing toothache or being acquainted with headache. What then do I know when I know what pain is like? Either I can say or display what it is

---

[25] A more radical incoherence is evident in the claim that 'an organism has conscious mental states if and only if there is something that it is like to *be* that organism – something it is like *for* the organism.' (T. Nagel, 'What is it like to be a bat', repr. in his *Mortal Questions* (Cambridge University Press, Cambridge, 1979), p. 166) Well – what *is* it like to be a bat? Rather like what it is to be a mouse, only with wings and an inbuilt sonar!

like, or it is ineffable. But if it is ineffable, then knowing what pain is like amounts to no more than to *have* or to *have had* a pain. But then the thesis that one can possess the concept of pain only if one knows what pain is like merely reiterates that someone who has mastered the use of 'pain' but has never had a pain does not know what the word 'pain' means, which is absurd. The criteria for possession of a concept, for mastery of the use of a word, consist in one's correctly using and explaining an expression, not in one's medical history.

One might wish to counter this by saying that unless one has, for example, suffered bereavement or undergone agony, one does not really *understand* what 'grief' or 'agony' mean. We may concede that we say such things – but suggest to the overhasty philosopher that the inverted commas be removed. It is not the *words* that we fail to understand, but rather is it the web of emotions, attitudes and behaviour into which the phenomena of grief and agony are woven. Undergo these terrible experiences, we may say, and your life will change; but not – and your mastery of English will improve!

One may feel cheated. Even if one concedes that one can master the concept of a toothache without having suffered one, still it seems evident that the blind cannot *fully* master colour concepts. Moreover, what limited mastery they can achieve is wholly parasitic on the skills of the sighted. Does this not show definitively that they 'lack the subjective experience of being red'? A subtle distortion of the truth is involved here. Misconceiving the character of concepts of sensation such as pain, we wrongly assimilate them to concepts of perceptual qualities (such as colour concepts) in thinking them to be defined by reference to samples. Reflecting further upon concepts of such perceptual qualities, and realizing correctly that, in the case of colours for example, the blind cannot fully master their use, we think that this amounts to saying that the blind lack the 'experiences analytic of being red, green, blue, etc.' (the deaf – the experiences of being shrill, melodious, soft, etc.) So having first erroneously projected the grammar and mode of explanation of colour concepts onto concepts of sensation, we now reverse the operation and misguidedly project the grammar and mode of explanation of concepts of sensation *thus misconstrued* upon the concepts of colour (and other secondary qualities)! What is difficult to grasp is that concepts of sensation are *not* explained by reference to samples at all, but by reference to behavioural criteria; and concepts of secondary qualities, such as colours, are defined by reference to (public) samples – *but not by reference to experiences* (let alone sensations). 'This,' we say, pointing at a ripe tomato, 'this colour is red.' We explain notes by, for example, striking a key on the piano: 'This note is F-sharp.' We give someone a morsel to taste: 'This', we explain, 'is bitter.'

At first blush, these familiar exercises seem definitively to *confirm* the empiricist conception. To know what 'red', 'F-sharp', or 'bitter' means, one must experience these qualities! So to think is to confuse a sample and its role as a standard for the correct use of an expression with an example of an item falling under a concept defined by reference to such a sample. What the blind lack is not an *experience* out of which a colour concept is 'distilled', for there is no such thing as distilling concepts out of experiences. Rather, they (tautologically) lack the capacity *to see*. And without the capacity to see, they cannot use a colour sample as a paradigm for the correct use of a colour predicate. The meaning of a colour word is given by specifying a rule for its use, in particular by an ostensive definition employing a sample. But to understand such an explanation of meaning, to grasp the technique of applying the expression in accord with its meaning, requires an ability to discern and employ the sample in its role as a standard of correct use. But if one cannot *see* a colour sample, and if one cannot discern the feature of which it is a sample, or distinguish it from samples of *other* colours, then one cannot employ it as an object for comparison by reference to which one's use of the expression can be justified and the expression explained. Hence one cannot master the use of an expression which is defined by reference to such a sample. (This is a *grammatical* point, not an empirical observation belonging to learning theory. Giving a correct explanation by reference to a sample, and applying an expression in accord with such an explanation are *criteria of understanding*.) It is no use giving a blind person a sample of Wellington blue or peach-blossom pink and asking him to bring items that are that colour. A perceptual *capacity* is here a precondition for full mastery of a *concept* – a capacity, not a private sensation, impression or experience. For colour concepts are not defined by reference to *experiences,* but by reference to public, visible samples – and to *use* these *as* samples, one must be able to see them.

Of course, the blind may achieve partial mastery of the use of colour words. They can ask for the blue vase and, knowing that it is a double-gourd shape, know that what you have given them (barring nasty tricks) *is* the blue vase. They can ask for a nice red apple, and knowing that red Jonathan apples are sweet, object rightly that you have given them a green (unripe) one by mistake. They may learn from others that the sky is blue, clouds are grey, and sunsets red. Their use of colour words may, to this extent, be correct, but it is essentially parasitic on our use, parasitic by way of hearsay, sinaesthesia, and a web of inductive correlations. What the blind cannot do, but we can, is successfully and regularly apply colour predicates to objects non-inductively, viz. to look at an object and say correctly 'That is red'. And they cannot use colour samples, e.g. of ultramarine or Waterloo blue, as objects of comparison; nor can they explain the meanings of colour words by pointing at appropriate samples (save in the case of antecedently known inductive correlations or hearsay). So they cannot participate in the normative activities distinctive of using something as a colour sample.

It is noteworthy that someone who was once sighted, yet is now blind, is *not* now any better off in respect of his conceptual competence than one who was blind from birth, save for the fact that he once *had* perfect mastery of the technique of using colour words and once enjoyed vision of the multi-coloured world around us. It is an illusion that the former, but not the latter, knows (ineffably) what red, blue or yellow are *like*.[26] The humble truth here is simple. One who was sighted, but who is blinded, might, if his sight were restored, *regain* his ability to use colour names *without fresh teaching*. But that does not mean that he really has the ability *in petto* all along, any more than a paralysed man has the ability to walk. Having (properly functioning) eyes is not an *opportunity condition* for exercising the ability to identify the colours of things. (Note, however, that there are borderline cases here.)

Concepts of secondary qualities are defined by reference to public samples, not private experiences. Samples of colour, taste or smell,

---

[26] Note, however, that there is an essential indeterminacy here. The person who has lost his sight may still insist that he remembers the appearance of daffodils, brilliant yellow against the green turf, or the fiery red of a sunset. But he can no longer say 'They look like *that* ↗'. Is there a point beyond which we can say 'He only thinks he can remember'? The normally co-ordinate criteria for another person's recollecting correctly come apart here, and the consequence is precisely this indeterminacy.

no less than samples of length (viz. metre rods, tape-measures, etc.) are to be found *in the world,* not in the mind. We do not use *experiences* to 'measure reality', either for length or for colour. We use public samples. We use them as part of our means of representation, also (occasionally) as elements of actual communication. They define an array of perceptual concepts. But to use them, we must be able to perceive them. Not only what is measured, but also what measures, must be discernible. Hence grasping these concepts requires appropriate perceptual capacities, not 'knowledge of certain kinds of experience'. And the concepts grasped do not, in the intended sense, have an 'experiential component'.

3 Phenol-thio-urea: a decisive argument?

The first three arguments all collapse. Yet the dispositionalist may well take heart from a notorious argument which seems, at first sight, to count decisively in his favour. The objectivist contends that secondary qualities are no less objective properties of things than primary ones. That an object is red or blue, sweet or sour, fragrant or acrid is wholly independent of our perception of it. Indeed, he insists, objects have whatever perceptual properties (primary or secondary) they have irrespective of whether we or any other sentient creatures exist or not. But this bold claim, the dispositionalist will retort, leads to incoherence. For reflect on the fact that it is perfectly conceivable that sugar might go 'from tasting sweet to us to tasting bitter overnight, *as a result of changes in our taste receptors'.*[27] Or reflect on the following bizarre phenomenon:[28] phenol-thio-urea apparently tastes bitter to 75 per cent of human beings, but is tasteless to 25 per cent of a standard sample population. By selective breeding the latter might come to displace the former completely. So phenol-thio-urea will be tasteless to all. Yet no change has occurred to the stuff itself! But this is incoherent, for it involves a substance having a certain property at one time, lacking it (or having a contrary property) at a later time, yet

---

[27] McGinn, *The Subjective View,* p. 10.
[28] J. Bennett, 'Substance, reality and primary qualities', repr. in C. B. Martin and D. M. Armstrong (ed), *Locke and Berkeley* (Macmillan, London), p.105.

undergoing no change. Similar arguments, it is held, could be developed for

the taste of any given kind of stuff, and also for colours, sounds and smells. [We can conceive such changes in us as would] . . . bring it about that no human being could see any difference in colour between grass and blood, and to do this would be to bring it about that grass was the same colour as blood. Similarly for other pairs of colours, and for tastes, sounds and smells.[29]

The evident incoherence is intolerable, and it is an incoherence into which we are led by the conception of secondary qualities as objective properties of objects. But if we see them for what they really are, the dispositionalist proclaims triumphantly, namely as powers to affect us in such-and-such ways, no incoherence results. For a disposition in an object to cause human beings to have a sensory experience of sweetness or bitterness, of seeing red or green, can indeed change as a result of a change *in human beings*. For the dispositionalist conceives of colours and other secondary qualities as essentially relational, and, to be sure, a change may occur in the relational features of an object through changes in the correlative relatum. Hence there is no incoherence in a substance changing from being bitter to being tasteless, from being red to being the same colour as grass, without any alteration in its monadic properties. And this proves that secondary qualities are dispositions (and hence relational); or so it seems.

Appearances, in this case, are deceptive. The case of colour-blindness will perhaps smooth the way for a re-orientation of our viewpoint upon the above characterization of gustatory qualities. The most common form of colour-blindness consists in an inability to discriminate red, green and grey (Daltonism).[30] We normal-sighted insist that grass and blood differ in colour. But if we all awoke tomorrow, having suffered from a uniform onslaught of red/green colour-blindness, we would find grass and blood, emeralds and rubies indistinguishable in colour. But *what* colour would we find

---

[29] Ibid.
[30] It is astonishing that the phenomenon of colour-blindness was not noted until the eighteenth century, when it was registered by the great chemist John Dalton, after whom it was initially named.

these objects and stuffs to be? Would they all be uniformly red, uniformly green, or uniformly grey? Is this an empirical question to be settled by experience? Could we not ask someone who suffers from Daltonism whether he sees emeralds and rubies to be red, green or grey? Obviously he could not answer. For he cannot explain the words 'red', 'green' and 'grey' correctly, he cannot uniformly pick out correct samples to explain what they severally mean. Nor can he employ the right samples as standards of correctness for the application of these words to coloured objects. Moreover he cannot correctly use or understand the use of samples in communicative acts, save *per accidens*. Does he nevertheless know, ineffably, how emeralds and rubies look to him? Should he say – 'They look like this ↗' – pointing with his mind's finger at an item, a 'sensory experience' or 'sensation of colour', visible only to his mind's eye? The simple fact is that he lacks one of the perceptual discriminatory capacities that is the foundation for the technique which we normal-sighted have mastered by the age of six, viz. the technique of using our common colour vocabulary. Hence in a very real sense he does not know what these words mean, cannot use them correctly in the way we do, and will characteristically eschew their use.

Nevertheless, in the land of the red/green colour-blind all will be well. Rubies, emeralds and clouds will correctly be said to be *gred*. And the colour name 'gred' in such a community will be explained indifferently by reference to samples which *we*, in English, would use severally and non-interchangeably to explain what 'red', 'green', or 'grey' mean. Yet none of their observations about coloured things are *therefore* false. Rubies are indeed gred, and so are emeralds; blood, clouds and grass are the same colour, viz. gred. In this community the geometry of colour concepts is, in this respect, *different* from that in our language, though no one would wish to deny that their expressions are colour words. Just as we do, so too do these speakers cut their grammatical suit to fit the cloth of their discriminatory capacities, although, of course, that is not to say that different communities with the same discriminatory abilities may not adopt different styles, all compatible with their discriminatory range. Their colour grammar leads them into no conflict with the truth, and it is no less justified than ours: for no grammar is justified by reference to reality.

What then happens when mankind becomes red/green colour-blind? Do grass, geraniums and clouds *change colour* as a result of this change in us? This is confused. What changes is not the colour of objects but the grammar of colour words. A change in our perceptual capacity effects a change in concepts.[31] For we lose the capacity to apply 'red', 'green', and 'grey' in accord with the technique of their use. We can no longer use samples of red, green, and grey severally and non-interchangeably as standards of correctness for applications of these distinct and mutually exclusive colour predicates. We cannot explain these expressions as before; we can no longer correct misuses as we used to, for we cannot respond to someone who says of an emerald that it is the same colour as a ruby by pointing at a sample of red and saying 'That colour is red, and the emerald is *not* that colour'. We have in effect lost the ability to use these different instruments of language *as* different instruments, and if we can no longer use them thus, then they *are* no longer those instruments of language. But we can recast our colour geometry. We can introduce the term 'gred' (or use 'grey', 'red' and 'green' as synonyms) and in so doing recast our concepts of sameness and difference of colour (and to that extent, our concept of colour itself). Now indeed grass *is* the same colour as blood, and rubies are the same colour as rain clouds, but not because they have changed colour, but because we have changed our concepts of colour.

What then of tastes? Cannot we capitalize on the clarification of the relationship between colour judgements, colour samples and the underlying agreement in colour discriminatory capacities to defuse the parallel argument concerning the taste of phenol-thio-urea and thus deflect the thrust of the dispositionalist's argument? At first glance the cases seem not to be parallel, and the account given of colour seems not to be extendable to this example at all. For in the case of colour-blindness as we have described it, the people suffering from red/green colour-blindness are quite generally incapable of distinguishing any green object from any red or grey one (of corresponding saturation). But in the case of phenol-thio-urea, it is just the bitterness of this specific substance that is indiscernible – other bitter things *can* be distinguished and the expression 'bitter' can be used correctly save with respect to this particular substance. This

---

[31] Of course, not overnight. If the change in the perceptual discrimination were reversed the following day, we would all heave a sigh of relief, and carry on as before.

appears to be akin to an inability to distinguish the colour of *this* ↗ tree (or perhaps of this kind of tree) from red and grey things, while leaving one's *general* capacity to discriminate green from red or grey intact. And in the face of such an eventuality, how could one capitalize on a move which depends upon being able to demonstrate a breakdown of *concepts,* a loss of mastery of the concepts of red, green, and grey on behalf of those suffering from Daltonism, and a corresponding confusion with respect to the concepts of bitterness and tastelessness?

Fruitful strategy typically requires an 'indirect approach'. So let us take a round-about route. Assume that half the population awakes tomorrow to find that they cannot taste sweet things – a spoonful of sugar is rather like a spoonful of soluble sand, gritty but tasteless to them; they can discern the texture of honey, but not its sweetness; and so on. So sweetened tea or coffee, confectionery, cakes and biscuits, ripe fruits and all the myriad foodstuffs that are sweet do not taste sweet to them. Is this not a form of 'taste-blindness'? Having lost their capacity to taste sweet things, to discriminate what is sweet from what is tasteless, what is sour-sweet from what is merely sour, what is bitter-sweet from what is bitter alone, are they not in the position of the red/green colour-blind, only in respect of taste? We might explain what it is for something to be tasteless by reference to a sample of water, and what it is to be sweet by reference to a sugar solution, but they cannot distinguish one such sample from another. We judge icing, sugar, saccharin to be sweet, and to differ in taste from water or pure alcohol, but they discern no difference in taste. Hence they do not, and cannot, apply the terms 'sweet', 'sour-sweet', 'bitter-sweet', 'tasteless', etc. as we do. So their grip on these gustatory concepts slips, and they can no longer participate in the practice of employing them.

Our phenol-thio-urea story is, however, more complicated than this. Its analogue, in the case of sweetness, would be a similarly *selective* 'blindness' to sweet things. One might suppose that a proportion of the population suddenly cease being able to discern the taste of sugar, but do not differ from us in respect of honey, saccharin and other similarly sweet things. Surely these people still have the same concept of sweetness as hitherto, still share our common concept of sweetness. But if, a week later, we too suffer an onslaught of this curious 'taste-blindness', then we, like them, will find sugar tasteless. So are we not back to square one? Is the dispositionalist's point not proven? For a change in all of us seems to have effected a change in the taste of things (or, more specifically, of sugar) even though no monadic property has changed. And this, the dispositionalist contends, can only be explained by reference to the fact that taste is a dispositional property, hence implicitly relational, hence alterable as a consequence of a change in us.

This is too quick. Philosophers should greet each other, Wittgenstein once observed, with the words 'Take it slowly!' So let us go over the ground again. When half the population suffers 'sugar-blindness' do they really retain their grip on the use of the expressions 'sweet' 'tasteless', 'bitter-sweet', 'sweet-and-sour', etc.? Do they really explain 'sweet' as we do, i.e. as it is to be explained? Do they, by and large, apply it correctly? This is by no means obvious. Sugar is a *stuff*, not a thing. It is an *ingredient* in innumerable sweet *things*. Hence 'sugar-blindness' is very unlike colour-blindness, for colours are not ingredients of coloured things. (The colour analogue of our imaginary 'sugar-blindness' would perhaps be 'chlorophyll-blindness'.) It is true that people who suffer from this defect could use a sample of 'artificially' sweetened liquid or food and say 'This is sweet' or 'The taste of this is (called) sweet'. And we will agree. But they will apply this explanation quite differently: the icing on the cake, they will claim, does *not* have *that* taste, indeed it has none. The sugared almonds, meringues, lollipops, etc., they will insist, are *not* sweet, for these sugared things do not have the taste of the chosen sample or samples by reference to which they explain what 'sweet' means. But such confectioneries are paradigmatic examples of sweet things, paradigmatic instantiations of what *we* call 'sweetness'. And while we might use any one of these items as optional samples to explain what it is to be sweet, what we call 'sweet', what 'sweet' *means*, they would not.[32] On the contrary, they would use any of these as samples to explain what they mean by 'tasteless' or to exemplify what they mean by 'not sweet'. We would

---

[32] As we would use any ruby, drop of blood, lump of vermilion, etc. as an optional sample to explain what 'red' means. For more detailed examination of the character of optional samples and similarly of *standard* and *canonical* samples, see G. P. Baker and P. M. S. Hacker, *Wittgenstein: Understanding and Meaning* (Blackwell, Oxford, 1980), pp. 198–9.

say that sugared edibles and otherwise sweetened things have the same taste (*ceteris paribus*), while they would say that they are *different*. We would say that sugared water has a different taste from pure water, they will say that both are tasteless. Is it still obvious that we and they are employing the same concepts? Is it not rather that all is falling into confusion?[33]

Confusion of tastes: I say: 'This is sweet', someone else 'This is sour' and so on. So someone comes along and says: 'You have none of you any idea of what you are talking about. You no longer know at all what you once called a taste.' What would be the sign of our still knowing? (Connects with a question about confusion in calculating.)[34]

But might we not play a language-game even in this 'confusion'?
– But is it still the earlier one?

What we have here, in our imaginary example, is an exemplary illustration of Wittgenstein's previously cited observation that 'if language is to be a means of communication there must be agreement not only in definitions but also (queer as this may sound) in judgments.'[35] In our imaginary cases of inability to discern sweetness and the different example of inability to taste sugar we have neither agreement in judgements nor agreement in definitions. In the latter case it is wholly misleading to claim that sugar (and all things sugared) change from being sweet to being tasteless overnight 'for' 50 per cent of the population, for sugar does not change its taste through a change in the gustatory discriminatory capacities of part of the population. But such a change may, as in the imagined tale, bring about a partial breakdown in communication. And this in turn may stimulate a shift in gustatory concepts and the emergence of new, different, language-games.

Common perceptual capacities, shared discriminatory abilities, are a *precondition* for a shared perceptual *vocabulary*. If some of us could not distinguish salty from sweet foods, others could not discriminate between sour and salty stuffs, yet others found sugared foods indistinguishable from unsugared ones, and so on, then we would

---

[33] Cf. L. Wittgenstein, *Zettel* (Blackwell, Oxford, 1967), §§ 366–7
[34] See below p. 158.
[35] Wittgenstein, *Philosophical Investigations,* § 242.

not have a *shared language of taste qualities*. Similarly, the onslaught of extensive *variegated* forms of colour-blindness would preclude a shared colour language. Neither the world we describe would change, nor would our descriptions of it change *in respect of truth or falsehood*. Rather confusion would supervene. Our *concepts* would change. We would adopt a different grammar of taste and colour (and *various* possibilities can be imagined); or we would abandon (part of) it altogether.

But there is no difference, in this respect, between primary and secondary qualities. We explain concepts of secondary qualities by reference to samples (whether they be optional or standardized), just as we explain simple concepts of measurement of length or weight, for example yard, metre, kilogram, by reference to samples (standard or canonical). These are part of our means of representation. It is important to remember that whether something is a sample or paradigm in an explanation of meaning is not an intrinsic property of that thing. It is a status conferred on it by us, by the way we *use* it as a 'measure'. We use the world (or, rather, bits and pieces of it), not our 'experiences' of it, to measure the world. But to use something as a sample, as a standard for the correct application of an expression, we must, tautologically, be able so to use it. This is no less true of samples of measurement (i.e. primary qualities) than of colours, tastes, sounds, etc. If, through some weird changes in physics, one could not lay rulers alongside objects (if they were repelled, like magnets) we would abandon our day-to-day concepts of measurement, for we would be unable to use them as we now do (and would replace them, very likely, by some more or less remote heir to our mundane notions of metre length or yard). In the cases we have examined above a change *in us* brings about an inability to use certain samples (of colours and of taste qualities) as they are to be used, and hence an inability to apply the corresponding perceptual predicates as they are to be applied, i.e. in accord with the rules for their use – rules which are given by reference to samples.

In philosophy a hairbreadth separates sense from nonsense. To be sure, we should immediately concede

how thoroughly contingent it is that we are in a position to say of anything that it is bitter or green or noisy or the like. The occasional failures of agreement bring home to us how dependent our public secondary quality terminology is upon the fact that we usually *do* agree in our secondary quality discriminations – the failures help us to realize that our notion of two things having the same colour, say, is only as secure as our ability to muster an overwhelming majority who see them as having the same colour.[36]

One may have found the right combination to the lock of a safe, but then go through the operation backwards, only to find that the safe is still stubbornly locked. It *is* thoroughly contingent that we construct our concepts of secondary qualities as we do; moreover, different cultures construct them differently despite common discriminatory capacities. But it is equally thoroughly contingent that we construct our concepts of primary qualities as we do, and we can imagine such changes in us or in the world as would cause confusion to supervene in respect of concepts of length, weight or velocity. Indeed, such considerations apply with equal validity to our *mathematical* concepts and number system, even though philosophers labour under the illusion that here we have, as it were, the hardest of the hard. If everyone disagreed in the results of their calculations, if whenever one checked a computation one always got a different result, if, while calculating a multiplication sum, one always forgot what digits one was working with or what number to 'carry over', then we would have no arithmetic or a very different arithmetic.

Calculating would lose its point if *confusion* supervened. Just as the use of the words 'green' and 'blue' would lose its point. And yet it seems to be nonsense to say – that a proposition of arithmetic *asserts* that there will not be confusion. – Is the solution simply that the arithmetical proposition would not be *false* but useless, if confusion supervened?

Just as the proposition that this room is 16 foot long would not become *false,* if rulers and measuring fell into confusion. Its sense, not its truth, is founded on the regular working of measurements.[37]

Wittgenstein sapiently adds 'But don't be dogmatic. There are transitional cases which complicate the discussion.' No doubt it is impossible to say in advance what counts as an aberration and what as a breakdown in concepts. Nor can one draw sharp lines to determine

---

[36] Bennett, *Locke, Berkeley, Hume,* pp.95–6.
[37] Wittgenstein, *Remarks on the Foundations of Mathematics,* 3rd edn (Blackwell, Oxford, 1978), p. 200.

at what point confusion supervenes. It is this, among a host of further misconceptions, that lends the example of phenol-thio-urea its deceptive allure. It is a substance we rarely come across. It is not a common ingredient of our daily foodstuffs. Hence the impact of this aberration on our shared language-game with taste predicates is minimal (but it is easy to imagine how this could be different, how this perceptual aberration might lead to massive disruption of our gustatory vocabulary). The guiding principles leading back to the highroads of sanity are clear. And the argument from subjective changes in our perceptual capacities to the alleged dispositional character of secondary qualities is as confused as the other arguments in support of the dispositional thesis.

4 Of mice and men and Martians

The phenomenon of colour-blindness is a fecund source of confusion. No sooner is one conundrum resolved than another springs up in its place. Most mammals cannot see chromatic colour. So how does the world appear to the humble mouse? If we try to picture this to ourselves, we are driven to think of black and white photography. Surely the mouse must see the world as it appears to us on black and white television screens. The rich symphony of colours we see in the rose garden is orchestrated for the mouse in subtle modulations of grey, black and white. And the bee, the entomologist tells us, can distinguish yellow, blue-green, violet and, strange to say, *ultra-violet;* but it is insensitive to red and orange. When we look at the blossoms of leopard's bane we see yellow, the mouse sees a shade of grey and the bee sees – who can say? It *reacts* to ultra-violet absorption and reflection, and a photograph of leopard's bane on ultra-violet-sensitive film reveals a pattern of markings invisible to us! And now the mind reels in confusion. For what colour is it really? If each species sees it differently, if even members of the same species see it differently, how can we say? What right could we possibly have to take man (if he is not colour-blind) as the measure of all things?

A small dose of science fiction can increase our confusion. For surely we can imagine that objects which look red to us might look green to Martians? From this we may well conclude that it is quite impossible to choose between the Martians and ourselves in respect of whose experience determines the colours of the objects in question. This apparent liberalism seems to push us remorselessly into a dispositional account of colours and other secondary qualities. Precisely this conclusion was drawn by Helmholtz in the nineteenth century:

> there is no sense in asking whether vermilion as we see it is really red, or whether this is simply an illusion of the senses. The sensation of red is the normal reaction of normally formed eyes to light reflected from vermilion. A person who is red-blind will see vermilion as black or as dark grey-yellow. This too is the correct reaction for an eye formed differently from that of other persons. In itself the one sensation is not more correct and not more false than the other, although those who call this substance red are in the large majority. In general, the red colour of vermilion exists merely in so far as there are eyes which are constructed like those of most people. Persons who are red-blind have just as much right to consider that a characteristic property of vermilion is that of being black.[38]

A dispositional account seems to relieve us from the intolerable pressure apparently exerted by considerations of species-specific discriminatory capacities as well as colour-blindness (or 'taste-blindness'). For if secondary qualities are like the dispositional properties of being nourishing or poisonous, then they are essentially relative.

This relativity implies that there is no genuine disagreement between us and the Martians when they call an object green which we call red; for all these colour ascriptions assert is that an object looks green to them and red to us. It is thus entirely proper to speak of objects as red with respect to perceiver x and green with respect to perceiver y.[39]

And what goes for Martians goes for mice! So, after all this, what colours does a thing really have? Strictly speaking 'as many colours as there are different ways it (systematically) looks'![40] In this sense, the dispositionalist concludes, objects have many contrary colours simul-

[38] Helmholtz, *Treatise on Physiological Optics*, (1866), repr. in translation in WW, p. 190.
[39] McGinn, *The Subjective View*, p. 10.
[40] Ibid.

taneously, just as a foodstuff may be poisonous (to species x) and nourishing (to species y). Rubies are red (to us), dark grey (to mice), and bright green (to Martians).

The illusions of reason are powerful indeed; they bedazzle the mind with false glare. To see the world from the correct logical point of view we must examine more closely the concepts in terms of which we conceive it. For here we confuse the tangled skein of our concepts with a wholly mythical veil of fluctuating, relative appearances. The veil is only as dense as our misunderstandings.

If, under the pressure of these puzzles, we are driven into construing colour concepts (and concepts of other secondary qualities) as essentially relational, we are committing ourselves to the idea that they must be defined by reference to subjective experiences. It is no coincidence that claims such as 'colour concepts have an experiential component' or that they are 'distilled out of experiences' trip lightly off the dispositionalist's tongue. It was argued above that these claims confuse the *capacity* to employ a public sample with the possession of a private sample – something that is 'given', indeed an experience. This point can be pressed further, and brought to bear on the present conundrum.

The dispositionalist argues that there is no genuine disagreement between the Martian who says that poppies are green and humans who insist that they are red. When we say that the poppy is red we simply mean that it looks red to us (to those whose visual organs are like ours); and there is no reason why it should not look green to a Martian, grey to a mouse, and ultra-violet to a bee. This commits him to explaining what it is to look red (or whatever) by reference to the *experiences* enjoyed when one looks at a poppy (for example). Hence, he argues, when Martians look at grass, they may have qualitatively identical experiences to those we have when we look at poppies! Wittgenstein's argument against the possibility of a private language demonstrates the unintelligibility of this tale, and although it has been briefly sketched above, we must make perspicuous its application here.

Waiving legitimate qualms about the use of the term 'experience' in the phrase 'the experience of seeing red', and granting that a normal-sighted person who looks at a poppy in daylight 'enjoys the experience' of seeing a red object, why can we not claim that this experience is to be taken as a *sample* for the correct use of 'red' or 'looks red to me and other normal human beings'? Clearly A's experience of seeing red cannot function as a *public* sample, for an experience is not, in *this* sense, shareable. I can see the poppy A sees, but I cannot have his experience of seeing it, any more than I can have his headache. And although there is such a thing as displaying or exhibiting an experience, there is no such thing as exhibiting an experience of seeing red (as one can exhibit a public sample of red) so that the *experience* can be used as an object of comparison or sample for the general, common, use of the colour word. Consequently, we would not know whether we all mean the same by 'red'; indeed, in one sense we would know that we do not, since A means *his* paradigmatic experience and I mean *mine*. And since his experience is not something I can have, we cannot mean the same.

One might attempt to sidestep this embarrassment by the suggestion that although experiences are unshareable, nevertheless they may be qualitatively identical. The 'scientific realist' may indeed argue that the extensive convergence of colour judgements makes the supposition of qualitative identity an 'inference to the best explanation'. But this is confused. First, if A's current experience of seeing red is to function as a sample for his use of 'red' or 'looks red', it is unclear what qualities that experience can intelligibly be said to *have,* which someone else's private paradigm could also be said to have. Certainly seeing something red neither looks red nor is red! Secondly, if the 'experience' functions as a paradigm, it cannot at the same time be said to fall under the concept it defines, for if it is what measures, the one thing it cannot measure is itself. (Just as the standard metre cannot be said to be one metre long!) No doubt there is such a thing as checking one sample against another. If my tape-measure gets drenched I can hold it up against my yardstick to check whether it has shrunk – here the yardstick measures and the tape-measure, no longer functioning as a sample, gets measured. But there is no such thing as juxtaposing A's seeing red with B's seeing red in the manner in which a pair of samples might be thus juxtaposed. So it makes no sense, in *this* context and with *these* presuppositions, to talk of identity. (Compare: A relates that he dreamt that he walked for a very long time at an unspecified season of the year, from dawn to dusk; B had a similar dream, viz. that he worked in a field at an equally unspecified date from dawn to dusk. Did A walk (in his dream) for longer than B worked (in his dream) or for the same length of time?!) Thirdly, it does, of course, make perfectly good sense to say that A and B enjoyed the *very same* experience of seeing the red poppy. It is, however, wholly confused to suggest that their experiences are *numerically* distinct but *qualitatively* identical, for that distinction does not apply here any more than it does to colours (or pains). But that their 'visual experiences' are or can be identical *presupposes* a criterion of identity which on the dispositionalist's tale is meant to be given by the experiences themselves.

An apparent fall-back position would be to suggest that each perceiver employs private paradigms for his own use alone – I may not know what you mean by 'red', but I surely know what *I* mean. This position too was undermined by Wittgenstein. Of course there can be private, i.e. unshared paradigms. I might, in writing my diary in code, introduce a private sample of length, e.g. my handspan = 1H, and use it to measure lengths. If no one was told what 1H was, then this measure would be unshared, though not unshareable. But the idea of using one's own 'experience' or recollected 'sense-impression' as a sample that functions as a standard of correctness for one's use of colour predicates presupposes the intelligibility of unshareable samples. And that, as Wittgenstein showed, and as we sketched out above (see p. 109), makes no sense. In this case there is no criterion for what counts as remembering the putative 'inner object' correctly, since a sample would itself be necessary to distinguish correctness from incorrectness in such a case. For the memory of an experience (whether veridical *or not*) presupposes the concept of the experience of which it is a memory. Moreover there can be no technique of comparing such an envisaged 'sample-experience' with anything, and consequently no internal relation between the putative explanation of meaning by reference to a 'private' sample and the application of the relevant expression. So the thought that our understanding of names of secondary qualities rests upon 'acquaintance with experiences' that function as 'private' samples is incoherent.

We can now return to Martians and mice and review the problem from a fresh vantage point. Does it make sense to suppose that objects which we see as red Martians see as green, or that objects which look red to us might look green to them? Note that we say of a person that something looks red to him both if he looks at an object and says 'That thing is red' and if he says 'That looks red' (to which he might add 'although I know it is not' or 'but I am not sure what colour it really is'). Something looks red to a person if, on looking at it, he takes it – or would, if not for collateral information, take it – to be red. But a person can take an object to be red only if he knows what it is for something to *be* red, i.e. if he possesses the concept of being red, knows what 'red' means. Seeing an object *as* red or green, an object's looking red or green to a person, is bound up with actual, tentative, or counterfactual judgement and discriminatory behaviour. So it makes sense to say that objects which we characterize as red look green to Martians or are seen as green by Martians only if the Martians know what it is for something to *be* green. And if they know what it is for something to be green, they also know that if it is green it is not also red! For a thing does *not* have 'as many colours as there are different ways it (systematically) looks'. That white surfaces systematically look pink under red light, bluish when blue shadows are cast upon them, greenish when viewed through green glass (all thoroughly systematic) does not make them anything other than white. If the criteria for the Martians' mastery of the concepts of red and green are satisfied, if we can establish that the expressions 'A' and 'B' in their language mean red and green, then it is trivially possible that *in certain circumstances* (perhaps when suffering from an overdose of this or that) red things might look green to them, and that they might, in this innocuous sense, see red as green. (But then so might we, in similar *or different* circumstances). If the Martians explain their colour word 'A' by picking out red samples and 'B' by reference to green samples, and if they typically apply 'A' only to red objects and 'B' only to green ones, then we have adequate grounds for thinking that they possess the concepts of red and green. If they then, having eaten some disagreeable food, report that red things suddenly look green to them, then that is intelligible.

This triviality is, of course, not what the dispositionalist wants. Is it not possible, he will retort, that for all the paraphernalia about public samples, red *systematically* looks green to them, and vice versa? Could it not be that when they explain 'A' by pointing at a ripe tomato, and 'B' by pointing at grass, nevertheless the tomato looks green to them and the grass looks red? No, this is not possible. Such a supposition would only make sense if it made sense to assign meaning to colour words by reference to 'experiences of seeing colours' employed as 'private' samples. But it does not. We can only intelligibly suppose that something red looks green to a Martian if we can establish that the Martian knows what it is to be red or green, and that in turn requires agreement in definitions (in the use of samples in explanations, justifications, criticisms and corrections) and agreement over a broad range of judgements. The supposition of systematic inversion, like the more general conundrum of spectrum inversion, is incoherent. This is just a special case of the principle that what may happen some of the time may well not be capable of happening all of the time. The incoherence consists in the fact that the imagined tale employs the concepts of looking red (or green, etc.) to a person while repudiating the very conditions which make the employment of these concepts intelligible.

What then of the humble mouse? Do we characterise its experience correctly by saying that it sees the world as we see a black and white television screen, that things look to a mouse to be black, white and grey, that it sees things *as* black or white or grey? No – this is a mirage of the intellect. A number of different considerations converge on this conclusion.

The first is quite general, applying to completely colour-blind language-users, but also bearing indirectly on animals. 'Black', 'white' and 'grey' are words which belong to our colour grammar. A colour grammar usable by someone totally colour-blind would not include these concepts. For paradigms of grey are, for us, precisely *not* correctly used as paradigms for chromatic colours (of relatively low saturation) and vice versa. Someone totally colour-blind can neither explain nor apply 'grey' as we do. We may characterize the picture on the black and white television screen as black, white and grey, but only because it stands in contrast to our chromatic characterizations of the multi-coloured objects of which it is a picture. For we are in a position to say that your dark blue suit looked black on the television screen, your pale blue shirt looked grey, and your light blond hair looked white. To say that a colour-blind person sees a range of similarly saturated pastels *as* uniform grey means no more than that he cannot distinguish these colours one from the other or from grey. And to say that he sees them as grey is a misuse of the phrase 'to see them as grey', for what does this person understand by 'grey'? What is it that he takes them to be when he takes them to be grey, how do they strike him when they strike him as being grey? So far the illusion; and yet there is a reality behind it. A totally colour-blind person can no more discriminate the colours of objects in the world around him than we can discriminate the (chromatic) colours of objects (excluding collateral information) by looking at a black and white television screen. That is what it is to be colour-blind. And this modest truth applies to the mouse no less than to the man.

Secondly, while it is trivially true that an animal that sees an object which is red sees a red object, it is far from being trivially true that the animal can see the colour of the object. That much is obvious enough. Clearly, we should pause before saying of an animal that a given object looks such-and-such a colour to it. To say this of a language-user amounts to saying that on looking at the object the viewer takes it (or would, other things being equal, take it) to be such-and-such a colour. To say it of an animal, however, requires a differential response on its behalf to the object it perceives which constitutes an analogue to a person's taking the thing to be such-and-such a colour. That in turn is justified only to the extent that its behavioural repertoire provides adequate grounds for so saying. We might indeed train an animal that was not colour-blind to manifest a differential response (bark, mew, or chirp) to grey objects (in contrast to red, green, yellow, etc. objects). Then we would be in a position to say that it can see (discriminate) grey. If we contrive, by a cunning arrangement of lights, to make a coloured object look grey, and the animal reacts to it as trained, we might with justice say the object looks grey to the animal even though it is not. (Note, incidentally, that there seems no room in the case of animals for the counterfactual addendum to account for something looking such-and-such a colour to a person even though he knows it is not so coloured.) But, to return to our mouse, this differential response is precisely what we cannot train colour-blind animals to elicit. For, again, they cannot discriminate between grey and chromatically coloured objects. *A fortiori* we cannot suppose that the multi-coloured objects around us look grey to a mouse.

Neither mice nor Martians provide us with any good reasons for espousing any dispositional conception of colours (and other secondary qualities) as relational. Such conceptions are rooted in misleading pictures of the relationship between the discriminatory capacities that are preconditions for concept-possession, colour concepts (or other secondary quality concepts) and the criteria for their possession, and true or false statements about coloured objects.

5 Turning the tables

Thus far we have allowed the dispositionalists the offensive, letting their arguments splinter in the onslaught. If our defences have been sound, then there is nothing to be said in favour of this conception of secondary qualities save that it interlocks with deceptive smoothness with other related misconceptions. Having examined a range of direct arguments in support of varieties of dispositionalism, it is time to turn the tables, to show that not only is there no good reason for embracing this picture, but also that it is radically incoherent.

Colours and internal relations

Secondary qualities, in particular colours and sounds, like primary qualities, display a rich array of internal relations. Colours can serve to exemplify the point. Red is a colour, and that statement, unlike 'Lions are carnivorous' is not a contingent truth. Scarlet is a shade of red; if anything is scarlet, it must also be red. If an object is red all over it is not simultaneously green all over. Being carnivorous often excludes being herbivorous, but not necessarily. Colour exclusion, however, is necessary, not contingent – we cannot even imagine something being both red all over and green all over simultaneously. Lions are larger than leopards. Black is darker than white. The two statements appear deceptively similar. But whereas we can imagine a leopard that is larger than a lion, no feat of the imagination will enable us to imagine black being lighter than white. And our failure does not stem from poverty of imagination, nor will daily exercises to strengthen our imaginative powers avail us. There are such colours as greyish-blue or yellowy-green, but there is no such colour as greenish-red, and one can guarantee in advance that astronauts will not find such a colour even in the farthest reaches of the universe. We are familiar with transparent red glass, or transparent green, yellow or blue glass; but we have never come across transparent white glass. And we never will.

What is the nature of these necessities? Wrongly viewed, they seem like descriptions of the essential, structural, features of the world (in respect of colour). It is in the nature of colours to exclude each other, one is inclined to think. But is this akin to the claim that there is no room on a chair for two people to sit down (see above, pp. 100–1)? Or is it like the claim that if something is one foot long, it is not also two feet long? And is the latter claim also a description of essential features of the world? One might be inclined to think of such propositions as metaphysical. But metaphysics is not a super-science, it is an illusory science. So-called 'truths of metaphysics' are not descriptions of the 'essential, structural, properties of reality', since they are not descriptions at all.[41] Metaphysics is a cloud behind which lies either grammar (and hence convention) or nonsense. If we are puzzled by the nature of such patterns of internal relations, to have recourse to metaphysics is to enshroud an unclarity in a mist.

An alternative tack is to suggest that such propositions are true in virtue of the meanings of words. But this is either absurd or unhelpful. For one surely would not wish to say that the meaning of the word 'red' precludes red and green from being coinstantiated over the same expanse. Do meanings of words have such power? How does the meaning of 'black' guarantee that black is darker than white? Does it do this in co-ordination with the meaning of 'white'? And how strange that 'noir' and 'blanc' should do the same? This is perspicuous nonsense, replacing a metaphysics of colour with a metaphysics of meanings. We might avoid that absurdity, yet still insist that red excludes green, that being white precludes being transparent, because of the meanings we have given these words. But now, although this may point in the right direction, it offers no explanation at all. Moreover, it is gravely misleading. For it is not *because* of the meaning of 'red' and 'green' that nothing can be red and green all over simultaneously, rather is it an *aspect of the meaning*, the use, of 'red' and 'green' that the phrase 'red and green all over simultaneously' is useless, has no application.

How does the dispositional theorist approach these questions? For

---

[41] For detailed defence of this claim, see L. Wittgenstein, *The Blue and Brown Books* (Blackwell, Oxford, 1958), pp. 44ff; and, for elaboration, P. M. S. Hacker, *Insight and Illusion*, rev edn (Oxford University Press, Oxford, 1986), ch. VII and G. P. Baker and P. M. S. Hacker, *Wittgenstein: Rules, Grammar and Necessity*, (Blackwell, Oxford, 1985), pp. 263ff.

if colours (and other secondary qualities) are really dispositional powers in objects to affect us, to cause us to have 'experiences-of-seeing-colours', then it is incumbent upon him to give an account of these internal relations. Of the large number of philosophers who have favoured dispositionalism, only one has tried to meet the challenge of accounting for the 'geometry' of colour in dispositional terms;[42] and none have tackled sound. The argument runs as follows: since colours are dispositions, there is nothing awry with the idea that something can be both red and green all over simultaneously, any more than there is with the supposition that a substance might be both nourishing and poisonous. For just as a food may be nourishing to species A but poisonous to species B (or nourishing in small quantities but poisonous in large), so too an object may be red for A and green for B, i.e. the same object may have the power to cause 'qualitatively distinct experiences' to different perceivers (or perceivers of different species). The real 'logical form' of 'no surface can be both red and green all over simultaneously' is 'no surface can look red and simultaneously look green to X'. This is held to contrast with primary quality incompatibility. For suppose that things could be round and square simultaneously – then theoretical and common-sense mechanics would break down and there would be no coherent description of how bodies are disposed to interact. These are 'ontological necessities'. But since colours are, it is held, irrelevant to the causal powers of objects, joint instantiation of red and green would have no such calamitous consequences – things would interact just as before. What would be impossible would be to *perceive* objects thus qualified, for we cannot imagine what it would be like to experience things as having contrary secondary qualities. These are not 'ontological' but 'phenomenological' necessities. The impossibility of being red and green all over flows from the phenomenological impossibility of something's looking both red and green all over to a normal human being. These phenomenological necessities are held to be 'laws of appearance' and Wittgenstein's authority is invoked in support of this claim:

But what kind of proposition is that, that blending in white removes the colouredness from the colour? As I mean it, it can't be a proposition of

---

[42] McGinn, *The Subjective view*, pp. 21ff.

physics. Here the temptation to believe in a phenomenology, something midway between science and logic, is very great.[43]

It seems that these necessities are 'quasi-logical relations, which arise from the subjective nature of the experience involved . . . We can grasp these laws of subjectivity only by enjoying the kinds of experience of secondary qualities from which they issue.'[44] For 'in coming to be a conscious perceiver you come to conform to a rich system of phenomenological laws governing how things can seem, these laws arising from the very nature of perceptual experience.'[45]

This is both incorrect and incoherent. It is incorrect in as much as Wittgenstein's name is invoked in support of a claim which he explicitly repudiated. The temptation to believe in phenomenology is one he was concerned to warn against. There is *nothing* between science and logic: 'There is no such thing as phenomenology, but there are indeed phenomenological problems', he observed.[46] The impossibility of certain colour blends is not confirmable or refutable by experiment. 'It would, however, also be wrong to say: "Just look at the colours in nature and you will see that it is so". For looking does not teach us anything about the concepts of colours.'[47] Goethe's *Farbenlehre*, interesting though it is, is full of 'absurdities',[48] precisely through failure to realize this. 'Phenomenological analysis (as for example Goethe would have it) is analysis of concepts and can neither agree with nor contradict physics',[49] for conceptual analysis can never agree with or contradict empirical facts or (coherent) theories.

The dispositionalist's phenomenological account is incoherent for the following reasons. First, as has been shown, since red and green, unlike being nourishing or being poisonous, are not dispositional properties and neither explicitly nor implicitly relational, there is no such thing as an object's being red *for* a person let alone red for one

[43] L. Wittgenstein, *Remarks on Colour* (Blackwell, Oxford), II, §3.
[44] McGinn, *The Subjective View*, pp. 34–5.
[45] Ibid., p. 37.
[46] Wittgenstein, *Remarks on Colour* I, § 53.
[47] Ibid., I, § 72.
[48] Cf. letter to Norman Malcolm, 16 January 1950, printed in N Malcolm, *Ludwig Wittgenstein: A Memoir*, 2nd edn (Oxford University Press, Oxford and New York, 1984), p. 125.
[49] Wittgenstein, *Remarks on Colour*, II, § 16.

person and green for another.[50] Of course, a surface (e.g. a white wall) may look red to A (looking through a piece of transparent red glass) and green to B (looking through transparent green glass). And, of course, no surface can look to a person to be both red and green all over. But that is no 'law of subjectivity'. There is *no such thing* as being red and green all over, *a fortiori* no such thing as an object's looking to someone *as if* it is both red and green all over simultaneously.[51]

Secondly, there is *no* contrast here with primary quality incompatibility. There is *no such thing* as being both exactly one metre long and also exactly two metres long at the same time. These words, thus combined, have no use. 'Is both round and square' (said of a two-dimensional shape), 'is red and green all over' are nonsensical combinations of words, like 'a southwesterly north wind'. Hence it is literally unintelligible to 'suppose' that things could be simultaneously round and square, or spherical and cuboid – there is nothing here *to* suppose. A logical impossibility is not a species of possibility; it is not, as it were, a possibility that is impossible. One cannot suppose (there is no such thing as supposing) it to be actual, for such forms of words are not *descriptions* of something that might be the case, nor are they descriptions of something that cannot be the case, for they are not descriptions of anything. It is therefore doubly unintelligible to suggest that if things could be both round and square (or spherical and cuboid) simultaneously, then the laws of physics would break down. The laws of physics are impervious to nonsense. They may 'break down' in all sorts of ways – but not through *objects* violating the bounds of sense. *That* is a distinctly *human* prerogative![52]

---

[50] Contrary to what is claimed by McGinn, *The Subjective View*, p. 37.
[51] But note that there is such a thing as liquid's feeling both warm and cold to a person at the same time, viz. feeling warm with a cold hand and cold with a warm hand, both simultaneously immersed. And *this*, interestingly, is intelligible despite the fact that there is no such thing as something's being both warm and cold throughout simultaneously. For, of course, the liquid does not feel as if *it is* both warm and cold (that would be unintelligible).
[52] But, to be sure, if one *must* play this game, there is little mileage in it for the dispositionalist. If something 'could be both black and white all over' it would both absorb all the light and also reflect it simultaneously, warm up in sunlight to such-and-such a degree and also not warm up to that degree! The slopes of nonsense are slippery indeed.

Thirdly, the dispositional theorist attempts to explain colour (dispositional) incompatibility by reference to 'subjective' incompatibility. We must immediately concede that nothing can simultaneously look red and look green all over to a person. But the dispositionalist owes an explanation of this impossibility. To appeal to 'phenomenological necessities' or 'laws of subjectivity' issuing from the very nature of perceptual experience is precisely *not* to explain, but rather to enfold an intellectual debt in obfuscating jargon. For if these 'laws of subjectivity' are empirical psychological laws about our experiences, then they are contingent and could be otherwise. It would be *intelligible* to speak of someone seeing something to be red and green all over (something's looking red all over and also green all over to that person at the same time), or to speak of encountering a black box that was lighter in colour than a white one, or of perceiving something to be reddish-green. But it is not. And if these 'laws' are logical, then they are not phenomenological. There is no logical space between empirical or scientific laws on the one hand and logical laws or truths of *grammar* on the other.

Jettisoning dispositionalism rids one of thse absurdities. Colours (and other secondary qualities) are objective properties of objects, no less mind-independent than shapes or lengths. Concepts of colours, as has been shown, are explained by reference to samples. An ostensive definition of a colour word by reference to a sample gives a rule for the use of that word. A sample which we use to explain what 'red' means is not correctly used also to explain what 'green' means,

---

It has been argued (J. Bennett, *Locke, Berkeley, Hume*, pp. 96ff) that while we know what colour-blindness is, we cannot imagine an analogous 'size-blindness', and that this supports the classical distinction between primary and secondary qualities. The argument is incorrect, since it turns on the mistaken supposition that the colour-blind and the 'size-blind' have mastered the *concepts* of sameness and difference of colour and size respectively. It is not that the 'size-blind' would wrongly *think* five-penny coins are larger than ten-penny ones but would be unable to rectify their error by looking and *seeing* that they are not, rather they cannot discriminate relative differences of size, and so would lack mastery of the *concepts* of sameness and difference of size. There is ample evidence that many creatures are exceedingly poor at shape- and relative size-discrimination. Were they language-users they would not be able to master our shape and size vocabulary. It is, of course, true that 'size-blindness' would be a far more grievous defect in a human being than mere colour-blindness and the consequent inability to master our colour vocabulary. But a high degree of 'size-blindness' has not impeded the remarkable evolutionary success of octopuses!

and vice versa; just as a sample used to explain what 'one metre long' means is not correctly used as a sample of what 'two metres long' means. That nothing can be red and green all over simultaneously is a statement of an internal relation which serves to exclude a form of words from use. It is a norm of representation, an expression of a grammatical rule. If something is correctly said to be red all over (i.e. this ↗ colour – pointing at a sample of red), then it is incorrect also to say that it is green all over, since it is not that ↗ colour (pointing at a sample of green). If we gave someone ostensive explanations of 'red' and of 'green', and he went on to say of an object that it was red all over (namely that ↗ colour) and also green all over (namely that ↗ colour), we should not understand what he was saying, and we would judge him not to have grasped the explanations we gave him. Similarly something which is just one metre long is not also two metres long (but exactly one half of a two-metre length). Our form of representation allocates no *sense* to such combinations of words.

That black is darker than white is a grammatical truth, not a 'phenomenological necessity'. Any ordered pair of samples used to give a correct explanation of the meanings of 'black' and 'white' may also be used to explain what 'darker than' means.[53] The statement of this internal relation functions as a norm of description: if one says that A is black and B is white, and goes on to say that therefore B is darker than A, then one has made a mistake and argued *nonsensically*. This is precisely analogous to counting thirteen nuts in pile A and twelve nuts in pile B and then going on to say that therefore there are more nuts in pile B than in pile A. To be sure, we say that it is *of the essence* of black to be darker than white, as it is of the essence of thirteen to be greater than twelve. (If you know that A is black and B is white, you need not look to see whether A is darker than B!) This merely means that what we call 'black' we also call 'darker than' what we call 'white'. (So too, if you know that there are thirteen nuts in pile A and twelve in pile B, you need not match them up to see whether there are more nuts in pile A than in pile B!) Essences are the shadows cast by grammar, and statements of essences, which are statements of internal relations, function, like propositions of mathematics, as norms of representation.

[53] Cf. Wittgenstein, *Remarks on the Foundations of Mathematics,* 3rd edn, pp. 75–6.

The use of *public* samples of colour (and, *pari passu*, of other secondary qualities) provides the key to the correct explanation of internal relations among colours (and other secondary qualities). Any attempt to reduce it to a *subjective* account of colour, which is required by dispositionalism, runs up against the insuperable objection that there is no such thing as a mental *sample,* no such thing as a private ostensive definition. Hence there is no such thing as explaining the meanings of colour words (even to oneself) by reference to private impressions of colour. A proper account of the 'geometry' of colour would be a lengthy and daunting task, which Wittgenstein began with all his characteristic subtlety. All that has been done here is to gesture in the direction of such an account. For present purposes the important point to note is that the dispositionalist has *no* cogent way of explaining the nature of this web of internal relations. But the objectivist about secondary qualities is faced with no such predicament.

The perceptibility of powers

If secondary qualities of objects were dispositions, they would not be perceptible. In the particular case of colours, for example, if they were mere powers, then colours would not be visible, i.e. it would be nonsense to talk of seeing the colours of an object. And if colours were not visible, then material objects and their shapes would be invisible. And this is a *reductio ad absurdum* of the dispositional thesis.

The route to this conclusion is simple. We may grant the dispositionalist that we do speak of perceiving powers or potentialities. One can feel *the elasticity* of an elastic cord by pulling it and feeling it stretch, as one can feel *the rigidity* of a steel rod by trying to bend it. In such cases a power is tactilely perceived by manipulating the object in question in order to find out whether the object will bend or stretch when pressure is exerted upon it or when it is pulled. One can indeed see *that* a round peg fits into a round hole, and that a square one will not fit. In this case one need not see the actualization of the fit, it suffices to see the shapes and relative sizes of the object in question – if the drawer is bigger than the book, then the book will fit into the drawer. Similarly, I can surely see *that* your Sheraton nest of tables is fragile, and to that extent it is legitimate to speak of seeing *the fragility* (i.e. the disposition) of the tables. The slender legs, absence of stretcher, delicate joinery, the slightly unstable way they stand, all betoken fragility. The tables *look fragile;* other things look robust and durable. So, if one knows what things that are fragile, durable, or robust *look like,* i.e. what characteristic appearance they have, it is possible for one to see that a given object is fragile, robust or durable. These possibilities turn wholly on the fact that the power or disposition is typically correlated with an array of visible features, for example shape, size, structure. Where this condition is not satisfied, as in the case of solubility, there it is senseless to speak of seeing the disposition or power of the object. One cannot see the solubility of sugar or the non-solubility of sand, but only see it dissolving (or not dissolving) i.e. see the potentiality actualized, and *hence* see, conclude, *that* it is soluble (or insoluble).

If we are to talk of a power itself (independently of its actualization) as being visible, then possession of the power must be well correlated with a certain array of visible features. To establish such a correlation, the power must be identifiable independently of those features. We typically ascertain the powers of objects by tests which provide conditions that will bring about the exercise of the power. One determines that a substance is soluble in water by immersing it in water, that it is brittle by striking it, that it is slippery by sliding on it. In the case of tactile perception of such powers as elasticity or plasticity, the manipulative perception of the relevant power actually effects a change in question which perceptibly realizes the relevant power. Hence it makes sense to talk of feeling its elasticity or plasticity. But colours are not like this. On the dispositionalist conception, the alleged power which we call 'red' is actualized by bringing it about that a person has a certain sensory experience, variously denominated 'a sensation of red', 'looking-red-to-A', or 'an idea (or impression) of red'. But this alleged experience is not itself the secondary quality, viz. the power *red,* any more than dissolving is solubility. Nor is such a putative perceptual experience a perceptual property of an object. Consequently it would only be possible to perceive the colour of an object if things which have this power-to-cause-experiences of such a kind typically possessed a *different* perceptible feature which was inductively correlated with this power. If, for example, red things typically tasted of tomatoes, then one might speak of tasting the redness of an object in the sense in which one can see its fragility (but, of course, only if tastes are not themselves powers!) Any account of our concepts of colours (and, more generally, secondary qualities) which leads to the conclusion that they are not visibilia (or, more generally, perceptibilia) is surely bankrupt.

There is, to be sure, a grain of truth in the suggestion that coloured objects have a power to affect perceivers in certain distinctive ways in virtue of their colour. If one stares at a scarlet circle in bright light and then looks at a white surface, one will have a distinctive green after-image. One might, on the pattern of the dispositionalist accounts, claim that the green after-image or the having of a green after-image, is a sensory experience. And one might claim that the scarlet circle has the dispositional property of causing such sensory experiences 'in' observers in such-and-such conditions. But, of course, that does not make *scarlet* a dispositional property. What I see, when I look at the circle, is the scarlet circle. I perceive its colour, not its disposition to cause perceivers to have subsequent green after-images. And no one would dream of *identifying* this power to affect one thus with the scarlet colour of the circle. The grain of truth is a very small one; and the large and rambling weeds of the dispositional account of secondary qualities cannot be grown from it.

5
Are Secondary Qualities Relative?

1 Absolute and relative descriptions of the world

Our culture is above all a scientific culture. We look to science both to formulate our problems and to provide solutions to them. Our paradigms of explanation are scientific, and our conception of understanding is modelled upon scientific understanding. The achievements of our sciences over the last four centuries are due in large part to their mathematicization. It seemed altogether plausible to the founding fathers of modern science to view mathematics as the instrument whereby the true nature of the world around us can be apprehended. It is hardly surprising that the triumphs of mathematical *physics* and its extension beyond the sublunary sphere to the macrocosm (thus displacing the old 'Geometry of the Heavens') should revive the Pythagorean myth that reality can be grasped only in the language of numbers. 'The chief aim of all investigations of the external world,' Kepler wrote, 'should be to discover the rational order and harmony which has been imposed on it by God and which He revealed to us in the language of mathematics.' Galileo sang a similar song:

Philosophy [natural philosophy] is written in that great book which for ever lies before our eyes – I mean the universe – but we cannot understand it if we do not first learn the language and grasp the symbols in which it is written. The book is written in the mathematical language . . . without whose help it is impossible to comprehend a single word of it.

An earlier version of this chapter was published in *Mind*, XCV (1986), pp. 180–97.

The conception was a powerful one. If the laws governing the physical universe are essentially mathematical, it seemed almost irresistible to conclude that what is quantitative and susceptible to mathematicization is *more real* than what is merely qualitative and perceptual. Kepler drew this conclusion. It was no less tempting, especially in the light of the corpuscularian hypotheses about perception, to conclude that qualitative and perceptual properties, i.e secondary qualities, are not objective properties of reality at all. As we have seen, Galileo and subsequently Descartes drew that conclusion.

In its classical form, which was adumbrated in chapter 1, this conception was a radically *subjectivist* one. Secondary qualities *as we perceive them* were held to be merely the effects on our minds of certain dispositions or powers of objects. 'Red', 'shrill', 'sweet', etc., are, as Galileo put it, 'nothing but mere names for something that resides exclusively in our sensitive body'.[1] In this form, the doctrine was firmly tied to a representationalist theory of perception. As is evident from the writings of many of our contemporaries, this metaphysical picture is no less powerful today than it was in the seventeenth century. Indeed, given the success of atomic physics in unlocking the secrets of the microcosm and its mathematical laws, its allure is even greater. The defects of this picture have been brought into view in previous chapters. Aware of at least some of its flaws, various philosophers have attempted to salvage something of that conception in keeping with the 'scientific world-picture' that informs it. Recently it has been argued that 'a distinction of primary and secondary qualities can be detached from the representational theory of perception, and when it is formulated independently of that, it emerges as of very great significance.'[2] One kind of account (but *not* the only possible one) which emerges from this detachment is a conception of secondary qualities as *relative*. Such an account can take various forms. The purpose of this chapter is to investigate a number of variations upon the theme of the relativity of secondary qualities. It is, to be sure, not immediately obvious what is meant by denying

---

[1] Galileo, *The Assayer,* repr. in A. C. Danto and S. Morgenbesser (eds), *Philosophy of Science* (Meridian Books, Cleveland and New York, 1960), p. 28.
[2] B. Williams, *Descartes: The Project of Pure Enquiry* (Penguin Books, Harmondsworth, 1978), p. 241.

that secondary qualities are *relational,* while insisting that they are *relative.* But we shall let proponents of this account speak for themselves.

On one conception,[3] the detachment of a distinction between primary and secondary qualities from representational idealism can be used to formulate a distinction between the world as it really is (and is described as being by natural sciences) and the world as it seems to us. This, it is held, is not to say that our conception of the world is totally unrelated to reality, but rather that it has features peculiar to us. But we need a conception of reality which is corrected for the special situation and peculiarities of human beings, a conception of the world as it is independently of all observers. Such a conception will leave out secondary qualities such as colour, taste, smell, sound or texture, for, though they are not relational, they are, in an important sense, relative. They are a function not just of consciousness, but of the peculiarities of individuals or species. However, in pursuit of genuine objectivity, 'what we want is to reach a position as independent as possible of who we are and where we started, but a position that can also explain how we got there.'[4] Scientific explanation of the kinds of processes that underlie the phenomena of colour explains why a thing should seem one colour to one person, another to another, or why it should seem coloured to members of one species, monochrome to members of another. In understanding these explanations 'we shall find that we have left behind any idea that, in some way that transcends those facts, they "really" have one colour rather than another.'[5] Our distinctions between what, for example, seems green and what is green are essentially based on agreement within the range of human experience. But 'human thought is not, in that limited sense at least, tied only to human experience: scientific and philosophical reflection can stand back from at least these peculiarities of our constitution'.[6] Secondary quality terms may not mention their human relativity, but they only too obviously display it to reflection.

This conception of the relativity of secondary qualities perspicu-

---

[3] Williams, *Descartes,* from which the following sketch is derived.
[4] T. Nagel, *The View from Nowhere* (Oxford University Press, Oxford, 1986), p. 74.
[5] Williams, *Descartes,* p. 242.
[6] Ibid.

ously reveals conceptual confusion. But before examining this specimen under a critical microscope, I should like to add a further one, which differs from it in certain respects and which elaborates it in others. This relativist picture can be pushed further by a certain construal of the relationship between our ordinary descriptions of the world around us and a scientific or 'absolute' description.[7] Our initial descriptions of the physical world, ontogenetically and phylogenetically, are couched in terms of the vocabulary of our perceptual experience. These perceptual concepts, it is held, are explained in terms of *our own perceptual capacities:* 'we normally acquire, and should normally explain, all expressions for observational qualities by reference to our capacity to recognize such qualities by unaided observation'.[8] It is within the framework established by these concepts that we distinguish between how things are and how they merely appear to be in respect of these perceptual properties. Such concepts, such characterizations of the world, are dependent upon 'the situation of human beings, located on the surface of a certain planet at a particular stage in its history, being of a certain size and having a particular range of sensory faculties'. But it is a fact, and an important one, that we strive to attain an *absolute* description of reality, a description of things *as they are in themselves,* independently of our modes of perception. An absolute description does not invalidate our ordinary *relative* descriptions, it does not show them to be *false.* But it transcends them. 'One of the things that a scientific theory aims to do is to attain an *accurate* description of things as they are in themselves, or as they really are, in this sense.'[9]

The alleged striving after an 'absolute description' of reality is manifest, it is argued, at the most basic level of common sense. Whenever we can, we give preference to such descriptions: this is evident in 'the interpretation of our essentially two-dimensional visual impressions as three-dimensional'.[10] For our vocabulary of assigning three-dimensional shapes to objects, our locating them in three-dimensional space is already an absolute, observer-independent

---

[7] The following account is derived from Michael Dummett, 'Common sense and physics' in G. F. Macdonald (ed.), *Perception and Identity,* (Macmillan, London, 1979).
[8] Ibid., p. 22.
[9] Ibid., p.16, my italics.
[10] Ibid. p. 33.

characterization of the world. For though shape, size, distance, etc., are observable, a purely perceptual judgement can always be overridden by *measurement*.[11] This shows that 'the practice of taking the physical world to admit of a description independent of viewpoint, and of regarding such a description as representing it as it actually is, is rooted in our most primitive experience of it'.[12] But it goes much further than that; for it also shows that the absolute description of the world for which we strive and which is embodied in the crowning intellectual achievement of our civilization, viz. the corpus of the physical sciences, is a natural extension of our common-sense conception of reality.

This thought can be reinforced, it is argued, by reflecting on our ordinary conception of colour. We all know implicitly, and 'will recognize on reflection, that colour predicates stand for essentially dispositional properties, for a propensity to present a range of appearances under a variety of conditions'.[13] This is evident in the case of such terms as 'shiny' or 'moiré', but is no less true of 'yellow', 'red', etc. The visual appearance of a uniformly coloured surface depends on its illumination, the angle at which light strikes it, and the position from which one views it. Its colour is just its propensity to appear thus-and-so from here (to A) in such-and-such conditions, or to appear so-and-so from there (to A (or B)) in such-and-such different conditions. But these considerations lead us immediately to an 'embryonic theory' which will *explain* these propensities as consisting in complex abilities to emit, reflect, absorb or transmit light. Thus physical theory grows out of, and is continuous with, common sense. What physics achieves is precisely that absolute description of reality which, in this case, transcends (*but does not falsify*) common sense. A physical theory of light gives an account of different kinds of light and different kinds of surface structures that explain appearances of colour, and, in conjunction with a physiological theory of perception, reveals the highly contingent character of our colour perception.

[11] Cf. C. McGinn, *The Subjective View* (Clarendon Press, Oxford, 1983), p. 11: 'there is an experience-independent criterion for whether the primary quality is substantiated, viz. measurement.'
[12] Dummett, 'Common sense and physics', p. 33.
[13] Ibid., p. 26.

Having arrived at this stage of understanding, we subsume the concept of light under the more general one of electro-magnetic radiation, and regard propensity to reflect, absorb or transmit radiation of different wavelengths as a more accurate replacement of the experientially based notion of colour. In doing so . . . we are simply remaining faithful to that quest for a description of reality in absolute terms that we have from the outset taken as a quest for a description of it as it is in itself.[14]

This picture has a mesmerizing charm. It apparently avoids the incoherences of the classical representationalist conception of secondary qualities, while constituting, it seems, a genuine advance in our endeavour to understand the world.

2   On the non-relativity of secondary qualities

Truth has dignity, but rarely charm. It is the illusions of philosophy, not its humble truths, that mesmerize. When, in doing philosophy, a picture holds us in thrall, we can shake ourselves free only by reminding ourselves of how expressions are used and explained, in what contexts and against what stable background they are applied. The problems confronting us are not empirical, and we neither want nor need a theory to resolve them, but only a patient scrutiny of the web of grammar in which we are enmeshed. We must look more closely at what is *called* 'a relative quality', what it is for something to be 'a function of consciousness' or 'dependent upon a viewpoint'. We must remind ourselves how, in our ordinary linguistic transactions, we do actually explain what names of secondary qualities mean. We can free ourselves from conceptual illusion, not by scrutinizing phenomena nor by consulting scientists, but only by disentangling rules of grammar.

Secondary qualities are not relative. Being poisonous may be said to be a relative quality, since a stuff may be poisonous to A but innocuous to B, poisonous to humans but nutritious to some other species. But being red is not a relative quality; 'This is red' does not mean 'This is red for me' or 'for human beings', although it may be that the colour-blind and members of other species cannot discri-

[14] Ibid., p. 35.

minate red. 'The traffic lights turned red' does not mean the same as 'The traffic lights turned red for me', let alone 'turned red for human beings'. Of course, the temptation is to equate 'is red' with 'looks red to normal human beings'. But that temptation should be resisted, for – as we have seen – it only leads to further confusion.

That this rose is red, that one yellow is not a 'function of consciousness' but a function of the pigmentation of the petals, itself determined by the genetically 'programmed' biological processes characteristic of those plants. That lemons are sour and dates are sweet is not a function of the peculiarities of individuals and species, but a function of the constituent citric acid on the one hand and sugars on the other. What *is* is a function of consciousness, and of individual and species-specific peculiarities, is *the capacity to perceive these qualities*.

Secondary qualities are not dependent on a 'viewpoint'. 'To be red', 'to be two octaves higher than middle C', 'to be acrid' are not properties relative to a 'viewpoint'. 'To be red' does not mean 'to look red from here', let alone 'to look red to N.N. from there'. Whether this ↗ note (striking the keyboard) is or is not two octaves higher than middle C is not dependent on who hears it from such a position in such and such circumstances. What *is* dependent upon 'viewpoint' is whether a creature who is not colour-blind (tone-deaf) can see *this* ↗ colour from *there* ↗ (hear this note from there) in *these* conditions. The capacity to perceive secondary qualities is a function of consciousness and of the species. The *opportunity* to exercise that capacity optimally (or at all) is dependent on circumstances of observation (as well as circumstances of the individual). Concepts which *are* 'viewpoint-dependent' are such as 'looks brighter than it actually is against *that* ↗ background', or 'looks deceptively near from here, since the middle ground is featureless'.

The argument in favour of the viewpoint-dependence of colour is a new variant on the dispositional analysis of colours. But this analysis is confused. It is, of course, true that a uniform red surface may have highlights at a given point when viewed from a certain angle and proximity. It may look darker at the corner, where a shadow is cast. It may look more brilliant at the edge, where it is adjacent to green. And so on. But it *is* uniform red. Artists apart, we rarely even notice these features of coloured objects, for we are rarely interested in these subtle modulations of colour appearance. We typically see *that* the object is a uniform red. But we could not even coherently describe the fleeting, circumstance-dependent appearances (relative to a viewpoint) unless we had concepts of colours whereby to characterize the object. For, as we have seen, our concepts of colour appearances are logically dependent upon our concepts of colours.

If secondary *qualities* are not relative, are the *concepts* of secondary qualities in some sense relative? Are they explained 'in terms of our own perceptual capacities' or by reference to 'our capacity to recognize such qualities by unaided observation'? This is confused. 'To be red' or 'to be F-sharp' does not mean 'to look red to most of us' or 'to sound like F-sharp to most of us'. We explain such terms by reference to samples. The explanations of the meaning of 'red', 'F-sharp', 'hot', 'sour', etc., make no mention of our perceptual capacities. That we have those capacities is a *precondition for possession of those concepts*. But it is not a characteristic mark of the concepts; it is part of the *framework* within which the use of these concepts is embedded, not a constituent element of their use. It is true that *mastery* of *some* of these concepts is manifest in applying them on the basis of observation alone. But the fact that I manifest my understanding of 'red' in unhesitatingly saying, on looking at an object in my vicinity, that it is red goes no way to showing that 'red' means 'what most human beings can recognize to be red'. Moreover, numerous concepts of secondary qualities are not thus applied. Few people can judge immediately whether this ↗ note is two octaves higher than middle C, or whether this ↗ is indigo. Typically we use samples as objects of comparison before applying or withholding the relevant concept. Finally, it is a misuse of the term 'recognize' to suggest that when I normally look at grass in daylight I *recognize* that it is green (just as it would be a misuse to say that I recognize my wife when I sit down to dinner with her).

I turn now to the scientific mystification involved in these relativity theses. First, as has been shown, the scientific explanation of processes underlying perception does not explain why *in general* a thing should seem one colour to A, another to B, coloured to men and monochrome to mice. This is a mischaracterization of colour-blindness and inter-species variation in discriminatory capacities. Neurophysiology explains why A cannot discern those colours which B discerns (for example because he lacks one of the three cone pigments in the retina). It explains why many mammals can discern no chromatic colour (because their retina contains no cone cells at all); i.e. it does not explain why the world 'seems monochrome' to them, but rather why they are colour-blind.

Neurophysiology may be said to explain the neural basis for aspects of our discriminatory capacities. It can give an account of the normal structure and functioning of the appropriate parts of the cerebral cortex, damage to which or malfunctioning of which will impair or destroy our perceptual discriminatory capacities with respect to secondary qualities. To the extent that these capacities are a precondition for possessing, being able to use, our colour concepts, this science explains (in one sense) not our colour concepts, but how it is possible for us to have colour concepts at all. But to just the same extent, it explains how it is possible for us to have concepts of length or shape, weight, mass or size.

There is a quite different sense in which a science can explain how it is that we have the perceptual concepts that we have. For just as it is true that if we lacked the array of discriminatory capacities that we have, we would not use our colour, smell, taste or sound predicates as we do, so too, if the world were unruly in certain specifiable ways, these concepts would become obsolete. If everything changed colour at great but irregular speed, or if objects were all iridescent or opalescent, our colour grammar would be of very little use. And, of course, scientific theories can explain why the colours of objects are relatively stable, why it is that most objects are not iridescent or opalescent. But, again, this applies to primary qualities no less than to secondary ones. For if objects around us pulsated constantly and irregularly, expanded and contracted incessantly like a Proteus gone mad, our concepts of shape and measurement would be utterly useless. And, to be sure, physics explains why solid objects have (or retain) stable shape and why quantities of liquid do not. In this respect primary and secondary qualities are on a par, and the availability of scientific explanations *in this sense* goes no way to demonstrating the relativity of either kind of quality or correlative concept.

It is a grievous error to think that a scientific account of the surface molecular structures of differently coloured objects, an explanation of the mechanism whereby photons of such-and-such energies are absorbed and others re-emitted, is an explanation of what colour *is* (let alone that it explains colour *away*). If someone were to ask us 'What is red?' we should rightly point at a sample and say '*That* ↗

colour is red'. If he were to insist impatiently that of course he knows what 'red' *means,* but that he wants to know what red *is* (or, *really* is), we should judge him to be confused. (Compare: 'I know what "square" ("bachelor", "one metre long") *means,* I want to know what being square really *is!*') A scientific explanation of the way in which molecules are arrayed in solid objects (as opposed to gases or liquids) does not explain 'what solidity really is', but only what the micro-structure of solid objects is. Indeed, it presupposes that we know perfectly well what it is for something to be solid; otherwise it could *not* explain what the microstructure of solid objects is. Similarly the physical theory of colours explains *(inter alia)* the molecular structure and light-reflective properties of objects which *are* such-and-such a colour. But it is (at best) misleading to call this an explanation of what red is; as if prior to the availability of such a theory people did not know *what red is,* even though they knew what 'red' means and so knew what it is for something to be red (namely to be *that* ↗ colour). For to know what it is for something to be red *is* to know what red is. And one may, indeed one must, know *that* before one can investigate the microstructural photo-properties of red objects.

One may react with indignation to this claim. Does this mean that colours are *inexplicable,* that science has nothing to say about colours? The indignation is as misplaced as the question. If the question is – what are colours? – then it is confused. For we all know what colours are and have known it since a very tender age. Is it red we are puzzled about? *This* ↗ is red (and we may point at a poppy, ruby, or ripe tomato). There is no explanation of the 'essential nature of red' that goes deeper than that. The hankering for a deeper explanation stems from projecting onto the *property* of being red requirements of explanation appropriate only for quite different categories, for exam-ple objects of certain types and stuffs of different kinds.

Is there then nothing here for science to explain? To think that would be no less confused. Physics can explain what colours are associated with light-reflective propensities of what kinds (and what colours are *not uniformly* so associated). It can investigate different kinds of light and their effects on colour *appearances.* Physiological psychology can examine the dependence of our perception of coloured objects and of our capacity to discern their colours even in changing light upon the context of overall frequency emission. And it can study the neural processes underlying our discriminatory capacities. In all these respects great advances in understanding have been achieved. But this is no more an explanation of what colour really is than an explanation of the shape of a candle flame (in terms of convection currents) or of a raindrop (in terms of surface tension) is an explanation of what these shapes really are. *A fortiori* such explanations do not explain *away* the property which, for example, poppies, tomatoes or rubies have.

What then of the contrast drawn between 'absolute' and 'relative' descriptions of the world? There is much confusion here. It is true that we 'strive for' *true* descriptions of states of affairs in the world around us, descriptions that characterize things as they are in themselves, independently of us or anyone else. It is also true that characterizing objects as being of such-and-such shapes, sizes, heights, etc., is describing them as they are in themselves. But it is not true that we attain such objective descriptions by interpreting our essentially two-dimensional visual impressions as three-dimensional. We do not have 'two-dimensional visual impressions' when we look at objects around us (save for after-images or, rather differently, when we look at a drawing of a cube and see it as a flat polygon). It is extraordinary that philosophers can persuade themselves that we do. One kind of reason that perhaps moves them is a battery of bad (and long since refuted) Berkleian arguments to the effect that distance is not 'immediately perceived' by sight. Another kind of reason is misconceived physiological psychology; we find distinguished scientists arguing, 'The fact is, of course, that the subjects of seeing are not objects themselves, but the flat images of them which hide within the pupil of the eye.'[15] But, of course, the fact is that we do *not* see our own retinal images; and from the fact that our retinal images are 'flat' (i.e. projected images on a concave surface) it in no way follows that our visual impressions are essentially (or even contingently) two-dimensional. We do not typically *interpret* anything, and certainly not our retinal images, when we look around us in normal circumstances. (Nor, *pace* speculative neurophysiologists, does our *brain* – for it makes no literal *sense* to talk of the brain interpreting anything.) The absurdity of the supposition that our visual impressions are two-dimensional springs into view as soon as we reflect on what it would

[15] C. Blakemore, *Mechanics of the Mind* (Cambridge University Press, Cambridge, 1977), p. 66.

be for a creature to have two-dimensional visual impressions, i.e. *to be unable to perceive depth*. Such a creature would, *inter alia,* not be able to *find its way around* by using its eyesight. It would not see semi-occluded objects as located *behind* occluding objects, and it would no more pick up a seen cup from a seen saucer than we would pick up a painted cup from a painted saucer. Mercifully, we are not such creatures.[16]

Furthermore, it is altogether mistaken to suppose that characterizing objects in terms of their secondary qualities is *not* a description of things as they are in themselves independently of observers. Objects do not become colourless or invisible when no one is looking at them; the tones of Beethoven's Fifth continue to ring out of the gramophone even when one leaves the room for a while; sugar is just as sweet in the bowl as it is in my mouth when I taste it; ice is no less cold when it is in the freezer than it is when it is in my hand. It is a fallacy bred of misinterpretation of scientific theory and of bad philosophy that the *esse* of secondary qualities is *percipi*. There are no grounds for denying that our descriptions of objects as coloured, noisy, rough or smooth, hot or cold, etc., are any less 'absolute' (observer-independent, characterizing the world as it is in itself) than descriptions of sizes, lengths, masses, and so forth. But cannot they be said to be less 'fundamental'? To be sure, these expressions do not occur in the explanans of a particle-physics explanation of a phenomenon which that science is competent to explain. If that is what is *meant* by the claim that secondary qualities are not 'fundamental' it is uncontroversial – but it also cuts no metaphysical ice. For it does not follow that secondary qualities are not 'absolute' qualities of those objects (as they are in themselves) to which we ordinarily attribute them. Nor does it follow that names of secondary qualities do not occur 'fundamentally' in sciences other than particle physics.

It is true that a scientific explanation of the reflective properties of coloured objects leads to a theory of light and a complex account of molecular structures and behaviour. But this does not involve 'abandoning' or 'transcending' the idea that things really have one colour

---

[16] But are not new-born babies thus? Maybe so – but it does not follow from the claim that the new-born cannot see depth that *our* visual impressions are 'essentially two dimensional', any more than it follows from the fact that the noises the new-born emit are inarticulate that our speech is essentially inarticulate.

rather than another. Of course, some sciences are concerned with phenomena for which colour ascriptions are senseless (the study of the fine structure of matter). Other sciences or departments of sciences are uninterested in secondary qualities (as demographers are uninterested in people's weight and accountants in their height). But lack of *concern* involves no ontological insight. Many sciences, on the other hand, are interested in, and do not 'abandon', the colours of objects. Geologists do not contend that copper sulphate deposits are not 'absolutely speaking' blue or coal not 'really' black. Ornithologists and botanists, distinguishing species of birds, their display and camouflage habits, or families of plants differentiated by their colour-markings, make no claim about the unreality or inferior objectivity of colour. Physiologists describing the appearances of cells under a microscope do not add, explicitly or tacitly, that they are not 'really' coloured.

Physics is concerned with classifying certain features of the physical world, with constructing predictive and explanatory theories, and with discovering general laws. It *starts* from ordinary descriptions of those features of the perceptible world. (Where else could it commence? Where else could it locate anything to explain?) These descriptions are not overthrown, shown to be false or only 'relative'. But, of course, they are sometimes not very *useful* for certain purposes which scientists have in constructing theories; concepts of hot, warm, cool, cold are indeed inadequate instruments for thermodynamics. Physics strives to discover general and precise laws, and, where possible, to make accurate predictions. For these purposes, it employs mathematical techniques. Not surprisingly, then, it often 'transcends' *descriptions* of objects in terms of secondary qualities (without, however, implying their relativity). But is a description of the colours of objects (or of the notes of Beethoven's Fifth) essentially inaccurate? Is the characterization of the Virgin's robe in a Botticelli painting as ultramarine inaccurate? What is the standard of accuracy here? If we were signing a contract with Botticelli, we might wish for a specific shade of ultramarine – in which case we could employ a sample. The robe, we might write in the contract, is to be this ↗ colour.[17] What would or could be more accurate? If what is desired is *exact* matching, is this inadequate?

[17] It would have been more common simply to specify a particular grade of ultramarine, usually identified by price.

Replacing the descriptions in terms of colours by such as are given in terms of spectral reflection curves is not a more accurate description of an object, but a different description, indeed a description (if so it be called) of an altogether different *kind*, for very different purposes. And those purposes are not to approach closer to being an 'absolute description of reality', but to construct theories of light, electro-magnetic radiation, physico-chemical structures of objects. These do not supersede, since they do not compete with, ordinary descriptions of the perceptible world.

Concepts of shape, size, length, height and breadth are importantly different from concepts of colour, taste, smell, sound and texture. But the relativist, intoxicated with deeply rooted myths about science and blinded by Pythagoreanism, misconstrues these differences. It is correct that our distinction between what seems green and what is green is, in one sense, essentially based on agreement within the range of human experience. We may agree 'how thoroughly contingent it is that we are in a position to say of anything that it is bitter or green or noisy or the like'.[18] Our concepts of secondary qualities are indeed dependent (as *shared* concepts of a common language) upon agreement in definitions (viz. rules for the use of names of secondary qualities, for example ostensive definitions) and agreement in judgements (applications of those rules). But, as we have seen, our concepts of primary qualities, in particular of measurement, are in the same boat. If whenever we laid measures against objects we got different results (perhaps because we could never remember how many times we had laid down the measure, or because we constantly misread the graduating marks, or because we all correlated the graduating marks with the measured object in a different way), then we would have no use for these concepts of measurement. Agreement in definitions and in judgements is a precondition of *any shared* concept. And regularity in application is a precondition of *any concept*. Such agreement and regularity depend both on our nature and on the nature of the world around us. Disruption of either could cause confusion to supervene. But this does not show our concepts to be 'relative'.

---

[18] J. Bennett, *Locke, Berkeley, Hume; Central Themes* (Clarendon Press, Oxford, 1971), p. 96.

It was argued that secondary qualities are 'recognitional', whereas primary qualities involve an 'experience-independent standard', viz. measurement. Again, there is a modest truth in this claim, but it is sorely distorted. It is true that my judgement that an object is a regular octagon (or 26 feet long, or 3 litres in volume), if made by merely looking at it, is correctible by measurement. My judgement that something is green, while not a matter of recognition, is, if correctible, correctible by looking again in better light or asking someone else. On the other hand my judgement that something is vermilion, indigo, or eau-de-Nil is typically correctible by comparison with a sample. Similarly, my judgement that something is B-flat or F-sharp is correctible and typically corrected by a tuning-fork or piano. Samples here function in a way analogous to measures.

It is obscure why measurement should be thought to be any more independent of experience than is the use of samples of sound or colour. As noted, we must be able to see (or feel) that the yardstick coincides with the measured object *thus*. Our methods of measurement, whether simple like yardsticks or highly sophisticated like spectrometers, would be utterly useless for different creatures (for example ant-sized homunculi) or under different conditions (at the centre of the sun, or in a black hole) or, if such are conceivable, for disembodied creatures. As previously observed, we use the world (or parts of it) to measure the world, but it must be usable, and we must be capable of using it.

It is striking that when philosophers think of shapes they instinctively hit upon geometrical examples. No doubt we encounter cubes, rectangles, triangles, etc. But examine the following altogether common judgements of shape:

He has his mother's smile (nose, eyes, mouth).
That is typical Chippendale (Hepplewhite, Sheraton) design.
This drawing has unmistakable Leonardesque strokes.
That cloud has the shape of a face.
Low's caricature captures the essential shape of Churchill's head.

In none of these cases is measurement seriously relevant to the judgement of shape. If the judgement is in error, a ruler or tape-measure would not serve to correct it.

At the heart of these confusions lies the venerable Pythagorean myth that 'all things are numbers', that, as Philoleus put it, 'Were it not for number and its nature, nothing that exists would be clear to anybody either in itself or in its relation to other things.' We continue to think that, in some sense, a mathematical description of features of the world is closer to capturing the essence of things, closer to picturing things as-they-are-in-themselves, than any other descriptions. But one cannot be closer to the truth than saying what is, without qualification, true. And that this rose is red, that note B-flat, are not 'less true', less accurate or more 'observer-dependent' than that this table is 3 feet long. It is, of course, true that measurements in microns are more precise than measurements in feet; but that does not make measurement in feet, yards or miles inaccurate. Moreover, such precision is not always a virtue, nor always intelligibly applicable. (Try measuring the height and width of an oak tree in microns!) And, of course, greater precision in describing the colours of things than is given, for example, by 'red' or 'blue' is available in the rich vocabulary of shades. This we can refine, by the use of samples: the Inter-Society Colour Council – National Bureau of Standards lists the names of 7,500 shades of colour, locating each on a colour solid.

It seems to us, in our Pythagorean moments, that mathematical concepts are, in some sense, more objective, less contingent on the peculiarities of their users and the vagaries of the world than perceptual concepts. In really inane moments, we include in the payload of rockets sent beyond the reaches of the solar system plaques on which are engraved mathematical theorems, as if we believed that Betelgeusians may not share our perceptual capacities and hence concepts, but if they can think at all, they will recognize our mathematical ones. But our mathematical concepts are just as dependent upon contingencies as any other concepts, though not always in the same way. If the world were less regular, if things multiplied, coalesced or disappeared at great speed with total irregularity, there would be precious little use for number concepts. And mathematics without any application would be merely a game with signs (not a description of a realm of Ideal Mathematical Objects). If our powers of surveyability were poorer, what we now call 'proofs' would no more be proofs than a row of digits stretching from London to New York is a numeral. If written signs (ink on paper, chalk on blackboard, scratches on slate) changed their shape constantly, our mathematics would shrink dramatically. And if we could never agree on proofs and computations, if people all got different results, if double-checking always produced different answers, if different mathematicians were never struck by the same aspects, analogies, patterns in extending mathematics, then there would *be* no mathematics. Finally, *our* mathematics is just one (mighty, remarkable, extraordinarily useful) calculus among many possible ones, indeed indefinitely many possible ones, limited only by the unclear limits of what we might be willing to call 'a calculus', 'counting', 'computing', 'measuring'.

All concepts are 'measures of reality'. Concepts of primary qualities are not privileged in comparison with concepts of secondary qualities. They are importantly different in many ways, play distinct roles in shaping our conception of the world, interlock in different ways with our concepts of space, material object and hence, too, time. But they are no 'nearer reality' than concepts of secondary qualities. At the end of the day, is not the philosopher's quest for an 'absolute' description of reality an illusory quest for a description of reality in terms of *true concepts,* concepts which in some ineffable sense, mirror reality? But there is no such thing. For no concept is *true;* nor do concepts *mirror* reality. Concepts create a 'logical space', not a place. And whether reality fills that space or leaves it empty, whether the proposition expressed is true or false, is up to the world. The philosopher seems to hanker for 'universal concepts', concepts usable and intelligible to any thinking being in any circumstances, independently of the world and of the peculiarities of the thinking being. But there is no such thing; or rather, if there are such concepts, they represent not the jewel in the crown of Reason, but the lowest common denominator of what we are willing to call 'expressing a thought', 'having a language', 'reasoning'. Indeed, is not the vision, pushed to its limits, one of characterizing the world without the 'limitations' of our conceptual scheme, imagining, as it were, that God's would be so much closer to things-as-they-are-in-themselves? It is no coincidence that the greatest of scientists thought that mathematics was the language of God: *cum Deus calculat, fit mundus.*

3 'Our best account of the nature of the external world'

Behind the philosophical positions we have been examining there often lurks a preconception about the privileged status of 'science' or of what the Vienna Circle called the 'wissenschaftliche Weltauffassung'. Though implicit in much of the discussion hitherto, it is worth bringing it into full view. It is commonly argued that

things as they are in themselves are as theoretical as the physicist tells us they are. The theoretical-scientific account may be incomplete and subject to revision, but it provides the best available view of what the world is like.[19]

If one thinks thus, it will indeed seem that one is forced to embrace *some* version of the classical distinction between primary and secondary qualities. That version may be subjectivist and representationalist, or relativist; but it must, it seems, hold secondary qualities not to be qualities of things 'as they are in themselves'. For

Modern physics . . . provides a basis for making the primary/secondary distinction. The primary qualities here become those properties that feature in a *physicist's* description of the world . . . . Colours, tastes and smells have no place in the physicist's description of the world. Thus while members of our list of primaries may have changed, this set of qualities still enjoys the privileged status of alone featuring in our best account of the nature of the external world (the scientific account).[20]

We have already noted that it is false that colours (things' having such-and-such colours) do not feature in causal explanations of natural (physical) phenonema. We also pointed out that the fact that secondary qualities do not occur in the 'ultimate' or 'fundamental' microphysical characterizations of material things shows nothing about the subjectivity or relativity of secondary qualities. This is not our current concern, which is rather to examine the supposition that 'science' gives us the 'best account' or 'best available view' of 'what the world is like' or of the 'external world'. By briefly examining it,

---

[19] B. Aune, *Metaphysics* (Blackwell, Oxford and New York, 1986), p.186.
[20] E. Prior, *Dispositions* (Aberdeen University Press, Aberdeen, 1985), p. 103.

we can gain further insight into the confusions which we are endeavouring to dispel, and perhaps fore-arm ourselves against seas of further troubles.[21]

First, as Ryle pointed out, there is no such thing as *the* scientific or theoretical-scientific account of the nature of the world. We speak, quite rightly, of *science,* as we speak, equally licitly, of *language.* But there is no more *one* science than there is *one* language. Just as our talk about language is talk about English, French, Chinese, etc. indifferently, so too our talk of science is talk about the various *sciences.* Palaeontology is no less of a science than physics, although it is not concerned to tell us 'what the world is really like'. The vulcanologist tells us about the nature of volcanoes, not stars or starfish; and the astronomer does not tread on the toes of the marine biologist, ecologist, or animal behaviourist. There is a multitude of different sciences, related to each other (if at all) in various distinct ways. Some are complementary, but the relation of particle physics to some parts of chemistry is very different from the relation of ecology to marine biology. Others, for example marine biology and astronomy, make little or no contact.

Of course, many philosophers and some scientists have dreamt of the essential unity of all the sciences, indeed of the *reducibility* (in principle, if not in practice) by derivation (with the aid of 'bridge principles') of *all* scientific laws to the 'ultimate' laws of particle-physics. This, in principle as well as in practice, is chimerical.[22] But it is true that physics (and chemistry), being concerned with the nature and behaviour of matter and energy in all their forms, have *a* concern with at least an *aspect* of everything there is that has a physical nature. That, however, is not to say that they have a concern with everything there is – no aspect of a legal system, for example, lies within the province of physics! Nor is it to say that the physical aspect of an object or type of object provides the basis for the most 'fundamental' explanation or 'account' of the character of that object. One can calculate the trajectory of a book flung from the window, its velocity

---

[21] Detailed treatment would require a treatise on the philosophy of science. For a more elaborate and elegant short account, see G. Ryle, *Dilemmas* (Cambridge University Press, Cambridge, 1954), ch. V.

[22] J. Dupré, 'The disunity of science', *Mind,* XCII (1983), pp. 321–46.

on impact and the damage it might do – but its being a *book* is incidental to the physics of the matter, and there is nothing *fundamental* about the free-fall or particle structure of books in relation to our study of literature. Indeed, among the very many kinds of interest and cognitive concern we have with respect to books, the 'physics of books' does not even occur (nor would one expect it to) and the chemistry of books is an interest largely confined to the conservator, and yields no more fundamental an account of the 'nature' of books or of a particular book than the bibliophile's, historian's, or – from case to case – the critic's, scholar's or general reader's.

Secondly, and connected with the first point, there is no such subject matter as *the world* which provides a single science (for example physics) with its object.[23] There is, of course, 'the world of physics', as there is 'the world of philately', i.e. the *domain* of a specific interest or concern. But the world, i.e. the totality of what exists, everything that obtains, takes place, or goes on, is not the subject of a single master-science which aims absurdly to 'explain everything'. The physicist investigates the *physics* of anything in the world, but not the botany, zoology, physiology or ecology of the creatures of the earth, let alone the history, psychology, economics or sociology of human beings and societies. Hence *no* science gives or even purports to give us a view of 'what the world is really like', nor is it intelligible that it should. The physicist, crudely speaking, attempts to give us a view of the physical nature of the world, the botanist tries to give us a view of the plants of the earth, and the palaeontologist endeavours to explain the character of fossils in the earth. And so on.

Hence, thirdly, it is misguided to suggest that physics 'provides the best available view of what the world is like' or gives 'the best account of the nature of the external world'. Tautologically, it gives the best account of the *physics* of objects, events, processes, etc. that have a physical nature. But, of course, that does not even touch upon the nature of much that deeply interests and concerns us. It does not give the best, because it does not give any, account of the extinction of the dodo, the effects of the Black Death, or the equilibrium of a

---

[23] See Ryle, *Dilemmas,* pp. 73–4.

given ecosystem. It is, quite rightly, silent on the rise and fall of empires and the causes of the Second World War, on the evolution of legal systems and the explanation of the House of Lords decision in DPP *v.* Smith, not to mention the character of the twentieth-century novel, the iconography of Raphael's *Dream of Scipio,* or the meaning of Wagner's *Ring.* Are things as they are in themselves 'as theoretical as the physicist tells us they are'? It depends what things, and what counts as 'in themselves'; also on how much of what the physicist tells us concerns domains in which he is illicitly trespassing.

Finally, it is altogether misleading to talk of 'a physicist's description of the world'. In the first place, the physicist does not 'describe the world', any more than does the physiologist. At best he describes the physics of the matter and energy (variously parcelled) of the world, as the physiologist describes the functioning of the organs or cells of a given kind of organism. In the second place, and more importantly, in the sense in which I may describe my room or the events I witness in the street, physics not only does not describe 'the world', it does not typically even concern itself with *describing* the physical features of things in the world. Rather, it constructs explanatory and predictive theories. Neither Newton's laws nor Maxwell's equations are illuminatingly characterized as *descriptions,* although from these formulae and an array of measurements one can predict and explain various phenomena.

I may describe a room thus: there is a Chippendale longcase clock against the west wall, with a pagoda hood topped with finials, a finely patterned mahogany case, rococo C-scroll spandrels, signed on the chapter ring by Robert Henderson who was active in London from the 1770s to 1790s; on the large Regency pedestal library table, which is veneered in burr-oak, lies a copy of Ryle's *Dilemmas . . . ,* etc., etc. What would a physicist's description of this room look like? Would it be the best available account of this little part of the 'external world'? Would it even *compete* with my common-or-garden description, which may be refined *ad libitum,* but not – to any purpose – in the direction of particle-physics.

It is tempting, in view of these reminders, to suggest that the common-or-garden description of an object, a specialist's (art histori-cal, architectural, antiquarian) description, a chemical analysis of its constituent matter, the physics of its mode of operation (a pendulum clock) or of its material constitution, are all merely different, nonconflicting descriptions of one and the same thing, descriptions that are given from different points of view. This can perhaps be said in *some* cases, but not in others. Ryle warned:

If the seeming feuds . . . between fundamental physics and common knowledge are to be dissolved at all, their dissolution can come not from making the polite compromise that both parties are really artists of a sort working from different points of view and with different sketching materials, but only from drawing uncompromising contrasts between their business.[24]

The remainder of this chapter will examine a final variant upon relativist accounts of perceptual qualities.[25] It is more subtle and sophisticated than the previous two, but pays no heed to Ryle's warning.

4 Relativity to points of view

The argument runs as follows: there is an irreducible relativity to a perceptual point of view built into all ascriptions of visual properties. For a thing which is red, i.e. *red-looking,* need not look red all the time to all observers under all circumstances. For example, a mountain may be red-looking from here now, and blue-looking from there later. A surface may look pink and smooth from a distance, mottled and grainy from close up, and different again under a microscope. In ordinary discourse, however, we implicitly take some range of perceptual conditions, i.e. a certain perceptual viewpoint, as standard. We introduce explicit acknowledgement of relativity only in cases of deviation; for example, we say, 'It looks purple in this light, but take it to the door and you will see that it is really green.' But the 'really' is relative to the standard viewpoint.

Sometimes, however (the argument continues), we shift the standard. For example, under a magnifying glass a green fabric may appear

[24] Ryle, *Dilemmas*, p. 81.
[25] See P. F. Strawson, 'Perception and its objects' in G. F. Macdonald (ed.), *Perception and Identity: Essays presented to A. J. Ayer*, (Macmillan, London, 1979), pp. 57–9, from which the following account is derived.

as printed with blue and yellow dots. Is it 'really' green or dotted blue and yellow? Or a smooth piece of skin vastly magnified is uneven and 'ridgy'. Is it smooth or 'ridgy'? Thirdly, blood under a microscope is mostly colourless. So it is *not* 'really' red? In all these cases there seems to be a conflict. But there is not really one, since the divergent judgements are made relative to different perceptual points of view.

This feature can be brought to bear upon scientific realism to reconcile it with our perceptual judgements. Descriptions of reality in terms of the concepts of physical theory involve a more radical shift of viewpoint, not from one perceptual viewpoint to another, but from a perceptual viewpoint to a non-perceptual, intellectual one. These no more conflict than do the shifts in perceptual viewpoint. Those very objects which from the perceptual point of view are, for example, brown, smooth and solid (the top of my desk) are, considered scientifically, quite different, viz. a congeries of electric charges widely separated and in rapid motion. The two points of view can be happily combined (for example, 'My solid mahogany desk top is, scientifically speaking, nothing but . . . ') without any contradiction. Once we recognize 'the relativity of our "reallys"' we realize that there is no genuine conflict.

This is a persuasive picture. But it will not do. The trouble starts, as so often in philosophy, before the beginning. As was observed in chapter 3, to say that something which *is* red *is* red-looking is to treat the verb 'to look' on a par with 'to taste' or 'to smell'. Something which is sweet is indeed sweet-tasting, i.e. it is, as far as its taste is concerned, sweet. That much is virtually pleonastic. Something which is acrid is acrid-smelling, i.e. it is, as far as its smell is concerned, acrid. 'Smelling' and 'tasting' occur here merely to emphasize the perceptual modality of the perceptual quality. If we say that red things are red-looking, blue things are blue-looking, etc. does this amount to no more than saying that they are, as far as their looks are concerned, red, or blue? Of course, as we have seen, this is not quite right. For 'the looks of X' is manifestly not used analogously to 'the smell of X' or 'the taste of X'. For objects do not have 'looks' as they have tastes or smells. We do speak of a good-looking woman, a Baroque-looking building, a healthy-looking baby, and so on. But 'an F-looking X' does not stand to 'an X which is F' as 'a sweet-tasting X' stands to 'a sweet X' or 'an acrid-smelling X' to 'an acrid X'. The phrase 'an F-looking X' displays very great diversity, depending upon what characteristic F is, what kind of object X is, and in what context the phrase is used.[26] Sometimes an F-looking X is an X which *is* F, as in the case of a beautiful-looking woman, sometimes it looks like one but is not, as with Churchillian-looking babies, and sometimes it looks *as if* it is F, as is the case with healthy-looking people, even though it may not be. What is parallel to sweet-tasting, i.e. being, as far as taste is concerned, sweet, is: being, as far as *colour* is concerned, red. Certainly red things are, tautologically, red as far as colour is concerned.

Forewarned and cautious, let us examine the next step. A thing which is red, it is held, need not look red to all observers at all times: for if irradiated with green light, it may look black. But *this* use of 'looks F' is quite different from the one considered above. 'A red object looks black when irradiated with green light', or 'looks black to someone wearing green-tinted spectacles' does *not* mean that it is, as far as its colour is concerned, black. Exactly the converse: as far as its colour is concerned, it is red, but it does not look thus under these aberrant conditions. But then to say that it *is red* does not involve an implicit relativization to, for example, standard lighting conditions and normal observers.

Let us re-examine the original examples. A mountain may look red from here now, blue from there later, and when we are clambering up it, perhaps neither. The suggested implication is that here judgements of colour are overtly relative. But this is wrong. First, the fact that an object looks blue now from here does not mean that it *is* blue relative to the here and now, and that it looks red at sunset does not mean that it *is* red at sunset. We manifestly do *not* relativize colour attributions, only apparent-colour attributions. Secondly, only in very rare cases do we attribute colours to mountains. They constitute one kind within quite a wide range of what one might call 'singularities' in the grammar of colour. A denuded mountain consisting of pure lapis lazuli would be a blue mountain. But, alas, there are none such. Admittedly, Ayers Rock and the cliffs of Petra are indeed red, denuded red sandstone (and in some lights they look purple!) But such exceptions apart we do not give any global characterization of the colour of a mountain as opposed to its mere appearance. The

---

[26] This will be examined in detail in the next chapter.

reason has nothing to do with a plethora of viewpoints or variable lighting, but with the size of mountains, the diversity of colours of a mountain's different areas, the fact that a mountain is only 'an object', on sufferance as it were, and that the different colours of different areas are attributable to individual objects or substances in their own right. The grass growing here is green, the heather there purple; these rocks are reddish, and the snow on the summit is white. Given such simple facts, it is pointless to attribute a colour to the mountain, even though it looks blue from a distance at noon, and red at sunset.[27]

The second example of the 'built-in relativity of the perceptual point of view' involved shifting from how a surface looks from afar to how it looks when closely examined, to its appearance under a microscope. Are these merely three different 'looks' of the surface? I think not. We reserve the nominalized 'looks' for rather different purposes. Do we not rather say that from afar the surface (a rock-face, perhaps) looks uniformly pink and smooth, but that when one approaches close to it one can see that it *is not* as it *looked* from a distance, but rather *is* mottled and granular. (Appearance under a microscope will be examined in a moment.)

If this is correct, it casts doubt on the next move in the argument. We do, to be sure, say such things as 'It looks purple in this light, but take it to the door and you will see that it is really green'. But it is far from obvious that this involves *tacit* relativization of colour ascription to, say, daylight and close proximity, coupled with explicit acknowledgement of relativity only in cases of deviation from this norm. For it is manifestly false that the object in the artificial light *is* purple, false that 'it looks purple' – if that means: is, as far as its colour is concerned, purple. On the contrary, the object *is* green, and in this neon light it looks purple *but is not*! In broad daylight, you will see not

---

[27] Similar 'singularities' apply to the sun. We do say that the sun was a fiery red at sunset. Does this mean that we think it changed its colour between five and seven o'clock? Or did it only look fiery red? If so, what colour is it 'really'? Some might say – yellow. But I suspect that we simply do not draw any distinction between real and apparent colour here. Similarly with the sea: we say that it is blue on a sunny day, though green in the shallows. But it is uniformly grey on a cloudy day. Should we say that it only looks blue, green or grey? What colour, then, is it really? Of course, the sea-water of which it consists is colourless. But no one would say that the seas of the earth are colourless. Again, I suspect, we do not apply the distinction between real and apparent colour to the sea. Nor do we need it in such cases. These examples differ from the example of mountains. They are similar in being anomalous.

that it *looks* green, but that it *is* green. Statements about the colours of objects are not statements relativized to standard or normal observational conditions; but rather normal observational conditions are optimal opportunity conditions for perceiving what colour things really are.[28] Nor are the circumstances and condition of the observer – his eyesight, his spectacles, his state of mind – involved either tacitly or explicitly in an object's being green. Rather they are involved in possession of a perceptual capacity and in the possibility of exercising it effectively here and now.

The third step in the argument purported to show that we sometimes explicitly shift our standard from the naked eye, to the magnifying glass, to the microscope. But there is no conflict between the varying colour attributions, for they are severally relative to different standards; or so it was argued. Legitimate doubts, however, remain. For is it correct to say that blood under a microscope is mostly colourless? Is it not rather that under a microscope one can see the constituent *particles* of blood and lymphatic fluid, and the latter is colourless? But colour is not an absolutely dissective property (unlike, for example, spatial relations). There is indeed no conflict between saying that blood is red and saying that microscopic examination of a drop of blood shows that its constituents are largely colourless. But this is not because the former judgement tells us how blood looks to the naked eye and the latter how it looks under a microscope and looks are relative. Rather it is that blood is *red*, and that fact does not entail that every microscopic constituent of blood must be red. It is perfectly consistent with blood being red that its constituent microscopic particles and lymphatic fluids are not uniformly red. Similarly it is consistent with skin being smooth that magnification by 100 should reveal 'ridges' and 'bumps'. Being smooth, like being red, is defined *in certain circumstances* but that does not mean that it is defined *as relative to those circumstances*. Two equally smooth surfaces may, under magnification, be shown to be microscopically quite distinct, without necessarily derogating from their

---

[28] Although here too there are anomalies: for example, what are the optimal conditions for perceiving the 'real colour' of a fish whose habitat is 1,000 feet deep, where it glows in a multi-coloured array, but which is a muddy grey when fished up on the deck? Cf. J. L. Austin, *Sense and Sensibilia* (Clarendon Press, Oxford, 1962), pp. 65–6.

equal smoothness. The moot question is: how do we define, how do we explain the meaning of 'smooth'?[29]

The magnifying glass remains an interesting borderline case. And it is a borderline case precisely because it operates at the borders of dissectivity. There is no doubt that if a Seurat canvas looks green from 20 feet and is revealed at 5 feet to be a mass of blue and yellow dots, then it is not (we do not count it as) green. It is, I think, equally clear that blood is *not* largely transparent and colourless. But what of a surface which is green at arm's length to the naked eye, but can be seen to be composed of minute dots of blue and yellow if one has an ordinary magnifying glass? Indeed, perhaps a few very keen-sighted people can discern the dots without the aid of the magnifying glass. Here I think we hesitate, for to be uniform in colour means that all constituent areas are visibly of that colour. That below the threshold of vision there may be colourless or differently coloured parts or particles does not imply that the surface is not uniformly coloured. *That* is what is meant by 'being uniformly red all over', we say, pointing at an object which *can be seen* to be thus. Nevertheless the determination of what counts as *visible* is vague. An ordinary magnifying glass is not so different from a lorgnette, and a lorgnette is just a kind of spectacles. And that seems to explain our hesitation. We can, and do, live happily with it.

If these doubts are justified then the final move to reconcile scientific realism with our ordinary descriptions of objects of perceptual experience is also questionable. Is it correct that my desk top, from a scientific point of view, is *nothing but* a congeries of electric charges (or whatever) widely separated and in rapid motion? Does this mean that 'from a scientific point of view' it is *not* brown, smooth, made of mahogany which consists of cellulose cells, etc.? Does it mean that from a scientific point of view it is not solid, but rather full of holes, or perhaps 'quasi-granular' – like a heap of sand whose grains are in perpetual motion? This cannot be right, for it involves a grievous misunderstanding of physical theory. To say that from a scientific point of view it is nothing but . . . is allegedly to say

[29] Bear in mind that under pressure from science and technological needs the term may undergo a shift of meaning. If a surface is smooth if and only if under a microscope it reveals no ridges and bumps, that, at any rate, is not what we mean by 'smooth', nor how we explain it.

that there is a 'point of view' (intellectual rather than perceptual) from which the desk *is not* brown, and presumably also, *not solid* either. But a shift from the perceptual concepts to the concepts of theoretical physics cannot involve *displacing* the former, nor does it involve abandoning them. After all, the physicist sets out to *explain* the microstructures of coloured or solid objects – not to demonstrate that from a certain intellectual point of view things are not 'really' coloured or solid at all. If he contends that, because my table is a congeries of particles relatively widely separated from each other, therefore it is not (from his point of view) solid, he is in grave conceptual confusion. For it immediately follows that *nothing* on earth *is* solid. So what was he trying to explain? Indeed, even if he contrived to pack these mischievous little particles closer together, he would not be making anything *more solid*! He surely cannot think that if only he could get the little beggars to touch each other and stay put, *then* he really would have something solid. The way in which my desk top can fail to be solid is not: by being composed of congeries of widely separated electrically charged particles, but rather: by consisting of rotten wood worm-eaten through and through; or: by being made of plywood with a cavity between topside and underside. Similar considerations apply to being brown. It is not the case that 'from a scientific point of view' the desk top is *not* coloured, that it is *nothing but* a surface of molecules with a propensity to reflect light of such-and-such wavelengths. On the contrary, what the scientists (physicists) investigate is precisely what are the surface molecular structures and light-reflective properties which are characteristic of objects *of such-and-such colour*. Were they to deny that 'from their point of view' things are coloured, they would be sawing off the branch upon which they themselves are perched. Of course, the 'nothing but' is gravely misleading. For it suggests that to deny this form of scientific realism is to embrace the view that colour (or solidity) is something *in addition to* . . . As if, for example, colours were ethereal veneers spread over the molecular carcasses of objects. But, of course, that is *not* the claim the objectivist (anti-relativist) is making. To be coloured, to be solid, etc., are *properties* of objects (not *parts* of objects). The task of the physicist is not to tell us what those properties essentially are, i.e. what it is to be red (or solid), what 'red' or 'solid' *mean*. His task is to discover what is the particulate structure, the light-reflective, electro-magnetic properties of the constituent matter of, say, red *things* which differentiate things thus propertied from otherwise qualified objects, for example green or transparent colourless ones. He investigates how molecules of solid matter are chemically bonded ('gaps' notwithstanding) in contrast with the structures of liquids or gases; or why a solid piece of metal should suddenly crack (through metal fatigue) or what chemical changes occur to make wood rot.

The physicist's story, properly understood, is *not* in conflict with our ordinary descriptions of the world around us, i.e. our ordinary characterizations of things as red or green, solid or gaseous, hot or cold, smooth or rough. Since there is no conflict, there is no need for the dubious relativization thesis. It was only an illusion, bred of misconceptions, that there was any genuine conflict in the first place. And we may not reconcile an illusion with reality by tampering with our concepts of what is 'real'.

6

In Defence of Appearances

1 Looks and appearances

The picture that informs the mainstream of Western philosophy represents the world as it is independently of our perception of it as being very different indeed from the familiar array of multi-coloured, noisy, odorous objects we apprehend around us. The colours, scents, tastes, textures of objects, the sounds they emit, the flashes, glows and glimmers of light they produce are not, as we perceive them, objective features of the world. Rather they are mere appearances. The world as it is in itself is not manifest to our perceptual experience, but only to reason incarnate in particle-physics. The natural state of man is to be enmeshed in the veil of appearances. It is not experience that can disclose the veil for what it is, but only philosophy – which, it is argued, can demonstrate to us how much less perception reveals to us than we think, and how much more limited our knowledge is of what lies before our eyes than we think it to be. So too, it is not perceptual experience that can penetrate the veil of appearances, but only advanced scientific theorizing aided by experiments employing refined technology.

Appearances of things, in particular secondary qualities as we apprehend them, are referred to, innocuously, as 'sensory appearances', and sensory appearances are conceived, not at all innocuously, to be *sensory experiences*.[1] Hence, as we have seen, strictly speaking, being red, loud, salty, hot, acrid, etc. are – on one construal – dispositional properties of objects, grounded in their particulate

[1] E.g. C McGinn, *The Subjective View* (Clarendon Press, Oxford, 1983), pp. 5ff.

structure (or – on another – actually identical with this structure). But colour, sound, smell, taste and texture *as we apprehend them* are sensory experiences, mere appearances to an observer, something with which we are 'acquainted . . . only from the first-person perspective'. Not only are we ourselves, but also the world as we perceive it is 'such stuff as dreams are made on'.

According to this conception, looking red, sounding shrill, smelling acrid, etc. are logically prior to, and partially definitive of, being red, shrill, acrid, etc. Hence expressions such as 'It looks thus-and-so to me' or 'It sounds to me just like so-and-so' are conceived as *descriptions* of sensory experiences, or of 'subjective appearances' conceived as experiential episodes. Ample reason has been given in previous chapters for thinking that this picture of appearance and reality, and of perceptual experience and its objects, is fundamentally confused. The remaining tasks of this investigation are, first, to shed some light on the distinction, or rather, distinctions, between appearance and reality; secondly, to make clear the role of such expressions as 'It looks thus-and-so to me', in particular to differentiate this role from that of a description of perceptual experiences; and finally, lest it be thought that it is being suggested that there is no such thing as perceptual experience, or alternatively that perceptual experiences are indescribable, we must investigate what can legitimately be called 'describing a perceptual experience'.

We shall begin by clarifying some of the features of our use of 'looks', 'looks as if', 'looks like', as well as 'appears' and 'apparent', inattention to which fosters philosophical illusion.[2] The fundamental notion underlying our use of 'look' and its cognates is the faculty of vision. 'To look' is first and foremost to direct one's sight. Hence the vast majority of prepositions that go with the verb are directional: to look forward, backward, ahead, sideways, down, about, after (as in 'He looked after the disappearing car'), round, into, over, through, up, out, in, etc. It is striking how all these directional phrases took on figurative meanings which became established in their own right, as in 'to look forward to the weekend', 'After this achievement, he never looked back', 'He looked down on his inferiors', 'We must

---

[2] J L Austin made a start on clarifying these concepts in *Sense and Sensibilia* (Clarendon Press, Oxford, 1962), ch. IV. The following discussion is intended to press on a little farther down the path he pioneered.

look into this question', 'I must look him up when I am next in town', and so forth. This fundamental use also commonly occurs imperatively (and rhetorically) with an indirect question, where it is assumed that the question can be answered or resolved *at a glance*. Hence 'Look how the polished silver gleams!', 'Look what is written on the noticeboard!' or 'Look who's talking!'

From this core the concept evolved offspring in various directions, five of which are particularly interesting both in their own right and in the way they are linked. First, when people look at visible objects and events, they typically manifest their emotions, feelings, attitudes, inclinations or purposes. We are extraordinarily sensitive to minute (as well as gross) changes in a person's facial demeanour. Hence we attach adverbs or phrases to the verb which are indicative of the feeling or attitude which accompanies or informs the looking, or of the manner in which one looks. So we speak of someone looking at something sadly or joyfully, attentively, keenly or inquisitively. And hence we speak of a person as having a sad, joyful, attentive or inquisitive look on his face.

Secondly we nominalize the verb, speaking of 'a look', not in the above sense, but signifying an act of looking, or a glance. Hence we may have a look at something in order to see whether it is thus and so. And we may see, at a glance, that it is. People may exchange looks: lovers exchange looks of joy, and a sympathetic person may cast looks of compassion upon his suffering friend.

Thirdly, associating the notion of looking with that of a position from which a certain prospect is in view, we speak metonymically of architectural features or features of a landscape looking in a certain direction. Thus we say that the windows look north, or that the southern slope of the hill looks over green meadows.

Fourthly, we apply the verb 'to look' not only to the act of looking, but also to the visible features (and further properties for which visible features are either symptoms or criteria) of the object of vision. Something or someone looks thus-and-so when he, she or it has the visible appearance of being thus-and-so. The *Oxford English Dictionary* suggests here a linkage between this concept and the manner of looking or expression with which one looks. For someone who looks attentively at something looks attentive, and someone who looks angrily at something looks angry. And, of course, there is also an important (but only partial) parallel here between sight and the other four senses. How something looks typically consists of those features of it accessible to looking, just as how it tastes or sounds consists of those features of it discernible by tasting or listening, although, of course, nothing in the domain of visibilia stands to seeing as sounds stand to hearing, smells to smelling and tastes to tasting.

In this important use, the verb may be followed by various parts of speech, and expressions of very different logical types. We speak of people looking elderly or youthful; beautiful or ugly; robust or frail; graceful or clumsy; intelligent or stupid; well or ill. As the years go by one may have to reconcile oneself to the fact that one looks one's age; after recovering from an illness one may be relieved to look oneself again; appropriately dressed, one may be pleased to find that one looks the part. The complexity here (and not only in the appearances of human beings) is very great. In some kinds of case it makes sense to ask 'In virtue of what (visible) features does so-and-so look thus?', for example, 'He looks ill – pale, haggard, with sunken eyes, breathing rapidly and shallowly', or 'It looks cold outside – there is ice on the ground, it is sleeting and a strong north wind is blowing'. In other cases it does not, for example, 'It looks red'. 'The row of beans looks straight', or 'It looks sunny outside'. Where the question does make sense, the kinds of answer display important heterogeneity, sometimes specifying symptoms, sometimes criteria and sometimes sufficient conditions.

What is visible to a glance, indeed what is merely visible, is not always the whole truth, and sometimes indeed is anything but the truth. Something may have features A, B and C, which make it F-looking, and yet not be F. So, unsurprisingly, we have the forms 'to look as if', 'to look like', 'to look as though', which are followed by nouns or propositional clauses. Something may appear to sight like something or other, but further investigation may be warranted. There is much diversity here, and grave confusions stem from unduly concentrating on one kind of case and generalizing from it. Some of this complexity will be surveyed below.

The final branch to be adumbrated involves nominalizing the use in which we say of an object or person which is or may be visible that it looks thus-and-so. Of such an object of vision we can say, in some kinds of cases, that it has *a certain look*. Of people we say that they are proud of their good looks; a person may wear the look of a humble apology, while another may have the look of an impudent rascal. We further generate such forms as: good-looking. A woman may be beautiful-looking or graceful-looking, a man handsome-looking. Rather differently, we say that people are wealthy-looking or sad-looking, and that animals are dangerous-looking or tame-looking: they look as if they are wealthy or sad, dangerous or tame – but a beautiful-looking woman does not *look as if* she is beautiful, she *is* beautiful. (Good make-up can make a woman who is *not* beautiful *look* beautiful, but it cannot make her into a beautiful-looking woman.) The nominalization is used also of inanimate objects or states of affairs. I may dislike the look of the medicine, be delighted that the yellow vein in the rock has the look of gold, and gaze longingly at the beautiful look of forbidden fruit.

This brief survey strongly suggests that the family of concepts associated with looking has as its root not a subjective experience, a 'sensory appearance' conceived as an experience of an observer, but rather that of a perceptual act – the exercise of the capacity to discern, by looking, how things are in respect of visual (and inferentially related) properties in the world. (It is, as we shall see below, misleading to conceive of the exercise of perceptual capacities as involving 'experiences' in the sense – perhaps itself dubious – in which philosophers call sensations 'experiences'.) It is by looking at things that we find out how they are. How things typically look constitutes the totality of their visual characteristics, i.e. those characteristics discernible by looking. 'How does it look?' one may ask someone peering through a chink, and the answer 'It looks F' in such a context, other things being equal, may not differ at all from 'It is F' (just as 'It tastes sweet' and 'It is sweet' said on sampling a foodstuff are used equivalently). *Here* both answers are used equipolently, even though in other situations – or even with a different intonation contour – they would not be. In so far as 'It looks F' and related phrases are used to report on the visual characteristics of the object in view, they are clearly not employed as descriptions of *experiences*. For those characteristics, discernible by looking, are not modifications of a perceiver's mind. A beautiful-looking tapestry, a graceful-looking Sheraton table, a Palladian-looking country house are thus characterized as having certain visible features, not as causing certain experiences 'in' observers. Whether something or someone is beautiful or graceful is a matter of how it looks, how it stands or moves, i.e. of visible characteristics. Whether a piece of furniture or architecture is in baroque or neo-classical style is something presented to sight; look carefully and you will see.

There is no 'gap' between being beautiful-looking and being beautiful. But with respect to the hosts of features which do admit of a gap between how things look and how they are, there are indefinitely many ways in which a disparity may occur, and many different ways to validate or invalidate first impressions. What colour something is we determine by looking, but something may look red yet be white – and we find that out by examining the illumination, shifting position, etc. and looking again. Something may look near but be distant, look circular but be elliptical, look large but be quite small. Deceptive appearances here can be rectified by closer scrutiny and by metric aids to sight. In such cases, typically, deceptive appearances are consequent upon lighting conditions, distance, proximity or lack of proximity to other objects, and so on. This may be contrasted with such examples as whether a building or piece of furniture is genuine Gothic, baroque, or neo-classical. For this is not only a matter of how it looks, but also of when it was made. This *may* be determinable by looking more carefully, though what one would need to look at *might* not be stylistic, but structural features. Whether someone is ill or well, angry or calm, intelligent or dull is not only, and sometimes not at all, a matter of how they look, but of their health, temper and abilities. These *need* not always be manifest. Yet people who are ill characteristically look sunken-eyed, hollow-cheeked, feverish and pale; those who are well are typically bright-eyed and of lively demeanour. Such visible characteristics correlate well, though not perfectly, with being well or ill. In the case of psychological states and dispositions the distinctive facial expressions, the angry look or the look of embarrassment, are – in appropriate circumstances – criteria for the corresponding psychological state or disposition.

Thus far we have concentrated on objects' looking F, where F is a property. Objects commonly have characteristic visible features and hence can be recognized (given adequate knowledge) by looking. But we often employ the comparative 'looks like' in connection with substances in both senses of the latter term. Gold and fool's gold are both shiny, yellow substances; iron pyrites looks like gold, has the visual characteristics of gold. But these two substances differ greatly in chemical character. Similarly with objects: in shape and manner a fox looks rather like a dog; a stick insect, when motionless on a branch, looks remarkably like a stick. Something looks like such-and-such if it shares an array of visual features with it. It does not, of course, follow that one might mistake it for that which it looks like, or even that it looks as if it *is* that which it looks like. Mary may look like her father, but she certainly does not look as if she is her father, and no one would mistake her for her father. John, on the other hand, may not only look like his twin brother, but also regularly be mistaken for his twin, just as fool's gold looks like gold and looks as if it is gold. But that it looks like rain does not mean that it looks as if it is raining, but as if it will rain.

It is, however, not only substances that can be said to 'look like' such-and-such, but also, in certain cases, properties. For we do say such things as 'That colour looks like magenta'. Yet there is a striking difference. If the colour looks like magenta, it looks as if it *is* magenta. But an oddly shaped cloud may look like a face even though it does not look at all as if it is a face, and a Ferdinand Bol may look like a Rembrandt without looking as if it is a Rembrandt. The reason is evident: substances may resemble each other visually in some respects, hence look alike in respect of those properties, while differing in other visible (as well as non-visible) properties and so not look at all as if they are of the same kind. But no more is either necessary or possible for a (nominalized) visible property to look as if it is F than that it should look like F.

What of genuine dispositional properties? They are active or passive powers, potentialities, not actualities. As noted previously, while dispositions do not have, and are not, looks or appearances, things with certain dispositions often also have typical looks. Hence some dispositions are, in a qualified sense, visible. One can see *that* a round peg fits into a round hole, although one cannot say that one sees its disposition. But one can arguably claim to see the fragility of spindly, thin, delicately jointed artefacts. And one can certainly say of such objects that they look fragile, or look as if they are fragile. For in such cases a certain array of visible characteristics correlates well with a given dispositional property. Of course, many dispositional properties are not regularly conjoined with non-dispositional visible features, for example being magnetic or conductive. Hence, for example, good insulators do not look as if they insulate well nor do they look as if they insulate poorly.

The range of visibilia is vast in category and type. The correlations between the nature and the non-visual characteristics of objects, substances, events, states, processes, conditions on the one hand and their looks on the other are very varied. They depend upon a multitude of different kinds of contextual features. Hence generalization is hazardous, and contempt for the specific case a sure route to error. The extent to which how something looks, reveals or is a guide to how it is will vary from case to case, be dependent upon circumstances and the nature of the particular case.

The roads across this rough terrain are littered with wrecks. Various once popular philosophical generalizations are most tempting. For example, that one only says that something looks thus-and-so if one is uncertain whether it is or not. Or: that how things are cannot be *assumed* to correspond with how they look. Or: that things which look thus-and-so, or look like a so-and-so, are things that might reasonably be mistaken for a so-and-so.[3] But the temptations should be resisted and the details of particular cases examined.

The exclamation, as the royal coach sweeps by, that the Queen looks regal, or that the lady in red looks beautiful in no way suggests or implies any uncertainty about the regal character of Her Majesty or the beauty of the lady. Nor does the total absence of a Gricean 'doubt-or-denial' condition[4] make for any oddity or misleadingness. There is no impropriety or violation of conversational convention about saying that the Canterbury quadrangle looks beautiful, even though one has no doubts about whether it is so or not and even though one's interlocutor has not suggested that it is ugly. The observation that some early Raphael paintings look like Peruginos but that such-and-such details nevertheless give away the hand of the budding master does not suggest any uncertainty about the paintings. It simply draws attention to obvious visual resemblances and to less obvious differences.

[3] Ibid., pp. 40–1
[4] H. P. Grice, 'The causal theory of perception', *Proceedings of the Aristotelian Society*, suppl. vol. XXXV (1961).

There is no more to being beautiful or graceful than generally looking so. With such visible characteristics of things, generally looking so *is* being so. If London looked its best at the Silver Jubilee, then it *was*, in respect of its looks, at its best. In such cases, the looks of things do not 'correspond' with how things are, they are themselves an aspect of how things are. Possession of such properties just is a matter of having certain visible features. In other cases characteristics which are, as it were, fully open to view do nevertheless allow for a gap between how a thing generally looks and how it is. This gap may obtain because of the complexity of the visual characteristic. It is typically filled in, not by electron-microscopes and scientific hypotheses, but by a second look or a more informed scrutiny. At first glance, one might say, this looks Gothic, but a second look reveals it to be Victorian. Superficially, this bowl looks K'ang-Hsi, but if you look carefully at the glaze and examine the foot closely, you will see that it cannot be. In other kinds of case the potential gap between how something looks and how it is may be generated by circumstances of observation, for example lighting conditions, distance and character of surrounding objects. Abnormal or poor lighting disturbs or distorts vision, as does an intervening disruptive medium such as rising hot air, water or flawed glass. Absence of middle ground affects our capacity to judge the size or distance of objects in view. And an object's adjacency to certain colours may variously distort its appearance. Although the deceptive appearance in these kinds of case is perfectly public, an object's looking F or looking like an F is not due here to its possessing an array of visible features G which things that are F have. Rather it is due to the circumstances of observation and is eliminated by changing them, for example by altering the lighting, shifting one's viewpoint or moving the object to another context. Different again are cases of visual illusion such as the Müller-Lyer lines or the Ponzo illusion. Here too, the fact that X looks like Y or looks as if it is a Y (a pair of equal-length lines look like unequal-length lines) is not a matter of X and Y having common visible features. (On the contrary, the Müller-Lyer lines, for example, do *not* have the relevant similarity, viz. inequality of length, in virtue of which they look like unequal-length lines.) But, unlike the circumstance- and context-dependent cases, more careful scrutiny, proximity, or better lighting are of *no* avail in dispelling the illusion. Only the *visible* juxtaposition with a ruler assures us that, for example, the lines are equal in length; and they persist in *looking* unequal. In short, whether 'looks', 'looks like', 'looks as if' introduce potentially deceptive features depends upon *what* it is that so looks, *how* it looks, in what *context* it looks thus, and what kinds of fault (accident, mistake, illusion, etc.) are in question.

2 The apparent and the real

The discussion thus far has concentrated upon 'looks' and its cognates, invoking 'appears' and 'appearance' only charily. However, it might be thought that the latter expressions are better suited to carry the burden of some version of any subjectivity thesis concerning secondary qualities. Philosophers do, after all, talk of *subjective* appearances, and some talk of 'sensory appearances' as if they were 'properties of experience' analogous to pains.[5] However, even brief examination of 'appear' and related terms confirms the primacy of what is *apparent to sight,* what is in *public view* accessible to all, and not of 'the kind of acquaintance with sensory experience which we have only from the first person perspective'. It is what is seen, not the *experience* of seeing that occupies stage-centre. In this respect *appearing* and *looking* do not differ.

It is striking, in view of philosophers' preoccupation with the contrast between appearance and reality, that the primary notion of what is apparent is that which is manifest, evident or obvious, not that which is deceptive or not genuine. The apparent is what meets the eye, is open to sight or plainly seen. (Hence we contrast the heir-*apparent* with the heir-*presumptive,* and hence too the natural extension of 'apparent' from what is manifest to the eye to what is manifest to the mind: to make God's word apparent is to make it clear and perspicuous, not to render it superficial and illusory.) Similar considerations apply to the verb 'to appear'. Something appears when it comes into view, either gradually becoming visible from a distance

[5] G. Evans, 'Things without the mind', in Z. van Straaten (ed.) *Philosophical Subjects, Essays presented to P F Strawson* (Clarendon Press, Oxford, 1980) pp. 98–9

or suddenly emerging from concealment. What appears to the eye is what is visible. On this simple theme, variations have evolved: one may appear, present oneself, before a tribunal; or one may appear on the stage; and one's books may appear on publication date. What appears in a document plainly occurs, is set forth or declared; such-and-such a word may first appear in Chaucer; numerous well-turned phrases appear in Wilde's plays; and many a crucial jurisprudential doctrine appears already in Ulpian.

Nevertheless, if to appear is to be manifest to sight (disregarding other perceptual modes, as well as generalized applications of 'appears') it is evident, apparent to the mind, that not *all* that is thus visually manifest is a reliable guide to how things, not themselves mere visibilia, really are. Hence we do contrast how things appear to be with how they actually are. 'Do not be taken in by *mere* appearances!' we urge. That contrast, wholly legitimate in particular cases, leads to philosophical confusion. Or rather, those contrasts, wholly legitimate in various kinds of particular cases, lead to confusion. A venerable philosophical tradition, contemptuous of the particular case, craving for generality, sets Appearances in general (with a capital A) off against Reality (with a capital R). Locked within a Veil of Perception, we seem to be condemned merely to speculate on what Reality, inaccessible to perceptual experience, is really like. Surrounded by Appearances, we try to derive broad generalizations about holistic relations between the world 'as-we-perceive-it' and Reality. And we construe scientific theorizing itself as a 'description of the world' that transcends Appearances, and hence as the 'best available description of reality'.

But the multiple distinctions, with respect to different features of the world and its categorially varied occupants, between appearing and being do not yield any all-embracing concept of Appearances that can be applied to everything we experience and then held over against Reality. The manifold distinctions between the visual or other appearances of things, of conditions, circumstances, states of affairs, events, and so forth are distinctions that apply *within experience*. There are not two distinct domains – Appearance and Reality – the former 'subjective' and the latter 'objective', the former sensed or experienced (and so mere 'experience', since what we experience are surely experiences!) and the latter inferred. The 'World' is not something which, in general, appears to us in a certain way (the 'phenomenal world') which we can then set over against 'Reality' (the object of our quest for an 'absolute', scientific, description of how things are). It is rather the totality of things that for the most part, *inter alia* appear to us in manifold ways – to sight, hearing, touch, smell and taste. But what *counts* as appearing and whether it *can* be contrasted with being will vary from case to case.

If a picture appears upside down on the screen that does not mean that it is not really upside down on the screen or that it is right side up somewhere else; it only follows that it should be looked at the other way round. If the cricket-team appears to be winning in the late afternoon it does not mean that it is not really winning, but only that it has not yet won. If Charles I on the scaffold appeared every inch a King, it does not imply that there was a hidden inch or two of unmonarchic character, though it may suggest that he did not always appear regal. The Evening Star is the first heavenly body to appear in the evening sky, but it does not appear to appear, it really is visible! If Laurence Olivier appears at the Old Vic as Richard III it does not follow that he is Richard III but it does follow that he is acting that role. And so on.

When one can contrast how a thing appears with how it actually is, then what *kind* of contrast is in question depends altogether on what particular category of object, event, state of affairs, etc. is involved, what context is under view and what kind of purpose is at hand. Thus, for example, Van Meegeren's *Christ at Emmaus* initially appeared to many art experts to be a Vermeer. Close scrutiny revealed a multitude of stylistic features inconsistent with Vermeer's known style, technical features incompatible with a seventeenth-century painting, and chemical substances introduced only in the nineteenth-century. It was not only the discovery, with the aid of a microscope, of cobalt-blue crystals in paint which should have been pure lapis lazuli that really penetrated to Reality! Moreover, this was detected by examining the paint under a microscope and identifying the cobalt crystals by their characteristic *appearance*! A competent cabinet-maker can make a chest-on-chest that will appear to be an authentic Chippendale piece. Only careful scrutiny of the joinery, the underside and drawers will show the later date of production. But would anyone suggest that the veneer is mere Appearance and the carcass Reality? Prince Hal, according to legend, appeared to all and sundry to be a worthless playboy, but he was revealed, after his father's death, to be wise, virtuous and heroic. His real character, so the story goes, was *then apparent to all*. The pedestrian over there appears to be about to cross the road; whether he will cross the road or not *remains to be seen!* This material, in this light, appears to be peacock green, but if you take it into daylight you will *see* that it is blue.

Even this tiny sample, taken from a boundless range of very different kinds of case, should suffice to engender scepticism about philosophical theses concerning global relations between appearance and reality. Three points stand out clearly. First, the predominant notions of how something or other appears are rooted in public visibilia, not in private sensibilia. Secondly, typically, where we can intelligibly contrast how something (initially, at first glance, here and now) appears and how (on further scrutiny, more thorough examination, patient waiting on events) it is, we do not contrast Appearances experienced by us and Reality that transcends experience. Rather we contrast what is initially seen or manifest to perception (and what might be inferred therefrom) and what is seen, perceived or apprehended subsequently, at a more thorough examination. Hence, thirdly, even where the contrast is between defeasible evidence manifest to sight (or, more generally, perception) and what is the case, a thing's appearing thus-and-so is not a matter of an observer's sensory states, but of evidence open to view, which, in some kinds of case and for various different kinds of reason, may be overridden by other perceptible evidence. There is nothing private or subjective about straight sticks looking bent when immersed in water,[6] or for that matter about stick insects looking like sticks.

It might be objected that this is going too far. For is not the question of what things really look like when no one is looking obviously foolish?[7] And if so, then surely the appearances of things

---

[6] They look like sticks bent at an obtuse angle, although by and large they do not look as if they are bent. Note that pennies, ever popular as philosophical examples, do not, save in very poor light and from a distance, look the slightest bit elliptical; nor do they look as if they are elliptical. They look just as any round flat object does when viewed from such an angle. The only thing that would look (and *be*) elliptical here is the outline of the penny drawn on a piece of glass interposed between oneself and the (round-looking) penny. And that outline itself may appear other (e.g. more or less elliptical) than it is; i.e. occlusion-shape itself is subject to a distinction between appearance and reality.

[7] See A. J. P. Kenny, *Descartes* (Random House, New York, 1968), p. 219.

are in some sense 'subjective'? This is confused. It is true that a beautiful painting does not look beautiful *to* anyone when no one is looking at it, but its appearance does not change when unobserved (only when differently illuminated). A good-looking woman does not cease to be good-looking when no one looks at her. A beautiful view does not cease to present a fine prospect when the tourists leave, but only when the sun sets. Sebastiano's Roman paintings look Michelangelesque even when the museum is closed. For an object to look thus-and-so does not require spectators – how things look when no one is looking is just as they look when someone is looking.

3 Subjective appearances

The appearance of an object is typically a perfectly public matter accessible to all who are equipped with the appropriate sensory capacities. Of course, we differ in our perceptual abilities and skills, as well as in the intellectual baggage that informs our perceptual judgements. Moreover, varying conditions of the observer affect the exercise of his perceptual capacities. Because there is a potential gap between the visible appearance, taste, smell, etc. of things and how they look, taste, smell, etc. *to* a given person on a certain occasion, we distinguish between how a thing looks (smells, tastes, etc.) i.e. what characteristics it presents to sight and how it looks *to* A, i.e. what, on looking at it, he discerns or would, other things being equal, take those characteristics to be. This distinction, or rather, these distinctions, are a source of extensive philosophical confusion.

A perceptual statement of the form 'A perceived M' or 'A perceived that *p*' is commonly so used as to entail that there is an M in A's perceptual field or that *p* is the case. Moreover, to perceive something by looking, listening, smelling, tasting or feeling is a way of acquiring knowledge or information; indeed, it is, in the venerable philosophical phrase, to acquire knowledge by or through *experience*. We contrast acquiring knowledge by experience with acquiring knowledge at second hand, by hearsay, through reading appropriate authorities or being taught at school, and so on. Knowledge acquired by experience in this sense is knowledge acquired at first hand, by sight, hearing, smell, taste or touch. Of course, knowledge acquired at second hand also involves the use of the senses – one must *hear* what another tells us about what *he* perceived and *see* what is written in a book describing the outcome of experiments which one has never seen. But in the case of acquiring knowledge by experience in *this* sense, what we thus come to know is, crudely speaking, what we perceive to be so.

Statements such as 'A saw the (colour of the) chair', 'A heard the (sound of the) car' as well as 'A perceived that such-and-such' can be said to identify or describe what A perceived. The one kind of sentence characterizes the object of A's perceiving as such, the other characterizes A's acquisition of perceptual information. But, we are inclined to think, if we can describe this, then surely we can also describe A's perceptual *experience,* how he was subjectively affected by the world's impinging upon his sensibility. And philosophers, moved by such a seemingly innocuous claim, have cast sentences of the form 'It looks F to A (or, to me)', 'It feels F to X' or, more generally (and artificially), 'It sensibly appears F to X' in the role of *descriptions* of perceptual experiences. Indeed, it has seemed to some philosophers that the statement that A has perceived something must entail, or incorporate as part of its truth-conditions, an appropriately corresponding statement describing a subjective perceptual experience.[8] Indeed, one is sorely tempted to claim that every perception, as it were, *contains* a perceptual or sensible experience described by 'It visually (auditorily, gustatorily, etc.) seems to X just as if . . .' Accordingly every seeing has a *seeming to see* as a constituent, every hearing incorporates an auditory experience described as 'sounding to A (or: to me) just, like . . .'[9]

We have moved, in the last two paragraphs, from uncontentious tautology to philosophical thesis. And on these foundations, philosophical castles are erected. (But there is a lurking suspicion that they are mere castles in the air!) Casting sentences such as 'It looks (sensibly appears) F to A (or: to me)' in the role of descriptions of

---

[8] Of course, what the 'appropriately corresponding statement' is will vary. *Normally,* things are as we perceptually apprehend them as being. But, of course, things may look thus-and-so to me, and I may know that they are *not* as they look.
[9] Cf. J. R. Searle: 'When I see a car, or anything else for that matter, I have a certain sort of visual experience. In the visual perception of the car I don't *see* the visual experience, I see the car; but in seeing the car I *have* a visual experience . . . the visual perception always has as a component a visual experience . . .' *Intentionality, an Essay in the Philosophy of Mind* (Cambridge University Press, Cambridge, 1983), pp.37–8.

subjective experience, philosophers have argued that such statements 'do not go beyond the available evidence', for they do not entail the objective existence of what is apparently perceived.[10] Unlike 'I see M' or 'I see that *p*', they give minimal hostages to fortune. Some philosophers have indeed argued that such (alleged) descriptions of subjective experiences are *incorrigible*. On this conception, in looking at an object (a painting, for example) and saying 'That is a Rembrandt' I am identifying or describing what I see, a public object visible to all, whereas in saying 'It looks like a Rembrandt to me' I am identifying or describing my visual experience. It then appears that while an 'objective perceptual judgement' is typically corrigible (for example – it's a Frans Hals, not a Rembrandt), a corresponding description of my visual experience is immune to error. So, it seems, when I turn my outer eye upon the world, I am at the mercy of the whims of fate and physics, but when I turn my inner eye upon the deliverances of my outer eye, what is revealed is fully and incorrigibly revealed!

It is tempting to think that expressions of the form 'It looks (sounds, smells, etc.) thus-and-so to me' constitute the *evidential grounds* for a person's knowledge of the world around him. For we are all, surely, empiricists enough to realize that our knowledge of the world is 'derived from experience', and if these kinds of expression are descriptions of experience, then surely they constitute the ultimate justifying grounds for our empirical judgements! Is it not plausible to argue that its sensibly seeming thus-and-so to me *presumptively implies* that things are thus-and-so?[11] Might one not invoke Wittgenstein's notion of a *criterion*, and suggest that things' sensibly seeming thus-and-so to me is a criterion for me to judge that that is how things are?[12]

An exhaustive investigation of these claims would take us too far afield, but the following discussion will touch on all. It is not

[10] Cf. A. J. Ayer, *The Central Questions of Philosophy* (Weidenfeld and Nicolson, London, 1973), pp. 81, 89.
[11] Cf. P. F. Strawson, 'Causation in perception' in *Freedom and Resentment and Other Essays* (Methuen, London, 1974), pp. 66ff.
[12] This line of argument is thinly intimated in Wittgenstein's *Blue Book* (Blackwell, Oxford, 1958), pp. 63–4, although it does not surface again (save perhaps in his *Philosophical Investigations* (Blackwell, Oxford, 1953) §354) for very good reason. I misguidedly toyed with the idea in 'Are transcendental arguments a version of verificationism?', *American Philosophical Quarterly* 9 (1972), pp. 78–85.

intended to be conclusive. If it leaves behind doubts that fester, it will have served its purpose.

The first question to be addressed is what conceptual transformation or transformations are effected by adding to descriptions of objects of perception the words 'It looks to me (or: to A) as if. . .' or, *mutatis mutandis,* 'It sounds (smells, tastes, feels) to me (or: to A) as if . . .' It is tempting to think that this operation transforms a description of objects of sensible experiences into a description of sensible experiences. And if we conceive of sentences of the form 'Such-and-such looks (smells, tastes, etc.) thus-and-so' as descriptions of *objective* appearances or phenomena, it is tempting to suppose that adding 'to me' or 'to A' transforms a description of phenomena into a description of phenomenal experiences. But before succumbing to temptation it is worth looking more closely at the uses of such sentences, their functions in discourse. For here too things are not always as they appear, and the *form* of a description may mask a use that is far removed from describing.

Suppose I ask someone to go to the window to see how many people are in the front quad, or to see who is at the door. He obligingly has a look and says 'It looks to me as if there are twenty or so', or 'It looks like a policeman to me'. Going by what is accessible to his view, in so far as he can discern, this is how he takes things to be. In similar circumstances, to assert 'There are twenty or so' or 'A policeman is at the door' is to make a statement about what, as it happens, one sees. It may be true or false. The assertion 'I see (or: I can see) twenty or so', or 'I see a policeman at the door' is a statement concerning what one sees, which explicitly acknowledges *that* one sees it. Such statements would be false, for example, if there are only fifteen people in the quad, or if it is a postman at the door, or if one had kept one's eyes closed and guessed. But the use of such utterances as 'It looks to me as if . . . ' differs markedly, at least in certain circumstances.[13]

---

[13] One must beware of being dogmatic here. 'It is F' and 'It looks F to me' do not *in general* mean the same, are not in general used in the same way, any more than 'on' and 'on top of' mean the same (cf. 'on the mountain' and 'on top of the mountain'). But it does not follow that they are not sometimes used equivalently (cf. 'on the table' and 'on top of the table'). As noted earlier, in some circumstances there may well be no difference between, e.g. 'It is red', 'It is red in appearance', 'It appears red' and 'It looks red'; so too, in certain circumstances 'It is F' and 'It looks F to me' are used equipolently, Synonymy is not an all-or-nothing context-independent matter.

Such utterances, in the various perceptual modalities, are not statements about how the object perceived is. It may not *be* F, but that is how it sensibly seems to me to be. Nor are they statements about the public appearance of the thing in question. The painting may not look like a Rembrandt, but that is how it strikes my untutored eye. The role of 'It looks to me as if . . .' (in such cases as are in question) is not to describe what is in view, nor is it to describe something other than what is in view, for it is not to *describe* anything at all. And what goes for 'It looks to me' goes for the other perceptual verbs thus used too. To a first approximation, such sentences, in the first-person present tense, are used as *expressions* of what one takes oneself to be observing. This, however, requires both clarification and refinement.

It is not surprising that such utterances are commonly conceived to be descriptions of subjective experience. We may surely concede that there is an obvious sense in which they are concerned with something 'subjective'. What appertains to the subject is that the utterance is an expression of how things strike the speaker on looking, listening, or otherwise sensibly investigating his environment. It is *his* impression that is thus expressed, consequent upon *his* looking, listening, etc. Other things being equal, *this* is what the speaker takes himself to be observing. It is not a coincidence that, if things turn out to be different from how they initially appeared to one to be, for example, if the man at the door is a postman, not a policeman, one would just as naturally say 'Oh, at first glance, I thought you were a policeman' as one would say 'Oh, at first glance, you looked like a policeman to me'. Nevertheless, to say 'It looks thus-and-so to me' is not to *state* that this is how I take things to be. And 'It looks to me like . . .' does not *in general* mean the same as 'On looking, I think it is . . .' For in certain circumstances I may say, 'Well, it looks like a so-and-so to me, but I know it isn't', but not, 'On looking, I think it is a so-and-so, but I know it isn't'.

'It looks (smells, tastes, etc.) thus-and-so to me' expresses how something perceptually strikes one. Other things being equal, this is what I would take myself to be observing. But other things are not always equal. Perceivers possess a vast array of knowledge and collateral information, and it often happens that something may look thus-and-so to a person yet *not* be taken by him to be so. 'It looks just like a Rembrandt to me,' one may say, 'but I know it is a forgery.' If not for the collateral information, I *would,* judging by its appearance, have taken it to be a Rembrandt. Again, 'From this distance, in this poor light, it looks to me like a donkey; but things are too indistinct to be certain'. Here I suspend judgement: this is how it strikes me perceptually, but in these circumstances perception is bound to be unreliable.

It is equally easy to see why first-person utterances of this form have traditionally enjoyed a claim to incorrigibility. My assertion, made after careful looking, that there are twenty or so people in the quad may be confirmed or disconfirmed by counting. Certainly I may be wrong in that judgement, as with 'I see twenty people in the quad'. But 'It looks to me as if there are twenty' cannot be faulted by counting and establishing that there are only nineteen, any more than 'It sounds out of tune to me' can be shown to be mistaken *about how it sounds to me* by testing to see whether it is out of tune. I cannot be mistaken in the same way in these cases. For avowing how things, on looking, strike me as being, i.e. how they look to me, can only be faulted on the grounds of insincerity (or through my not understanding the words I utter). Here 'truthfulness guarantees truth'. There is no more room for error on my part here than there is in the case of the utterance 'It hurts' or 'I have toothache'. If I say of a painting that it looks like a Rembrandt to me, then, other things being equal, it does indeed look thus to me, and my saying so is a criterion for its being so, even though it is not a Rembrandt and perhaps does not even look much like one.

Error, of the kind to which utterances such as 'There are twenty people there' or 'I can see twenty' are susceptible, has no foothold with respect to such utterances as 'It looks (sounds, smells, etc.) thus-and-so to me'. Nor do doubt or ignorance get a grip here, for although I may hesitate to say how the music strikes me, or whether the painting looks like a Rembrandt to me, my hesitation does not stem from *ignorance of what it looks or sounds like to me* (though it may stem from my lack of expertise). For it is not as if it either looks (sounds) thus-and-so to me or looks (sounds) such-and-such to me, but *I do not know which.* Rather is it akin to my hesitation over whether I intend to visit London tomorrow – it stems not from ignorance but from indecisiveness. What is necessary is not information about what I already intend or how the object already strikes me as being, but rather what is needed is *a verdict or decision.* I may err in my judgement about how an object looks (objectively, publicly) or how a piece of music sounds, and I may correct my judgement, for example 'That church looks Norman . . . No, I am wrong, it looks more like the Transitional style'. But this should not be confused with the incoherent idea of making a *mistake* about how something sensibly strikes me as being. I may, indeed, withdraw or revise what I say, but that is not because it struck me thus-and-so but *I did not notice that it did!*

The use of first-person present tense sentences of the kind in question very obviously displays extensive affinities to the kinds of utterance which, in the wake of Wittgenstein, have been called 'avowals'. The exclusion of error or ignorance here makes no room for knowledge. The apparent incorrigibility of 'It looks to me as if . . .', 'It sounds just like . . . to me', etc. is no rock upon which to build epistemic castles. When asked who is at the door or how many people are in the quad, I may look out of the window to see. I do not know incorrigibly who is there or how many there are. I can say that it is a policeman or that there are twenty, and I may be right or wrong. I can also say that it looks to me as if there are . . . , that it *strikes me* thus-and-so; and in this I cannot be *mistaken*, but not because I am incorrigibly well-informed about myself. Indeed, 'I *know* that it looks to me as if . . . ' is either nonsense or just an emphatic way of saying that it really does strike me thus, just as 'I know I am in pain', if it means anything, is just an emphatic way of saying that I am in pain.

It should, however, be stressed that while there are affinities between such expressions of how things strike one perceptually and avowals (for example, of pain), there are also important differences. 'It looks to me as if . . .' or 'It sounds like an M to me' do not stand to seeing or hearing as 'I am in pain' or 'It hurts' stand to being in pain. Expressions of how things perceptually strike one are not in any sense replacements of primitive perceptual reactions (although, as we have noted, there are such reactions, for example to glare, bitter tastes, deafening noise). Avowals of pain are partial replacements of, or outgrowths from, natural or primitive pain-behaviour. Expressions of how things perceptually strike one are outgrowths from, indeed are results of grafting upon, descriptions of what is perceived. They presuppose mastery of the use of such descriptions. We first learn to describe what we perceive and to say that we perceive it, and hence learn to answer the question of how we know that that is how things are. Later we learn a new articulation, which is used in rather special circumstances: we learn to give expression to how things strike us perceptually.[14] But such utterances, which presuppose mastery of, and the prior intelligibility of, descriptions of what is perceived, do not constitute the grounds or 'foundations' of such descriptions.

I may claim that the painting at which I am looking is by Rembrandt, but my evidence for such a claim is not that it looks to me like a Rembrandt. That something looks thus-and-so *to me* cannot be said to be something I *know* (or something of which I can be ignorant) as I can know evidence supporting a certain conclusion. To say how something perceptually strikes me is not to adduce my evidence for its being so. In some cases the question of *evidence* does not arise ('I did not have *evidence*, I saw it with my own eyes!' is sometimes wholly appropriate). In other cases, it does; for example, the provenance of a painting, the characteristic brushwork, the way in which this or that feature is painted, the composition, etc., these are evidence for the authorship of the painting; but not 'It looks to me as if it is by Rembrandt'. The role in discourse of the latter kind of utterance is not to provide a justification for a claim to knowledge. Nor would it be accepted as such. If my attribution of the painting is challenged, I can defend it by reference to the provenance, brushwork, composition, etc. but not by reference to how it looks to me. Expressions of how things perceptually strike one are misconstrued when assimilated to epistemic support or answers to the question 'How do you know?' or 'What grounds are there for that?'

Such utterances as 'It looks thus-and-so to me' or 'It sounds like a so-and-so to me' indeed do not go beyond the available evidence, but that is not because they remain within the bounds of the available evidence; rather, because they play no forensic role in one's own case. Frequently, an expression of how something perceptually strikes me involves *backing away* from the available evidence, because of lack of confidence and recognition of one's lack of expertise, or because of countervailing considerations (poor lighting conditions, etc.). Note, however, that if a Gerson, a Rosenberg, or a White says 'It looks like a Rembrandt to me' *that* is pretty solid ground for *me* to stand on. My

[14] Cf. L. Wittgenstein, *Zettel* (Blackwell, Oxford, 1967) §§ 423ff.

avowal of how a painting strikes me cannot logically be evidence or grounds *for me* to judge whether things are as they strike me, and, given my ignorance, very poor evidence for anyone else. But an expert's impression, or, in less recherché cases, a competent observer's impression in optimal conditions, is indeed reasonable evidence for someone else to rely on.

Like avowals, so too expressions of how things strike one perceptually display a first/third person asymmetry. 'It looks F to him', 'It sounds to him like . . .', etc. *can* be said to be descriptions. They are true or false propositions. In the case of such utterances, we can distinguish truth from truthfulness. One can know, or be ignorant of, whether things look thus-and-so to him, and one may make a mistake in judging the noise to have sounded to him like a so-and-so. The utterance 'It tastes sweet to me' rests on no criteria, but 'It tastes sweet to him' is asserted on the grounds of his observed behaviour, including what he says. It is important to note that a person's saying 'It is sweet' (or 'It is hot') on tasting (or feeling) something constitutes a proper ground for saying 'It tastes sweet to him' (or 'It feels hot to him'). He need not say 'It tastes sweet to me' (or 'It feels hot to me') in order for the third-person statement to be justified.

Expressions of one's perceptual impressions, of how things strike one perceptually, have therefore been miscast by philosophers. They cannot fulfil the role of an Atlas on whose shoulders all our empirical knowledge rests, nor can they play the part of a Sibyl whose pronouncements are incorrigible. Far from being the hardest of the hard, such utterances are soft and elastic, *designed* to give way, not to stand firm. Because there is a sense in which they cannot be faulted, philosophers have been inclined to view them as epistemically flawless. But their flawlessness is that of a perfect shadow, not of a perfect solid – they can (with the previous qualifications) support nothing.

4 Descriptions of perceptual experiences

Descriptions of the perceptible appearances of things are not, contrary to what many philosophers have argued, descriptions of subjective experiences. Even where there is a divergence between how something looks and how it actually is, its deceptive appearance is public and manifest to all. An early Ferdinand Bol *does* look like a Rembrandt, and there is nothing 'subjective' about that! Similarly something may smell of fish or decay without being a fish or decaying, but its smell, though perhaps deceptive, is no experience, but rather publicly accessible to experience. To say that the back-firing of a car sounds like a gunshot is not to make a psychological statement about oneself.

Conceding that descriptions of appearances are not descriptions of experiences, it is, as noted, tempting to construe expressions of how things strike one perceptually as descriptions of *perceptual experience*. For even if the previous argument is correct in pointing out affinities between such *first-person* sentences and avowals, it was conceded that *third*-person sentences such as 'It looks thus-and-so to him' *are* descriptions. Are they then *not* descriptions of his perceptual experiences? And while a case may have been made out that epistemic terms behave anomalously in relation to 'It perceptually seems to me as if . . .', it was not made evident why such avowals are not nevertheless *descriptions* of one's (subjective) perceptual experience. Why should we not claim that in saying 'It looks like so-and-so to me' I am describing my visual experience, describing how something struck me visually? After all, one might remonstrate, *something* must count as a description of one's perceptual experience, on pain of denying that there are any perceptual experiences, or, equally absurdly, of holding perceptual experiences to be ineffable.

Our final task is to try to defuse this objection. We must clarify why it is misleading to characterize first-person *expressions* of how things strike one perceptually as *descriptions*, and why it is misleading to characterize third-person descriptions of perceptual impressions as descriptions of perceptual experiences. Something does indeed count as a description of a perceptual experience, but it is not located, as it were, in the logical space in which we are fumbling.

It is no coincidence that philosophers are inclined to think that in saying 'That is a Rembrandt' or 'That foreshortening is defective' one is identifying or describing what one sees, but that in saying 'It looks to me like a Rembrandt' or 'That foreshortening looks defective to me' one is describing one's visual experience. Our confusions are rooted in grammar and jargon; in particular in the jargon, popular in philosophy and psychology, of 'perceptual *experiences*'. It seems innocuous enough to say that seeing something is a visual experience, hearing something an auditory experience, and so on. Such a perceptual experience, we continue, is something one *has* : one has a visual experience, that is, one sees something. And surely one can describe what one *has* – such as a pain![15] Pain, we are inclined to say, is clearly an experience, and it can surely be described as sharp and stabbing, or dull and nagging. Equally, it seems, it must be possible to describe what one has when one has a perceptual experience. And what better form of words for this purpose than 'It looks (smells, tastes, etc.) thus-and-so to me'! For such forms of words 'render the perceptual judgement [that things are thus-and-so] internal to the characterization of the experience without actually asserting the content of the judgement. And this is really the best possible way of characterizing the experience.'[16]

We have already seen ample reason to doubt whether 'It looks (smells, tastes, etc.) thus-and-so to me', 'It seems to me just as if . . .', 'It sensibly appears to me as if . . .', and other similar candidates, are correctly cast in the role of descriptions of anything at all, let alone in that of descriptions of perceptual experiences. We are misled here by our own grammatical prestidigitations. In the first place, the *representational form* of ownership, viz. '*having* a perceptual experience', brings perception into deceptive isomorphism with sensation, viz. '*having* a pain'. But to see or hear something is not,

---

[15] In the heyday of sense-datum theory, it was a commonplace that phrases of the form 'looks thus-and-so to me' stand for 'a peculiar experience' (cf. C. D. Broad, *Scientific Thought* (Routledge and Kegan Paul, London, 1923), p. 236). Even when phenomenalism was subjected to justifiable criticism, the concept of describing visual experiences was still gravely distorted. A. M. Quinton, for example, wisely urged that phrases such as 'It looks thus-and-so to me' are not usually used to describe experiences, but for quite different purposes. However, he added, we can and do describe experiences, only it 'is a sophisticated procedure, and one seldom called for' (Quinton, 'The problem of perception', *Mind* LXIV (1955), p. 35), and engaged in typically by painters. This is curious, for what painters, unlike the rest of us, are abnormally sensitive to are not their experiences, but the appearances of things they experience. A painter will attend to, while most of us will not notice, the shadows and reflected colours cast upon and by objects, the sheen and shimmer of things, the highlights and modulations. What he paints is how things look, and that is not a description of an experience, but – if a painting is a description at all – then of what is experienced.

[16] P. F. Strawson, 'Perception and its objects,' in G. F. Macdonald (ed.), *Perception and Identity: Essays Presented to A. J. Ayer* (Macmillan, London, 1979), p. 44.

save formally, to *have* anything, any more than to have a pain is to *own* anything. And the formal similarity, as we shall see, engenders confusion. Secondly, the nominal 'visual (auditory, etc.) *experience*', unlike the verbal forms it replaces ('see', 'hear', etc.) induces the wrong picture of what *counts* here as a description. For the typical paradigm of describing what is signified by a nominal is describing an *object*. Thirdly, there is indeed such a thing as describing a sensation, and we are prone to think (quite wrongly) that describing a sensation is very *like* describing an object – only a 'private' object accessible only to its owner! These misleading features work hand in hand, enmeshing us ever more firmly in confusion. So we are misled by the similarity in surface grammar between 'Describe something!', for example something seen or visually experienced, and 'Describe your visual experience!' After all, we might insist, a visual experience is something – it must be describable (it is not nothing, and it surely is not ineffable!). We are equally misled by the similarity of form between 'Describe your pain!' and 'Describe your visual experience!' Since one *can* describe one's pain, describing one's visual experience must be logically similar; or so we think.

These superficial analogies and similarities mask from sight fundamental logical differences between describing objects, describing sensations, and descriptions of perceptual experiences. The latter differences comes into view when we juxtapose 'Describe your pain!' with 'Describe your seeing John!' (as opposed to the misleading form 'Describe your visual experience of John!' (?) or, worse, 'Describe your visual experience of seeing John!' (!)). These differences spring into focus when we juxtapose 'Describe your toothache!' with 'Describe your seeing that John was in the room!'. At the very least it becomes clear that the formal isomorphism of the philosophically favoured forms masks deep incongruities. Back to the rough ground of familiar usage, and we feel the friction engendered. It then becomes evident that in our striving for generality we are prone to be deluded by our ill-chosen, grammatically convoluted examples. For we then fail to notice differences. In particular we do not attend to features of the uses of the word 'experience' and hence also differences in what may be called 'a description of an experience'.

The concept of an experience is rooted in the notion of a test or experiment. To know something by experience was, originally, to know by experimental observations or tests. Thence the notion branched in several directions. An object subjected to experiences (experiments) undergoes and typically does (by way of reaction) various things. As people too are subjected to tests, they too undergo experiences. And since one learns much by observing both things and people subjected to experiences, one is naturally also said to learn *by* and *from* experience. Given that in *learning by experience* one learns *by seeing, hearing or otherwise observing* tests or experiments and their outcomes, it is natural enough that we should come to speak of 'perceptual experience'. But, in philosophical contexts, with caution!

If one speaks of having had some hair-raising experiences during the war, one is typically talking about one's adventures, what one *did* and *suffered*. To describe those experiences is to narrate those activities and escapades. If one speaks of having had to put up with some unpleasant experiences in hospital, one is typically talking of what was done to one. To describe these unsavoury experiences is to describe what one consciously underwent (for what was done to one under anaesthetic is *not* an experience one suffered). Philosophers are inclined to say that pain is an experience, and we might readily, unthinkingly, concur. But is this right? And what, if anything, counts as describing it? Pain is, to be sure, a sensation, as is a tickle or an itch. Are tickles and itches experiences? If one has a pain in one's knee, or if one's back itches, one does not have an experience in one's knee or back; and if the pain is a throbbing one, it does not follow that the experience is. One may be said, in a stilted fashion, to experience the pain or itch, i.e. to be subjected to it. For, as argued, pains belong to the category of passivity : one suffers them, experiences them or *has* them (when conscious). But although there is such a thing as describing a sensation, for example : 'It is a dull throbbing pain which is exacerbated by moving my arm, but is not too bad when I lie down', it is by no means obvious that describing a sensation is the same as describing the experience of having or suffering the sensation. To describe the *experience* of having an attack of angina pectoris is not, or not only, to describe the characteristic pain ('like iron bands squeezed right around one's chest, and a sharp pain running down one's arm'), but rather to specify one's fear as one has it, to report what one thinks in those terrible moments, to relate what one does when that frightening pain occurs. To describe one's pains and to describe one's experience of undergoing certain pains, of suffering or being subjected to them while undergoing medical treatment, for example, is altogether different.

If one thinks that describing one's pain is an instance of describing one's experience (for surely, one thinks, one experiences pain, and *what* one experiences are experiences!), then one will be inclined to look for a straightforward analogue, in the grammar of perception, of describing one's sensations. After all, one may reason, why should describing one's perceptions of objects be any more problematic than describing the objects of one's perceptions? I can, to be sure, describe what I see, but surely I can also describe my visual experience as such. 'We want an account,' the philosopher may urge, 'which confines itself strictly within the limits of the subjective episode, an account which would remain true even if [you] had seen nothing of what you claimed to see, even if [you] had been subject to total illusion'.[17] And this, he may contend, is given by such forms of words as 'It sensibly seems to me just as if . . .', or, less artificially and more specifically, 'It looks to me just like . . .' or 'It sounds to me like . . .', and so on. The function of such operators on descriptions of objects perceived is, one may think, to transform descriptions of what is perceived into descriptions of perceptual experiences.

We argued, in the previous section, that these sentences typically (though not uniformly) are used, in the first-person present tense, to *express* how things strike one perceptually. They arguably share with avowals a variety of anomalous features with respect to epistemic terms, and they typically have no evidential status for the perceiver's justification of cognitive claims about objects. As we noted, someone might still insist that for all that, these sentences *describe* how things perceptually strike one. This, however, would be misleading. First, reflect on the actual use of requests such as 'Describe how the so-and-so strikes you as being'. A very wide range of responses is imaginable, depending on the character of the object in question, the point of the request and the context. Typically, the speaker will want a specification of a range of associations ('The sonata strikes me as eery, the sounds seem to drop from a great height, crystalline and pure'), or aesthetic response ('It strikes me that the lintel is too low and the windows a little narrow, giving the façade a rather mean and

[17] Ibid., p. 43

skimped look'); sometimes it will call for a judgement of (literal) taste ('A little more salt, and it will be just right') sometimes for sensivity and perceptiveness – a refined response to subtle nuance. Obviously in *most* cases, the identity of the object is taken for granted. If I ask you how the Mozart sonata I just played strikes you, I surely do not want you to reply 'It sounds to me just like a Mozart sonata'. But though the kinds of answer are very diverse, none seem to qualify for the title of description of *perceptual experience*.

Secondly, it is very misleading in a philosophical context even to suggest that *expressions* of how things strike me, telling someone that something looks, sounds, smells thus–and–so to me, are *descriptions of anything*. To tell someone what I think is mischaracterized as describing my thoughts, and to declare one's intentions is not to describe them. So too to report that something looks thus–and–so to me is not to give a *description* of something, in particular not of an experience. (This issue here does not just concern linguistic propriety, but a sharpened awareness of differences in language-games.) I describe what I am acquainted with, but I am not *acquainted* with my thoughts, intentions or perceptual impressions.[18] If one *is* tempted to call 'It looks (sounds, smells, etc.) thus–and–so to me' a *description* rather than an *expression,* one should contrast how one learns to describe an object to another person with how one learns to tell another person how things look (smell, taste, etc.) to one (i.e. to convey to another how things strike one perceptually), and one should compare how one improves one's descriptions of an object with how one improves one's reports of one's impressions. I learn to describe objects by learning to observe them carefully, to scrutinize them for telling detail; I can improve my descriptions by learning more about the objects in question, and hence looking at them with a more expert eye. But my report of, or expression of, how something strikes me perceptually does not involve perceiving, observing or scrutinizing anything *other than* the object perceived, in particular *not features of the perceptual impression it makes on me*. I can improve my reports of how things strike me perceptually by observing the objects I perceive (*not my experiences!*) more attentively, and *thinking*.

[18] See L. Wittgenstein, *Remarks on the Philosophy of Psychology*, vol. 1 (Blackwell, Oxford, 1980), § 572.

What should be said of the corresponding third-person sentences: 'It looks (sounds, etc.) thus-and-so to him'? These we conceded to be descriptions, to rest on evidential grounds, to be confirmable or disconfirmable, and so on. But are these descriptions of a person's perceptual experience? That would be exceedingly misleading. For, in the first place, such sentences describe a person's perceptual *impressions,* and how things sensibly strike a person is misleadingly conceived of as an *experience.* Secondly, the logical space of 'a description of a perceptual experience' is already taken up by something quite distinct.

Bearing in mind the fact that the term 'perceptual experience' is legitimately introduced into philosophical discussion only as a general term to avoid the circumlocutory form 'seeing, hearing, tasting, smelling, or feeling' (these being ways of learning how things are 'by experience'),[19] the request to describe a person's perceptual experiences is a request to describe a person's seeing, hearing, tasting, smelling or feeling something. The order 'Describe A's tasting coq-au-vin' would certainly not be satisfactorily complied with by saying 'It tasted salty to A', let alone by 'It tasted to A just as if it were coq-au-vin'. The former would be an answer to 'How did it taste to

---

[19] There are many other, less legitimate reasons. It is tempting to argue that perceiving an M and having an hallucination of an M involve the same 'perceptual experience', the one caused by M, the other not so caused. It is true that A, who suffers an hallucination, typically thinks that he perceives an M. It does *not* follow that he is having the same experience. Seeing and hallucinating are no more the same experience than seeing and dreaming that one sees are the same experience. They are so different indeed that they do not even *look alike,* for no *observer* would mistake Macbeth's having an hallucination of a dagger for Macbeth's seeing a dagger! The presence of a dagger in his visual field is a criterion for the latter, whereas the absence of a dagger in his visual field is a criterion for the former. And the absence of a dagger does not look like the presence of one! Do the 'experiences' not look alike to Macbeth? No, for he cannot see his seeing or his hallucinating. Of course, one does not say *that one sees* such-and-such on the basis of any criteria, but it does not follow that there are no distinguishing criteria between 'the experience of' seeing an M and 'the experience of' have an hallucination of an M. What is, trivially, true, is that there is a complete and unmistakable distinction between seeing M and having an hallucination of an M, but one who suffers from an hallucination is not in a position to draw it. He may, as Macbeth did, realize that the dagger he seemed to himself to see was but 'a false creation, proceeding from the heat-oppressed brain', but he cannot *see* that there is no dagger before him. In our reflections upon the first-person case we confuse the absence of any criteria of identity with the presence of identical criteria, and conclude, quite wrongly, that the *experiences had* are the same.

A?' or 'What did the coq-au-vin taste like to him?, the latter (perhaps) to 'What did A take the dish to be?' We would not describe A's first seeing the Sistine Chapel by saying 'It looked to A just as if it were the Sistine Chapel'. Rather would we comply, in the first example, by saying 'A sampled the dish, chewed reflectively, rolled his tongue around his mouth, smacked his lips and exclaimed delightedly . . .', and in the second by: 'A entered the Chapel, looked around in amazement and gasped; tears came to his eyes and he stood awestruck . . .'. A description of A's seeing, hearing, tasting, smelling or feeling, i.e. of his 'perceptual experience', is a description of what he did when he perceived the object, of the circumstances in which he perceived it and of his responses, affective, conative and cognitive, to whatever he perceived.[20] Where the term 'experience' connects up with perception in a non-trivial manner (i.e. not merely as abbreviating 'seeing, hearing, smelling, tasting and feeling) is here. We do say such things as 'Hearing Callas sing was one of the most wonderful experiences of my life', but, note, hardly 'auditory experiences', rather 'operatic experiences'. 'Tasting that Chateau Rothschild,' the wine connoisseur may gush, 'was a delightful experience.' Seeing, or more commonly looking at or watching; hearing, or more typically listening to; tasting, but more probably eating – are naturally referred to as *experiences* when they are, in some manner, remarkable, most commonly because of their hedonic character (delightful, enjoyable, pleasurable; or distasteful, revolting, disgusting) or because they impress us as out of the ordinary, bizarre or wonderful. 'Describe the experience' sits comfortably here. Complying with the request would involve describing what was perceived and how it struck one *affectively*. One would describe how what one saw or heard *impressed* one, but not by way of a sense-impression ('She sounded to me just like Maria Callas' would not do at all), rather by specifying what was remarkable, uncanny or awe-inspiring.

It is noteworthy that the first-person present tense case is different. 'Look at this ↗ (or even: watch this) and describe your seeing', unlike

---

[20] Of course this is, in many cases, altogether awry. 'Describe A's seeing the flash of light', as opposed to 'Describe how A responded to seeing the flash of light', is anomalous precisely because 'seeing' there does not signify a continuous state or process.

'Look at this ↗ and describe what you see' is clearly anomalous. I can say or describe what I see, but that is no more a description of my seeing than reporting what I ordered is a description of my ordering. I can, on looking, tell you what something looks like to me, how it strikes me visually. But such expressions of perceptual impressions, as we have seen, are mischaracterized as descriptions, and are clearly not descriptions of looking or seeing. I can, of course, comply with the request 'Tell us about your first seeing the Sistine Chapel' or 'Describe your first hearing Callas sing'. This, answered in the *past* tense, would correspond with the third-person case above, for example 'I walked in, looked around, saw the great frescoes and was overwhelmed with emotion. Tears sprang to my eyes . . .' etc., etc. But why is a parallel route blocked in the present tense?

A number of reasons might be ventured. First, 'seeing' in 'Describe your first seeing X' is obviously not a verb but a verbal noun. Hence there is no *suggestio falsi* that one is being called upon to describe an *activity*. But 'Look at this ↗, and describe your seeing' carries precisely that misleading implication. And since seeing is not activity, there is nothing to describe! Secondly, matters are not improved by substituting 'looking' 'watching' or 'scrutinizing' for 'seeing', since though these are activity verbs, it is unclear what the instruction 'Describe your scrutinizing' calls for. After all, I cannot *see* myself scrutinizing; all I can do is say that I am fixing my eyes on . . . , that I am attending carefully to . . . , etc. But no one would call such reports 'a description of a perceptual experience'. Thirdly, if I were asked to watch *this* or listen to *that*, and say what I thought about it, express my responses to it, I could, of course, do so. But, again, this explicit emoting would hardly justify the expression 'a description of an experience', let alone 'a description of a perceptual experience'.

Is there, then, *no* such thing as a description of a current perceptual experience in the first person? That would be going too far. But what we can come up with is far removed from what the philosopher hankers for. At the oculist's I might say, 'I see the first line clearly, but the third line is indistinct, and beneath that everything is blurred.' So too, at a party, after having had one too many, I might say, 'Everything looks double.' Of course, *these* uses of 'looks' are not an expression of how, on looking, I take things to be, but rather a report of how my seeing is *distorted* or defective, viz. indistinct, blurred, double, etc.[21] If one *is* to call this 'a description of one's visual experience', then it must be borne in mind that in the case of normal vision, there is nothing *in this dimension* to describe!

Philosophers, and some psychologists too, will protest. Having reduced visual sensations to the sensation of a blinding glare that impedes vision (see above, pp. 94ff), we are now reducing our current visual experiences to defects of vision such as seeing indistinctly or in a blurred manner, etc. But that seems tantamount to denying that when people normally perceive things with normal sense organs, they have perceptual experiences![22] And is that not outrageous?

It would be, if it were so. But all that has been denied is the philosophers' characterization of the role of certain sentential forms; we have simply drawn attention to what they are actually used for. To deny that 'It looks (sounds, tastes, etc.) thus-and-so to me' is a description of a perceptual experience is not to deny that one can legitimately use the phrase 'perceptual experiences'. (Similarly, to deny that 'I love you', 'I adore Beethhoven', or, differently, 'I regret that I cannot come', 'I am delighted to hear your news' describe *emotional experiences* is not to deny that one can legitimately use the phrase 'emotional experience'.) One might say here, following parallel tracks to Wittgenstein, that the expression 'perceptual experience' *as construed by philosophers*

is a degenerate construction of our grammar (comparable in a sense to tautology and contradiction). And this grammatical monster now fools us; when we wish to do away with it, it seems as though we denied the existence of an experience.[23]

---

[21] One might compare this with the contrast between 'I remember that you picked up the book' and 'The morning after the night before I remember what little I remember very unclearly'.

[22] It is sometimes even suggested that the *facts prove* that there are visual experiences, e.g. the phenomenon of so-called 'blind-sight'. 'Those who doubt the existence of visual experiences . . . might want to ask themselves what it is that we have that such patients lack' (Searle, *Intentionality,* p. 47). This is as confused as trying to prove the existence of negative numbers by reference to debts. What the blind-sighted lack is normal vision. (And what those who are in the red have is debts, not negative integers!) But, of course, there are such things as visual experiences; and, to be sure, the blind-sighted lack visual experiences – they cannot be said to look at, scrutinize or watch visibilia, *a fortiori* take no pleasure in so doing, nor are they revolted by being presented with visually offensive objects or events.

But we have not denied that people enjoy perceptual experiences, viz. that they see, hear, smell, taste and feel things and thus come to know things about their environment by experience. Nor have we suggested that perceptual experiences are ineffable; far from it – we have reminded ourselves what a description of a perceptual experience is. Of course, we have denied various claims: for example, that perceptual appearances of things are perceptual experiences; or that a description of appearances is a description of experiences; also that expressions of how things perceptually strike one are descriptions, and that descriptions of how things strike someone else are descriptions of his perceptual experiences. But to repudiate these claims is not to deny the existence of anything.

It is not the task of philosophy to affirm or deny the existence of things, but rather to clarify what assertions or denials of existence signify, if anything. Ontology is as defunct as metaphysics. It is not philosophers who make discoveries about the furniture of the world, but empirical scientists. The task of philosophy is to check the inventory for double counting, to clarify the list-making principles when confusions arise (in science and philosophy alike) through miscategorization or cross-classification. This chapter has attempted to fulfil that task for such concepts as sensible appearances and perceptual experiences. The perceptive reader will have noted that if the account given in the final two sections is on the right track, then the (philosophical) causal theory of perception, in its classical and contemporary forms alike, is in ruins. This I deem to be a highly satisfactory conclusion. But to make it perspicuous, to show what follows from the collapse of that venerable house of cards, to clear the ground of the debris, is a task for another occasion.

---

[23] L. Wittgenstein 'Notes for lectures on "Private Experience" and "Sense Data"', *Philosophical Review*, 77 (1968), p. 34.

Index

Index